W9-BKP-185

THE
GREENING OF
PROTESTANT
THOUGHT

WITHDRAWN

THE
GREENING OF
PROTESTANT
THOUGHT

Robert Booth Fowler

The University of North Carolina Press

Chapel Hill & London

© 1995 The University of North Carolina Press
All rights reserved

Manufactured in the United States of America

The paper in this book meets the guidelines for permanence and durability
of the Committee on Production Guidelines for Book Longevity of the
Council on Library Resources.

Robert Booth Fowler is Hawkins Professor of Political Science at the
University of Wisconsin–Madison.

Library of Congress Cataloging-in-Publication Data
Fowler, Robert Booth, 1940–
The greening of Protestant thought / by Robert Booth Fowler.
p.   cm.
Includes bibliographical references and index.
ISBN 0-8078-2205-1 (alk. paper). — ISBN 0-8078-4517-5 (pbk. : alk. paper)
1. Human ecology—Religious aspects—Protestant churches—History
of doctrines—20th century.   2. Protestant churches—United States—
Doctrines—History—20th century.   3. United States—Church
history—20th century.   I. Title.
BT695.5.F68   1995
261.8'362—dc20   94-48277
CIP

99 98 97 96 95   5 4 3 2 1

❧ CONTENTS ❧

❧ PREFACE ❧

This book is about Protestant environmentalism in the United States in the twenty years after the first Earth Day, in 1970. It examines the extent to which ecological concerns permeate the elites, institutions, and general membership of Protestantism, while paying due attention to the varieties and divisions in Protestantism. It mainly addresses Protestant thought and how Protestant theologians and activists have formulated versions of a green Protestantism that addresses the environmental crisis and fends off numerous critics from within the larger environmental movement. It makes a special effort to look at Protestantism and the environment with a consciousness of Protestantism's many sides, including the world of Protestant fundamentalism. It also pays close attention to the setting of Protestant environmentalism, its relationship to science, its connections with broader social and political thought, and how it compares with the earlier Protestant civil rights movement.

Chapter 1 addresses the status of environmentalism within Protestantism today, and Chapter 2 covers the history of green Protestantism. Chapters 3 and 4 explore the differing interpretations within Protestantism of the meaning of the Bible in regard to the creation (the environment). Because the Bible is the central foundation for Protestantism, how it is interpreted in regard to creation is, predictably, both crucial and controversial. Chapter 5 describes and analyzes the intense debate both within Protestantism and between Protestant thinkers and their secular critics over the Christian environmental record.

Chapters 6 through 9 consider the various theologies by which green Protestants connect their faith with the earth. There is today an often fascinating and sometimes fierce argument among Protestant thinkers as to how Protestants should respond to the ecological crisis. There have been many alternatives proposed, from the traditional stewardship theology to creation theology to process theology to ecofeminism and beyond.

Finally, Chapters 10 and 11 examine the practical sides of Protestant environmentalism: the goals, policies, and strategies for change that Protestant thinkers advance. These chapters report and critically reflect on ecological Protestantism's usual objectives—a sustainable society, a just socioeconomic order, and a godly community—as well as its common vehicles for change—the church, the state, and (sometimes) politics.

I want this book to do more than tell the story of modern Protestant environmental thought, important as that is. I mean for this account to be analytical and critical in the best, most supportive sense. The world of environmental thought in Protestantism and elsewhere reflects the great commitment that underlies the entire enterprise. This reality is understandable, and I could not be more sympathetic. But there is also a distinct need for serious analysis of the claims and perspectives of Protestant environmentalism, in order not to undermine them but to strengthen them. It is no secret that enthusiasm does not necessarily yield a strong analysis. Sometimes it works to impede one.

Unless otherwise noted, all biblical quotations are from the Revised Standard Version.

I have tried to study Protestant environmentalism from many angles. I have gathered and analyzed public opinion data, denominational publications, theological writings, denominational statements, political arguments, and policy proclamations. I looked and read everywhere I could. My study of Protestant publications was financed by the Lilly Foundation.

Along the way I have had a great deal of help. Some people consented to interviews in person or by telephone by myself or my research assistant, Laura Olson; others shared their insights or encouragement in conversations or by mail. Some stimulated my work more than most through talks they gave or through papers they shared; I acknowledge them at appropriate points in the text, but I also want to mention them now: Joe Bowersox, Thomas Derr, Calvin DeWitt, Adolf Gundersen, Jim Guth, Lyman Kellstedt, Sallie McFague, John Meyer, Larry Rasmussen, Paul Santmire, Mark Thomas, Vernon Visick, Loren Wilkinson, and Keith Yandell. I am confident, unfortunately, that this list is not complete.

Others helped by reading parts of this manuscript. They were a blessing to me and to this project, suggesting ideas and correcting tenses, though they bear no responsibility for this work's errors. Thanks to Charles Anderson, Joe Bowersox, Jill Carnahan, Donald Downs, Kate Gurney, Andy Murphy, Finessa Ferrell-Smith, Adolf Gundersen, Ben Marquez, John Meyer, Kristin Novotny, Laura Olson, Polly Schloesser, Dave Siemers, and Marion Smiley. Alice Honeywell is both my favorite Protestant and my favorite environmentalist and she contributed more than anybody to this project. I am lucky to have found her.

THE
GREENING OF
PROTESTANT
THOUGHT

✜ INTRODUCTION ✜

This is a book about Protestant thought and green politics. Over the past twenty-five years, increasing numbers of Protestants—as individuals and as churches—have perceived the onset of an environmental crisis and the importance of attending to it. Their response has included the development of Protestant thinking that addresses the environmental situation, its dilemmas, and its difficulties. This study concentrates on the emergence of this Protestant thought—a process that has been an important step in both the political development of the environmentalist movement and the religious and political history of contemporary American Protestantism.

The greening of Protestant thought from 1970 to 1990 and beyond is a fascinating story that, because of my previous research on other aspects of Protestantism and politics, I believed I could undertake.[1] Almost from the beginning, I learned that in light of the broad consensus within Protestantism on the importance of God's creation—the environment—and the need to act to rescue it, generalized complaints about "the almost total obliviousness of organized religion toward the environment" are just plain wrong.[2] This judgment has even less to do with modern Protestant thought in the United States. It is more accurate to say that the larger, and largely secular, organized environmentalist movement has simply ignored Protestant concern with the ecological crisis. When a more accurate perception will occur is anyone's guess, but there are already some signs of change, as Roderick Nash illustrates in *The Rights of Nature: A History of Environmental Ethics.*[3]

This study concerns the thought of Protestants primarily but not exclusively. Protestant thinking is hardly hermetic today, and the boundaries of this book must be equally fluid. The main focus remains on Protestantism, but whatever their grounding, thinkers and ideas that have influenced Protestant environmentalism receive the attention they are due. For example, I explore the creation theology of several non-Protestants, and I consider several thinkers, including a number of process theologians, whose adherence to Christianity, not to mention Protestantism, is much-debated.

A similar spirit governs the book's approach toward its time period. The year of the first Earth Day—1970—marks a logical beginning point.

To what extent Protestantism was committed to environmentalism before 1970 has since then been the subject of controversy: what is the legacy of historical Protestantism? The burst of interest among Protestants around 1970 did reflect a similar shift of attitudes in the larger, secular culture, but it also built on previous Protestant environmental thinking, which had both ancient and recent origins.

It flowed as well from the considerable, disquieting controversy that broke out in the 1960s and 1970s when some secular environmentalists arraigned Christian thought and practice regarding the environment. Suddenly Christianity—and Protestantism as the major expression of Christianity in the United States—came under an attack that some green Protestants joined. Environmentalists pointed their fingers at Christianity, accusing that faith of being a major cause of the ecological crisis.[4]

The year 1990 was a convenient ending place in a project that has no obvious or logical terminus. This book freely discusses contemporary materials from time to time; but the pre-1970 and post-1990 writings used here are employed mostly in order to fashion as accurate a picture as possible of Protestant environmentalism from 1970 to 1990.

Over these two decades there were major changes in Protestant environmentalism; the degree of interest in Protestantism about the environment also varied significantly in that block of time. Much of the 1970s, for instance, saw major engagement with the issue. In the later 1970s and well into the 1980s, interest trailed off. In recent years, however, the 1980s pattern has reversed. Environmentalism in Protestantism is back as strong as ever, or stronger.

The book confines its attention largely to the United States. Occasionally I gratefully draw on the work of scholars in Canada or discussions about or from involved Europeans. There was and is much to learn from comparative experience and perspective.[5] The decision to deal primarily with Protestantism in the United States, however, reflected the overwhelming abundance of material. Looking to broader horizons promised to lead more to despair than to insight.

This book also tries to be flexible in how it characterizes the religious outlooks of the Protestants it explores. It is important when discussing Protestant religious ideas not to slip into a simple dualism and identify Protestants as either religious liberals or religious conservatives. Certainly it is wise to avoid intensely contested labels within Protestantism, such as "orthodox." There is a rich spectrum of religious opinions, particularly among green Protestant thinkers, and this book respects that variety. Religious liberals and conservatives do exist, but there are many variations among them and more than a few definitions of liberal and conservative. On this matter, as on so many others, the label "Protestant" implies less homogeneity than may first appear. This may be an age in which denominationalism is in decline, but division among Protestant thinkers has definitely not disappeared. Protestantism remains a large, sprawling, and wonderfully diverse entity.

Thus there is no single eco-theology or set of political beliefs among Protestants. This statement is true of various individuals and also of whole sectors of Protestantism, especially in the contrast between liberal and fundamentalist Protestants. A good portion of this book speaks to this diversity and underlines how rich, complex, and pluralistic Protestantism is. It encourages caution in making general statements about green Protestantism and about Protestantism and politics.

I distinguish among Protestants primarily by two means: self-identification and doctrine. The doctrinal distinction I employ most often is attitude toward the Bible, a distinction closely connected with Protestant self-identification. I define more liberal Protestants as those who employ the Bible as an important part of their faith, as a document that is inspired by God but that is also a historical and cultural work. Liberal Protestants do not contend that the Bible is somehow the full truth of God or that it is true in all aspects. I define evangelicals and especially fundamentalists as those who place greater stress on the Bible as the word of God, sometimes (as among fundamentalists) the completely inerrant word of God.

This book also addresses the relationship among Protestantism, Protestant environmentalism, and the larger culture. This concern takes several directions—for example, exploring the relationship between Protestant environmentalism and science and aspects of broader contemporary political and social thought. My assumption is that green Protestantism can be understood only when set in its overall intellectual environment.

As an important part of its comparative enterprise, this study specifically considers environmentalist Protestant interactions with the larger, and largely secular, environmental movement. This case study will illustrate both the connections and lack of connections that exist today. Much of green Protestantism marches in tandem with the broader movement. Indeed, there is little doubt that the broader movement has powerfully influenced Protestant environmentalism. At times it does seem as if some Protestant participants "merely appropriate religious language and metaphor for the promotion of the cause."[6]

Motivations, however, are tricky things to characterize, and the fact is that green Protestantism has very much its own voice. This has been obvious in its struggles over theology, the Bible, the history of Christianity, and much else in relation to the environment. It is especially noticeable when considerations of hope and history emerge. As we shall see, Protestant environmentalism can often match the pessimism of much of secular environmentalism. Yet it has something unique, a hope in history and the future because of God, that is quite missing from secular environmentalism. This hope does not substitute for human action or relieve the acute sense of crisis, but it is part of what provides a distinct cast to Protestant ecological thought.

The book also considers the marked gap in Protestant environmental thought between its theological reflections and its policy analysis and political theory. Theological fecundity and diversity properly define much of green Protestant thinking. Yet important questions must be raised about Protestant environmentalism's political and social theory and its specific societal goals, policies, and strategies of change. This book engages some of these problematics because they are essential to probing deeper into this Protestant thought and its implications.

One purpose here is to provide the perspective that comes from comparing green Protestant thought (and action) with other Protestant movements of recent decades. Specifically, I compare environmental Protestantism with the Protestant involvement with the Gulf War and, in much more detail, with the civil rights movement of the 1960s. These comparisons are developed in chapters 10 and 11 and focus on both the means and the goals adopted by the movements. In the process they draw on the growing literature of the Protestant civil rights movement.[7]

The political force and elite support of the Protestant civil rights movement appears to have been, at least for a short time in the 1960s, far more intense than that mobilized for environmental goals to this point. On the other hand, Protestant environmental thought is far more developed; many at the National Council of Churches were simply too busy in the 1960s to explore civil rights with the theological richness and rigor that is more and more evident in green Protestant thinking. However, many of the same goals and means of change (except—and it is a big exception—civil disobedience) characterize both movements.

Environmentalism in a Protestant Setting

Again, this book assumes that Protestant environmental thought can only be appreciated in relation to the larger movement and its intellectual themes. One of the most important concerns their mutual attitudes toward science. Both share a good deal of antagonism toward science—though not always for the same reasons. Much Protestant environmentalism teems with accusations that science (and technology) are principal causes of the current ecological situation. The same is of course true of much of secular environmental thought, as expressed in such historical treatments as Carolyn Merchant's *Death of Nature* or in classic arguments such as Bill Devall and George Sessions' *Deep Ecology.*[8]

At the same time, whether this fact is acknowledged or not, science often appears to be the ultimate authority among some Protestant environmentalists. Its findings are used to substantiate the claim of a current crisis, to provide the basic outlines of nature (of the biological and physical worlds), and to model the good society. This pattern parallels what is evident at least as strongly in the literature of the larger green movement. Whether the issue is about animal rights or "respect for nature," the image of animals and nature comes from scientific findings—or is sincerely believed to be based in them. There is plenty of room to debate whether such scientific claims actually have their origins elsewhere (for example, in political or ethical or religious ideals).[9] But in fact, science is often taken as the central authority.[10] The irony is that in a world where idolatry of science is often attacked, there are some signs that it is also practiced.

Both green movements also have deeply mixed attitudes toward philosophy. Both, as we will see, are pervaded by a sense of overwhelming crisis and, at times, an almost desperate urgency for action to meet environmental problems. In this light, both outlooks contain those who are impatient with abstract philosophizing, and both suffer from underdeveloped philosophical thinking. Yet I would insist that both the larger movement and Protestant ecological thought represent exciting frontiers in contemporary thought. There may be a good deal of ambivalence about philosophy, but much energy is also devoted to thinking seriously about how to understand the environmental challenge in a sophisticated manner.[11]

This energy is equally apparent among those who advance one or another view of the proper direction in which environmental change ought to proceed. As we will discover, Protestant environmentalist thought is quite diverse and often creative in its formulations of alternative stewardship theologies, as well as in such eco-theologies as creation and process theologies or ecofeminism. There is a great deal of philosophic life present as well, of course, in the larger, mainstream environmental movement. The "intrinsic worth" arguments of J. Baird Callicott, the neo-intuitionism of Paul Taylor, the natural rights views of Roderick Nash, even the radical "confessions" of Dave Foreman all illustrate the point.[12]

There is widespread ambivalence also regarding politics—that is, the pushing and shoving for interest and ideal in public life. In part this ambivalence reflects the sense of crisis in all environmental thought: the idea that we know what should be done and we must get on with it. In part it reflects a mutual interest in a goal of human community that parallels something of what environmentalists often conclude nature is like, a world where harmony is far more prominent than change or conflict; in part it expresses a distaste for liberal politics and the individual self-centeredness and capitalism that are widely condemned in environmentalist thought, religious and otherwise.

This ambivalence about politics is not always obvious, yet it unfolds soon enough. Often politics either disappears in any conventional sense—especially among many ecological radicals, such as Christopher Manes in *Green Rage*—or becomes transformed into an affirmation of decentralized community life, as in John Dryzek's *Rational Ecology*.[13] And this attitude, I will argue, is repeatedly on display in green Protestant writings, despite endorsements of the value and the necessity of "politics."

But the similarities are not only in the realm of ambivalence. For example, one of the most powerful themes in both Protestant and secular environmentalism is commitment to a community ideal. Indeed, this ideal overwhelms any other social and political possibilities. Community is the central political concept of environmentalism today, and its many proponents tightly link it to an equally holistic natural world.

Community is, of course, a complex and, particularly in this age of celebration of community, fascinating subject. This book will have a fair amount to say on the subject in exploring images of community in Protestant thought, in modes of scientific thinking, and in broader environmental and other political theory. All the nuances and variations aside, however, there can be no underestimating how central the community theme is in Protestant social thought and how closely it parallels a similar emphasis (albeit in somewhat different language) in the environmental movement as a whole.

Also widely shared is an image of nature as a steady state, interactive and yet diverse, one in which all parts are somehow in equilibrium. Such a view is, in fact, far from self-evident, though it is often presented as such. As we will see, there are other understandings of the nature of life and the universe that challenge this understanding of nature. In the process, they raise questions about crucial assumptions that underline both Protestant and other environmental thought.[14]

Yet despite such similarities, it remains true that there are major differences between the environmental thought found in Protestantism and that found in the broader green movement over the past twenty-five years. There is a unique realm of green Protestant thought, granting the diversity that is within it. After all, Protestant environmental thought is built upon its Protestant and Christian religious foundations. It normally takes for granted the existence of a Creator God and the divinity of Jesus Christ; it works with and from the teachings of the Bible (however interpreted); it deals with the Christian environmental record. It also concentrates a good deal on Christian theology. Some of it is quite familiar in Christian terms; some of it may not be, but that does not mean it is not a product of—or in accord with—standard Christian ideas. Moreover, while some Protestant thinkers' theology of creation is far from the mainstream, they understand Christianity as a living religion that should and must change to meet new conditions in God's created universe.

As Protestant eco-theory uses the language and the images of Christianity, it often speaks in a different language than that of the larger environmental movement; and that language often betrays different values as well as alternative foundations. The values are not to be dismissed. For while the movements share some ideas, such as their focus on community, there are also differences, some of which this book will accent. One crucial example is the role of hope. In the language of Protestant environmentalism, no matter how grim the crisis analysis nor how stern the injunctions to action, there is almost always an invocation of the hope that rests with faith in God. This faith may guarantee nothing about the fate of the earth, but the love of God and of God's ultimate blessing is integral to Protestant views.

Similarly, some Protestant considerations on how to make change are largely confined to Protestant thought. This is most apparent in its emphasis on churches as a vital agent of change. While secular environmentalism and its Protestant ally may share a faith in government, coupled with ambivalence about politics, there is quite a difference in the role each assigns to religion, religious people, and religious institutions as means of change. This difference should not surprise anyone, but it should induce caution before confident assertions that green Protestant thought is merely a stepchild of the larger movement.

Broader Settings

As this book proceeds, it will frequently attempt to place Protestant eco-logical thinking in the context of broader intellectual developments as well as the thought of the larger environment movement. It is important and enlightening to consider some similarities and differences with current intellectual directions in American thought, especially American political thought.

One is surely the matter of science in our age. Protestant environmental thought has several conceptions of science, and it is of some value that they be set in a context of current perspectives on science. At a number of points this book does just that. It explores, for example, how Protestant images of science fit with the rising perceptions of complexity science, most recently explored by M. Mitchell Waldrop.[15] Some eco-theologies, such as process and creation theology, fit surprisingly well, but the more steady-state vision of science that is dominant in most Protestant thought does not.

The fact is that in most green Protestant discussions science and its findings are treated as givens. Yet the extent to which the findings of science are socially constructed rather than "facts" is now much debated. Whether they are subjective constructs or not, such possibilities challenge characteristic Protestant assumptions about what science is and what it knows about the ecosystem. In this context, I found it fruitful to reflect on feminist analyses of science, some of which are decidedly skeptical of the certainties of science. Of course, this material is relevant to the chapter on ecofeminism, but the book applies feminist analyses more broadly than that; for the issues are really about what science is, how it is developed, and what basis it has for its authority and its findings. Among others, this book draws from work by Evelyn Fox Keller and Donna Haraway.[16]

A second larger intellectual setting in which this work places Protestant ecological thought is the broader philosophical situation—in particular, foundations for interpretation and values. After all, one of the most interesting aspects of Protestantism is its longtime tradition of interpretation. There is no doubt that Protestantism itself and the hundreds of years of disagreements that have characterized its history have often been rooted in conflicting interpretations of the Bible.

From this perspective, there is nothing new about the increasing post-modern emphasis on interpretation, though the more extreme claims, such as that there is no text or that all is interpretation are a bit much for most Protestant theologians. To be sure, liberal Protestant theologians are more frank in emphasizing the interpretivist task than some evangelicals and fundamentalists are, but few Protestant thinkers of any persuasion conclude that to interpret means to announce the validity of whatever may be in the eye of the beholder.

Much of the broader intellectual world today has, we might say, caught up with Protestantism—including Protestant environmentalism—in stressing the importance of interpretation. And the fact is, Protestant ecological thought is resolutely foundationalist. While much social and political theory today resonates with support for a nonabsolutist base for values, this stance is not much in evidence in Protestant environmentalism. Broader intellectual currents may affirm that values are social constructions or are the results of pragmatic choices. They may assure us that we can be "without foundations" or find a safe guide in the irony of Richard Rorty or the postmodern Nietzsche.[17] But in Protestant ecological thought there is scant echo of any of these concepts. There one finds an assurance about truth, religious truth and, as we will see, truth about nature as well—sometimes unrecognized and often undefended, but present nonetheless. It is a significant and interesting contrast, one that again underlines that Protestant thinking is no simple shadow of current intellectual fashion.

Finally, since this project focuses a fair amount on political thought, it is important to have some perspective on Protestant environmentalism's ideas and how they accord with developments in American political thought. This too is a complex subject, and in this work only certain points can be and perhaps need be made. Two particular political themes present in American political thought percolate through green Protestantism. One is a general uneasiness with liberal political thought, which is defined as the Western tradition, with its emphasis on the individual, rational thought, human freedoms, and capitalist economics. The second is an affirmation of the value of community as *the* objective in political and social—and environmental—reconstruction.

The work of such theorists as Alasdair MacIntyre and Michael Sandel form an intellectual setting now dominated by skeptics of liberalism, one alive as well in Protestant environmentalism.[18] Some contemporary theorists bemoan the rampant individualism that they see in modern liberalism, as William Sullivan does. Others denounce what they prefer to describe as deadly narcissism, a term used by Christopher Lasch. Still others emphasize the collapse of commitment in love and marriage, as does Ann Swidler. Yet others attack the disintegrative effects of the liberal market, as does Alan Wolfe.[19]

Each of these emphases appears among green Protestant thinkers as they too struggle with what seems to many of them to be a world that is selfish and confused and unable to respond in a coherent, communal fashion to the crisis of the age that environmental degradation poses. The same is true when we look at what Protestant environmentalism seeks as an alternative political outlook—above all, building of community. While there is no full agreement on the repudiation of liberal values—or even on what liberal values are—there is among green proponents a broad consensus on the great political good of community.

This book will explore the Protestant environmental affection for community—in nature and in society—in the larger intellectual setting, where community is the concept of the age.[20] It grants that there are exceptions to the cult of community in our era, to be sure, including defenders of traditional liberal values. There are others who worry about the conformist dangers of community, including some postmodernists and feminists, though many of them try to come as close to the community ideal as they can without sacrificing individual diversity.[21]

Yet the call for community resounds everywhere in contemporary American intellectual life, and green Protestant political thought cannot be understood outside this context. It is routine among secular environmentalists such as John Dryzek. It is also the answer for Alasdair MacIntyre and for Robert Bellah. Jean Bethke Elshtain recommends it, as do Kirkpatrick Sale and Jane Mansbridge. The list seems endless.[22]

Inevitably, there is intense disagreement over what kind of community would be best. Even in this secular age, there are a good many thinkers who speak for religious community. There are those who, inspired by the work of J. G. A. Pocock, advocate community in the spirit of the American revolutionaries, republicans seeking a public life of common norms and people committed to a public good.[23] There are participatory communitarians, such as Benjamin Barber, and traditionalist ones, as Allan Bloom was. There are feminists who advocate community, such as Susan Griffin, and populists, such as Harry C. Boyte and Frank Riessman.[24] The subdivisions are almost as numerous as the possibilities, but this profusion only underlines the dominance of the community motif in contemporary American political thought. One of those subdivisions—only one, but very much a part of the whole—is the celebration of community in Protestant religious thought on the environment.

What is interesting in this case, however, is that the focus on community within Protestant environmentalism is far from just another sign of how closely many Protestants share the spirit of the age. After all, community is and always has been a central political and social value of Christianity. For green Protestant thinkers, the focus on community reflects a powerful intersection of traditional Christian values, the demands of ecological crisis, the holistic images of ecological science, and participation in current political thought. All these roads lead toward community as the political and social "answer"—and few green Protestants dissent.

Critical Reflections

In this study of the thought of Protestant environmentalism, attention falls on the arguments and perspectives of theologians and analysts from 1970 to 1990 and beyond. The work respects what green Protestants have perceived and argued and seeks to share that story with others.

This book, however, is also a critical study. It is critical in the sense that it undertakes an overall interpretation and develops certain themes. But it is also critical in that it engages some of the claims that emerge from the fascinating world of Protestant ecological thought. Such a perspective proceeds with the assumption that a critical analysis is a valuable part of understanding what Protestant environmental thought has been about. It honors rather than diminishes that thought by constructively exploring its premises, strengths, and limitations along the way.

There are some important questions that deserve and receive attention. One is the relationship between science and Protestant environmentalism. How plausible are Protestant images of science? Which views are adopted and which are not? What are some of the reasons for the assumptions about science, the conclusions drawn from it, and the ambivalent attitudes that many green Protestants hold toward it? These matters merit critical examination, and they receive it in this work.[25]

Another such matter is the Protestant environmentalist engagement with community. What kinds of problems and difficulties does this transformative ideal have? How grounded is this ideal in nature or philosophy as opposed to religion? How realistic are its conceptualizations and analyses? How much of the enthusiasm is based on misunderstandings about the natural universe, or on a nostalgia rooted in present aspirations rather than past realities?[26] Green Protestant thought's affinity for community holds much worth exploring, and for that reason it deserves and demands critical analysis.[27]

The attitudes toward politics and government that permeate much of green Protestant thought also merit critical reflection. As we will see, Protestant environmentalism tends to view politics—the give and take, the pushing and shoving that comprises public life—very dimly. On the other hand, government rates as a surprisingly uncritical good. What is the place of politics, as distinguished from government, in Protestant environmentalism? What accounts for green Protestantism's tendency to believe that politics can disappear into the worlds of community, science, and religion? What is the significance of the affirmation of such a secular institution as government?[28]

In short, there is much to explore in the story of Protestant environmentalism from 1970 to 1990 and beyond. This book begins the story by describing the rise of environmentalism within Protestantism over the past twenty-five years.

PROTESTANTS FACE THE ENVIRONMENT

This chapter considers several important background elements to the greening of Protestant thought from 1970 to 1990 and thereafter. It tells part of the story of the shift by institutional Protestantism as the denominations moved toward encountering the environmental problems of the age. It reports the pattern of Protestant public opinion on environmental concerns. It discusses the two central assumptions that have greatly affected Protestant changes: the sense that the earth is in crisis and the perceived hostility from the larger environmental movement toward Christianity. Finally, it identifies some of the limits of the greening of organized Protestantism and of Protestant opinion—especially among fundamentalists. In short, the goal of this chapter is to explain some of the dimensions of the greening of organized Protestantism, and of Protestants as a people, to provide a context for the Protestant intellectual debates on which this book concentrates.

The Whirl of Action

Environmentalism has increasingly secured a place among the leadership, formal institutions, publications, and intellectual centers of Protestantism. The greening of institutional Protestantism is a fact, and its reality has quickened over the past decade. Denominational elites, clergy, and bureaucrats led the way. It took time: sometimes ecological concerns were peripheral to other agendas at denominational headquarters, often just part of one busy staffer's assignments. Sometimes they loomed more important to Protestant elites than at other times—for example, in the 1970s and in recent years as opposed to the early 1980s. But although it has not satisfied those who want far more attention given to the green cause, change over the past twenty-five years has been real.

Thus, while there has been a sharp rise in the amount of attention given to environmental education at Protestant colleges, critics complain that the effort does not begin to match what present exigencies demand. The same applies to Protestant seminaries and theological schools, where, until the late 1980s, there were rarely any courses attending to ecological theology. And, of course, there are distinctions—often profound ones—between manifestos about the environment and serious commitments to encourage change. Still, by the late 1980s there was a significant engagement between established Protestantism and ecological concerns.[1]

There is no neat chronology, nor is there any simple way to illuminate all the steps toward an engagement with the environmental cause that took place between 1970 and 1990 or since. There were, however, several important pioneers. One, for example, was Joseph Sittler, who began the task of alerting fellow Protestants to the need to preserve the environment. His main serious thinking about environmental theology took place in the 1950s and 1960s. A Lutheran and theology professor, Sittler wrote many essays, such as "A Theology for Earth" (1954) and "Ecological Commitment as Theological Responsibility" (1970), that are frequently cited as having been influential on others.[2]

The Faith-Man-Nature Group, which formed in the mid-1960s, represented another band of pioneers. This group operated in association with the National Council of Churches, which provided both the original impetus and subsequent support. It was designed to create a liaison between religious thinkers and scientists. Among those connected with the group were H. Paul Santmire, Philip Joranson, Richard Baer Jr. and Frederick Elder, all of whom became prominent in the world of Protestant environmentalism. The group's dissolution in 1974 was something of an indicator of success, for its agenda had spread throughout much of mainline Protestantism.[3]

The association of the early Faith-Man-Nature group with the National Council of Churches, home of religious and political liberalism within Protestantism, was no accident.[4] For much of the past twenty-five years, concern with environmentalism has been notably greater within liberal Protestantism than anywhere else. Leaders and bureaucrats in the National Council of Churches and its many mainline Protestant denominations have been at the forefront in defining and promoting a religious ecological agenda. The National Council of Churches in particular has proceeded in a number of directions. For two decades it has manifested policy interest in ecological matters. As early as the middle 1970s the council had an agenda directed to energy policy and the environment, and it has now broadened its environmental focus, as evidenced in its recent publication *101 Ways to Help Save the Earth*. Along the way, numerous conferences, discussion groups, and subagencies have demonstrated a continuing interest in environmental policy as well as theologies of ecology. The council's Eco-Justice Group has sponsored *The Egg: An Eco-Justice Quarterly*, a publication of the Center for Religion, Ethics, and Social Policy at Cornell University. Among its editors have been William Gibson and Dieter Hessel, workers in the vineyards of Protestant environmentalism. A string of Protestant environmentalist books have also appeared from such mainline presses as Fortress and Abingdon.

The World Council of Churches (with which the National Council has been intimately involved) has also been quite active. Since the late 1970s, the World Council has sponsored a series of projects and conferences under the title Justice, Peace, and the Integrity of Creation (JPIC). In 1990, the JPIC conference held in Seoul, Korea, garnered significant publicity. Each has taken place with the cooperation and encouragement of several organizations, including the National Council of Churches.[5]

There is no doubt that the National Council of Churches, the World Councils of Churches, and particular Protestant denominations—especially mainline denominations—have all had longstanding roles in the environmental cause. So have some individual Protestant churches all over the country. Resolutions in support of ecological concerns show that environmental consciousness has often been on denominational agendas, though at times other evidence has been scant. By now there have been a tremendous number of these resolutions. Some denominations adopt one or more every year they meet. Such resolutions routinely justify their concern in theological terms, of course, but most of their words go to favored policy directions and preferred strategies to implement them. The topic mentioned most often has been energy policy, but among an almost limitless array of others are land use, pollution, world hunger, and general lifestyle challenges.[6]

Every mainline Protestant denomination has taken stands—the Episcopal Church, the United Methodist Church, and all the rest. The Presbyterian Church has been especially busy lately, approving an elaborate statement titled "Restoring Creation for Eco-Justice." Originally drawn up by the Presbyterian Task Force on Eco-Justice, this document deals with current abuses of nature, overpopulation, and general human injustices. It was only the latest effort in a practice that stretches back to 1971, when the 183rd General Assembly of the Presbyterian Church began urging strides toward "environmental renewal."

Similarly, the United Methodist Church's General Conferences have approved a plethora of resolutions on such topics as toxic wastes, sea law, and the general wisdom of environmentalism. Similarly, the more liberal Lutheran denominations, before and after their unification as the Evangelical Lutheran Church, established a considerable record of environmental stands. For example, the American Lutheran Church adopted a statement titled "The Environmental Crisis" at its General Convention in 1970. This four-page, single-spaced document declared the responsibility of Christians as stewards of God's creation, detailed the environmental problems of its time, and made concrete suggestions about how to tackle them. Other statements followed, such as the 1980 General Convention declaration called "Theology of the Land."

Numerous other examples could be cited, especially from among mainline Protestant denominations. The American Baptists have adopted a series of proclamations announcing their commitment to Christian environmentalism. A 1988 "Policy Statement on Ecology" and a 1990 declaration titled "Individual Lifestyle for Ecological Responsibility" are typical. They speak in familiar terms of the ecological crises in our age and the theological and practical duties that they hold Christians should follow.

The Church of Christian Science has long taken a vigorous public stance in this area, and so has the Society of Friends. By now almost all major Protestant denominations have spoken out, including the largest, the distinctly nonliberal Southern Baptist Convention. Though in recent years internal strife has captured its attention, the SBC's Christian Life Commission witnessed in the environmental area at least as early as 1977, when it published "The Energy Crisis and the Churches."[7]

A number of mainline Protestant presses have published books that proclaim the gospel of Christian environmentalism. This practice is illustrated by the recent publication of James A. Nash's *Loving Nature: Ecological Integrity and Christian Responsibility* by Abingdon and Dieter Hessel's *After Nature's Revolt: Eco-Justice and Theology* by Fortress.[8]

Some denominations have had in operation for some time now, often twenty years, departments or subdivisions that try to go beyond statements of concern or commitment. This is true, for example, in the Evangelical Lutheran Church, the United Methodist Church, and the Episcopal Church. Sometimes these agencies have done tangible work, while at other times they have existed mostly on paper. Some are primarily educational; others emphasize legislative lobbying.

Many denominations have also sponsored retreats on environmental issues and developed materials on Christianity and ecology for camps and other gatherings. The Presbyterian and Methodist churches have been leaders in this area. For example, the Department of Environmental Justice and Survival within the United Methodist Church has prepared videos, such as "For Our Children," that give quite detailed advice on how Methodists can make a political impact regarding environmental issues. Another such video, "Creation's Caretakers," constructs a theological argument for eco-justice in rural America. Some institutional infrastructure is in place, especially in mainline Protestant denominations, providing a range of settings and materials for those who want to wrestle with the theological issues of the environment and for those who are ready to act.[9]

Other Protestant groups besides those associated with liberal Protestantism are also awakening to the environment as a Christian issue. The change is best symbolized in the new attention given to environmentalism within the pages of the evangelical magazine *Christianity Today*. While the liberal Protestant magazine *Christian Century* has discussed the environment and Christian responsibility many times over the past twenty-five years, *Christianity Today* has moved much more slowly. In the 1970s there was virtually no mention of environmental issues at all in *Christianity Today*, and later the environment was discussed only with real ambivalence. Today things have changed: *Christianity Today* has joined the environmental cause, or what it judges to be the Christian environmental cause.

In the last several years, William Eerdmans, a major evangelical publishing house, has begun to publish books on Christian ecology, complete with vigorous advertising campaigns in such liberal Protestant publications as *Christian Century*. The contrast here with Zondervan, which publishes more conservative evangelical wares and has done much less on green Christian topics, illustrates the continuing ambivalence about environmentalism among conservative Protestants.

The movement of evangelicalism as a whole, however, and *Christianity Today* in particular, is real. It exemplifies the most significant current trend within organized Protestant environmentalism: the emergence of vigorous evangelical support for the ecological movement. The Protestant environmental cause today is no longer solely a child of mainline Protestantism. It increasingly draws on energy also generated from within the evangelical world.

Some expressions of this development are recent, and no one can be sure of their eventual significance. This is also true of the efforts of several people—various liberal Protestant leaders, a few scientists, and Ron Sider and others long associated with Evangelicals for Social Action—who over the past several years have tried to come together to tackle environmental issues. Whatever its fate in the long run, this endeavor became a public sign of some evangelicals' desire to share the ecological gospel with the larger community.[10]

Another expression of the rise of green evangelicalism is the Au Sable Institute, headquartered in Mancelona, Michigan. Its educational programs, which stress environmental science and Christian faith, have already touched many people. The institute has an especially active relationship with the evangelical Christian College Coalition. Under the leadership of evangelical Calvin DeWitt, a professor of environmental studies, this basically evangelical institute (though its governing board and its participants are not all evangelicals) has played a major role in legitimizing an ecological Christianity within evangelical circles.

Also relevant is the North American Conference on Christianity and Ecology (NACCE). When it was established in 1987, NACCE was something of an offshoot of the evangelical Au Sable Institute. As an umbrella group for a number of Christians committed to caring for the earth, it has represented a potentially important organizational vehicle for Christian ecology. The conference has welcomed all who call themselves Christians to its ranks, but it has been largely a Protestant group, one where both evangelical environmentalists and more theologically liberal Protestants have interrelated.

The NACCE's first conference, which took place in North Webster, Indiana, in 1987, generated a good deal of publicity in Christian periodicals. There were disagreements between evangelicals and other Protestants (often those attracted to "creation" theology, which is discussed in chapter 8). Perspectives varied, but what resulted was a series of conferences in which evangelical and other Christian environmentalists met, talked, and argued with and learned from each other. The conferences also brought about the creation of a journal, *Firmament: The Journal of Christian Ecology*, which reflects NACCE's policy in its interdenominational and inclusive essays and authors.[11]

While NACCE's orientation stymied those who want unambiguous theological direction or strong consensus on paths of action, its very existence has been a sign of growing Protestant sensitivity toward an ecological Christianity. And it also demonstrated evangelical involvement in environmentalism.

As this book unfolds, it will consider at some length how the green movement within Protestantism compares with the civil rights movement within Protestantism in the 1960s. Undoubtedly, one area that is distinctly different is the growing strength of environmentalism in evangelical circles. For several reasons, the best of which was opposition to churches' being involved in politics, there was much less evangelical Protestant involvement in the civil rights crusade. The green movement seems to be proceeding more gradually, with more and broader local support and with much more effort to provide a solid theological grounding than did the Protestant civil rights involvement. In these ways, the green movement in Protestantism may prove more enduring than did the civil rights movement, which had a moment of intensity in the middle 1960s and then faded.[12]

The Setting

Two crucial background factors help in understanding the greening of official Protestantism and the directions it has taken. First, the greening has occurred within a climate of suspicion created by both secular and religious environmentalist critics of Protestantism—indeed, critics of all Christianity. To them, the painful truth is that Christianity has been more a cause of ecological problems than an ally in resolving them. The second factor is the overwhelming sense of ecological crisis that permeates Protestant environmentalism. Both of these factors have powerfully influenced the orientation of contemporary Protestant ecological thought. One illuminates its evident tone of defensiveness; the other explains its drive toward swift and sweeping action. Also, both underline eco-Protestantism's close connections with the larger movement.

Tim Cooper accurately observes that in the United States "Christians in the Green movement often appear to be on the defensive, faced with accusations that Christianity is at least significantly to blame for the present crisis, if not its main source."[13] Indeed, there is no way to comprehend the Protestant discussion of environmentalism without an appreciation of this defensiveness surrounding much of Protestant environmentalism.

More than a few critics outside the ranks of Protestantism insist that Christianity is, or was historically, somehow different than—and alien to—the ecological cause. Ian McHarg and Roderick Nash typify this attitude. McHarg accuses Christianity of promoting attitudes of "dominion and subjugation" toward nature, and Nash argues that Christianity has held innumerable false beliefs hostile to nature, such as the idea that wilderness is "a cursed land, the antipode of paradise."[14]

Similar charges emanate from within the house of the Protestant faithful. The most famous came from Lynn White in his classic 1967 *Science* article, which declared that Christianity had a great deal to answer for to friends of the earth. White argued, for example, that Christianity had long upheld a tragic dualism between humanity and the rest of nature that was disastrous for both. And when Christianity did not actively put nature down, its obsessive anthropocentrism caused it to ignore nature's existence. "Christianity is the most anthropocentric religion the world has seen," White claimed.[15]

White's complaints shaped a good deal of the discussion within Christian environmentalism from 1970 on. Some rallied to his point of view, while others dissented. Either way, though, his judgments have remained distinctly audible. Along with others who are sharply critical of the Christian witness on the environment, White's perspective has been both a challenge to the greening of Protestantism and a powerful stimulant spurring it on.[16]

The sense of crisis that permeates Protestant environmentalism is the second factor in the general setting that has strongly influenced Protestant ecological thought. In the past twenty-five years, Protestant writings about the earth have had that sense of crisis—and maybe that alone—in common. Marching in step with the secular ecological movement, they endlessly proclaim that the environment is in terrible crisis. With few exceptions, this perception is the foundation for Protestant engagement with the environment.

The announcement of crisis has come from many parts of the Protestant religious community, whether in statements by the Presbyterian Church or arguments by process theologians such as John B. Cobb Jr.[17] The language is often dramatic, driven by the conviction that a response is urgent. It reminds the reader of the pronouncements of Old Testament prophets. Thus we read of the "monstrous ecological crisis," learn that planet Earth is "on the verge of a breakdown," and hear about the "slaughter of the planet earth."[18] More than a few Protestant environmentalists feel "agitated, angered" and "guilty" and suggest that everyone else should feel that way too.[19]

At the same time, there is rarely much indulgence in pessimism. Protestant ecological language can wax apocalyptic, but it rarely gives way to depression or even serious despair. Hope is more common and stands more as an expression of religious faith than as anything else. The hope rests on the assurance that though "we deserve God's condemnation, . . . God acts with justice and mercy to redeem creation."[20] In this view and on other topics in green Protestantism, Jurgen Moltmann's theology has been influential, and his *Theology of Hope* is widely cited.[21]

Hope is also grounded in assumptions about humans and human action—above all, the assumption that people can make a difference for good. Though it may deserve to be, humanity need not be doomed if it decides to act. Environmental Protestantism hardly has a sanguine or cheerful outlook, but many of its advocates are convinced that Christian servants, if they listen to God, can win the battle for the earth.

The nature and contour of the ecological crisis, however, are often not entirely clear. The crisis is so self-evident among environmentally minded Protestants that analytic discussion about it is too rare. What often substitutes for such an analysis is a string of illustrations of the crisis. Pollution, toxic waste, energy problems, nuclear dangers, diminishing resources, and population growth are familiar entries.[22] Equally familiar is the usual secular tone of reflections on the crisis, whether the topic is the environmental situation in general, its meaning for our culture, its demonstration of human error, or the uncertain prospects of the twenty-first century.[23]

Yet many Protestant theorists, of course, have much more to say on this issue. For them, the crisis is in good part a religious crisis: "the ultimate basis of our ecological difficulties" is "in our spirituality itself."[24] The deterioration of the earth becomes for them a story about the death of God's creation and about human failure to live by and for God. From such a perspective, the ecological situation is not only about pollution or the other recognizable items on the crisis lists. It is about "caring for God's Creation."[25]

Thus, the crisis is considerably more complex than it may first seem, and hardly a crisis in the same terms as it is to the larger environmental movement. The crisis of earth is a crisis of creation and of humans as servants of God and God's creation. This is the core of green Protestantism as distinguished from the conventional analysis of ecological problems. It is what makes Protestant thought about the environment specifically religious. Overall, Protestant environmentalism speaks of today's ecological situation in both secular and religious terms. What that means, and what the balance is between these two languages, constitutes a significant part of the story this book tells.

Limits to Crisis

Yet by no means have Protestants always rallied to the environmental crusade. Over the past twenty-five years some Protestant periodicals have indeed given a mixed message about the ecological crisis. In some years, such as the early 1970s and the late 1980s and thereafter, publications such as *Christian Century* and some mainline Protestant denominational journals made environmental issues a significant part of their agenda. But there have been leaner years too, years when the environmental crisis almost disappeared in Protestant periodicals.

Within the capacious house of Protestantism there are also places where the seriousness or even the existence of an ecological crisis has encountered challenge. For a long time, the evangelical *Christianity Today* represented a soft expression of this outlook. It argued that the glass was half full rather than half empty; there was a crisis, but there was also environmental progress that measurably reduced the crisis. Popular ecological consciousness had spread, car emissions were way down, and other good things were happening that rarely got the attention they merited. As we already noted, however, things have changed at *Christianity Today*: it has taken a sharp, if not uncritical, turn toward an ecologically minded Protestantism.[26]

Both relative neglect and relative denial have flourished within Protestant fundamentalism. This is true not only among those who speak the language of end times but also among others, including "theonomic reconstructionists," those who advocate following God's biblical laws in modern life as much as possible. One of the most vexing problems that green Protestants confront today is, in fact, a lack of solidarity. Here as in so many other areas, Protestant fundamentalists do not drift with the flow and do not intend to do so. Their story will be told in chapter 4.[27]

From another direction, far from fundamentalism, others have cast doubt on Protestant orthodoxies about the ecological situation in the modern era. Writers within this skeptical perspective have declared that "no crisis is self-evident" and that it is sad how many have rushed to announce a terrible crisis without first asking searching questions. Instead of performing probing analyses, they argue, Protestants have too often chosen to develop an "eco-scare kit."[28]

Yet the significance of such dissents from the overall Protestant intellectual consensus should not be exaggerated. After all, the critics' numbers are small, and their group is not growing. They garner little sympathy among lay or activist Protestants. The movement is almost entirely in the opposite direction. The assumption of ecological crisis is absolutely integral in modern Protestant environmentalism, and its impact has been vast.

The Supportive Public

We know too little about the realm of individual Protestants and local churches—the substantive texture of Protestantism as it exists day to day. As a result, we do not know how much Protestant environmentalism has gone from theory to practice on the local level. We know more about the attitudes of the U.S. public in general—and Protestants in particular—regarding the environment.

From one angle, the greening of official Protestantism proceeds within the context of a highly supportive public. Protestant environmentalism is no lonely cause that attracts only the alienated or deals with a repeatedly negative public reception. To be sure, such a positive setting can disguise the reality that theory and practice often conflict. It can also direct one away from the fascinating and perhaps costly disagreements among Protestants who share an environmentalist Christianity. But at least there is little doubt that public opinion, Protestant and otherwise, shares ecological concerns and also supports government legislation to encourage protection of the environment. In this instance, Protestant elites are in touch with both the general public and their own laity.

Over the past several years there have been a number of studies of public opinion regarding the environment. As is always the case, these studies use diverse questions and often have contrasting purposes. They also employ various methodologies. Sometimes they are comparative and sometimes they deal only with the U.S. publics. Some seek to gain knowledge about the full range of the American population, others of particular groups, such as Protestant religious activists or African Americans. While they are rarely neatly comparable, they do not need to be to illuminate the basic situation. Together these studies show there is general support for environmentalism, a finding that is nowhere in dispute.[29]

A glance at a few especially interesting studies gives color to the picture. Consider the famous and rather complex *Times-Mirror Study of the American Electorate* of the late 1980s. It found popular approval of increased spending for environmental improvement across its dozen or so categories of citizens (with one exception) and at roughly the same rate among almost all of them. The greatest approval came, perhaps predictably, among those the study described as "1960s Democrats"—voters whose sensibilities were fashioned in the 1960s, when the ecological movement first began stirring. The one exception was among those citizens the study called "Entrepreneurs." Close to half of them endorsed increased spending for environmental matters, but more did not.

The *Times-Mirror* study acknowledged that there was some resistance to more governmental spending on environmental needs, due mostly to a fear that government costs for ecological renewal might be prohibitive, not to disregard for the environment. There was more resistance to environmental regulations when they were perceived to impede economic growth, but a majority of U.S. citizens rejected relaxing regulations in this instance also. The "1960s Democrats" were the least willing to relax environmental standards, while the "passive poor"—those in the most desperate economic shape—produced a modest majority prepared to move toward relaxing regulations.[30]

Adolf Gundersen's impressive study of citizens and the environment leads to similar conclusions about public attitudes. Gundersen argues that the data show that people are fairly consistent on environmental issues, though it would be a mistake to assume that the origins of this agreement are simple. His reading of the data also suggests that the American public has been gradually growing more sympathetic to serious environmental action. Yet Gundersen also recognizes public ambivalence, especially citizen disquiet over a too-powerful government and consequent reluctance to leap to radical new actions.[31]

Diverse articles and research reports have established that there are some variations within the population. Youth, for example, lead the way in support of environmental values and action. While this finding is not surprising, others are distinctly more controversial: for example, some data indicate that women are more ecologically sensitive than the general population and that African Americans are less so. Studies have also long noted the relevant class dynamics. There is a positive association between environmental activists and a middle-class background, though within the broader public, class standing and attitudes toward the environment are generally not correlated. Caution is in order here; no hard and fast generalizations connecting environmental attitudes to class can be made. Even the correlation between middle-class backgrounds and environmental activism is less strong than it may seem. The same class picture exists among activists in almost all political causes.[32]

For this study, of course, environmental views of Protestants in particular (white Protestants, in most studies) are of special interest (though, after all, more than half the general public identifies itself as Protestant). Their attitudes are clear. Self-identified Protestants claim to be distinctly proenvironment, and they often self-consciously identify with a "stewardship" outlook, believing they are called to look after God's creation. Specifically, studies confirm that there is overwhelming Protestant support for present or increased government expenditures for upgrading the environment. There is no significant deviation from this finding among members of any major Protestant denomination.[33]

Laura Olson's research on these attitudes as expressed in recent National Election Study data confirms others' findings. Olson found that the majority of self-declared Protestants were prepared to authorize increased spending for the environment and were in favor of strong government enforcement of environmental standards. When Olson probed more deeply and divided Protestants by denomination within the limitations of NES data, she discovered some variations among Protestants. Those identifying with mainline Protestant denominations (Presbyterians, United Church of Christ members, and Episcopalians) favored the most increased spending, while those associated with denominations with a large number of both religious liberals and conservatives (the United Methodist and Evangelical Lutheran churches) were somewhat less enthusiastic. The least enthusiastic group comprised Protestants in identifiably fundamentalist and evangelical denominations and all of the Baptists, though this group too gave majority approval to increasing expenditures. Olson's analysis suggests that the shift by evangelicalism's leaders toward more ecologically sensitive positions finds both an echo and some dissent among the laity.[34]

Others have reported data that notes this division within Protestantism, one that is best described as a matter of degree within a generally proenvironment group. The best guide to the contours of the division appears to be knowing how much a given Protestant believes the Bible is absolutely true. The more "fundamentalist" Protestants are in this sense, independent of other variables, the lower they will be, relatively, on assorted indices of environmentalism.[35]

By far the best and most up-to-date study is by James Guth and associates.[36] This research reports and assesses contemporary scholarship on public attitudes toward environmentalism and concludes that among clergy and informed laity, "evangelical self-identification is strongly associated with less support for the environment."[37] Moreover, in general the term "doctrinal conservatism" is consistently connected with relative coolness toward environmentalism. They also report, however, that data on mainline Protestants is not as full as it might be, while on the whole, "those who do not share the Judeo-Christian religious tradition—the Seculars—in fact are the most pro-environment."[38]

Some important questions about the relationship between Protestants and the environment cry out for more study. We need to know what

Protestant opinion on the environment is in more detail, more depth, and over time; to explore the differences among Protestants in more detail; to see whether people translate general attitudes to specific policies; to examine what the implications are for Protestants when environmental goals clash with other popular goals; and to ask whether Protestantism as a religion has actually affected Protestants' environmentalism or vice versa. And these questions are only a start. Nonetheless, we know at this point that most of the laity and much of institutional Protestantism hold general proenvironmentalist attitudes, while the largest dissent can be found among fundamentalists.

There has been too little systematic survey information available on "activist Protestants," defined as those likely to belong to Christian action organizations. One recent study, however, has taken us a long way toward greater knowledge in this arena. John Green, Jim Guth, Lyman Kellstedt, and Corwin Smidt studied five thousand religious activists (overwhelmingly Protestants) who were involved in one or more of the following groups: Bread for the World, Concerned Women for America, Focus on the Family, JustLife, National Association of Evangelicals, Pat Robertson's PAC, and Prison Fellowship.

The list contains some diversity, but most of the organizations appeal to both theologically and politically conservative Protestant activists. In fact, the majority of respondents identified themselves as Republicans. Yet when asked if they would be willing to pay more or even sacrifice jobs for increased environmental protection, the majority said they would, and less than 20 percent said they would not. Those who did not rank environmental concerns as a major national problem or did not have liberal attitudes on the issue once again tended to be religious fundamentalists.

In general, it was impossible to distinguish among these activists in terms of their attitudes regarding the environment on the basis of their degree of religiosity.[39] This finding parallels a similar broad consensus among activist Protestants and ordinary Protestants on the environment. This consensus within Protestantism is extensive and crosses most other distinctions among Protestants. This is why concern with green Protestantism has been quite unlike some other agendas of mainline Protestant leaders. It is not at all an elite-only phenomenon, though of course the complex and diverse articulations of environmentalism that this book considers are hardly the products of the typical Protestant.[40]

The greening of Protestantism has moved rapidly in the past twenty years. Consensus is broad. Most of institutional Protestantism has rallied to the cause; public opinion, among Protestants as in the society at large, is also sympathetic. There has been significant movement toward environmentalism among evangelicals, though fundamentalism remains an arena in which there is much less enthusiasm.

This book now turns to the substance of the greening of Protestant thought, especially its intellectual history from 1970 to 1990. This account begins where it must—with the fascinating and important struggle within Protestantism over what the Bible, its classic source of truth, teaches about the environment. Now as in the past, most roads in Protestantism lead back to the Bible.

THE BIBLE AS (CONTESTED) FOUNDATION

For almost all Protestants, the Bible is crucial in the debate over the environment within Protestantism. It is the one road that must be traveled, the starting point (if not always the ending point) for addressing creation and the environment. This is especially true among evangelicals and fundamentalists who speak from traditions that determinedly assert that the Bible in all its dimensions is, or is very close to, the literal word of God. But more theologically liberal Protestants also affirm that the Bible was inspired by God and invoke it in considering the environment. While some judge it only modestly useful in discerning the proper intersection between religion and the environment, others give it more weight. Few ignore it altogether.

As a result, no serious discussion of the greening of Protestant thought over the past several decades can ignore the diverse and sometimes clashing Protestant views about the ecological teachings of the Bible. The issue here is not whether the Bible is the inerrant truth of God but what the Bible teaches about the relationship between God, humans, and the earth. It is also about what the faithful should make of what the Bible enjoins.

The arguments proceed on two levels. What is the substance of the environmental teaching in the Bible? And how fertile is the Bible for constructing an environmental Christianity? This chapter and the next explore the several arguments on these questions, the two main issues that ricochet throughout writing by environmentalist Protestants on the Bible. They reveal the outer walls and the inner workings of Protestant thought on the environment.

Attention to the Bible is, of course, not unique to Protestant Christianity, nor are arguments about the significance of any particular section of the Bible. The Orthodox and Roman Catholic churches have their own ancient traditions of biblical interpretation and its attendant controversy. Nevertheless, the Bible continues to play an enormous role in Protestant thinking—regarding creation and much else. After all, Protestantism was born with the belief the Bible reveals God's truth, and modern Protestant thought on the environment continues to take the Bible very seriously.

Scholarly Perspectives and Secular Criticisms

There was a considerable scholarly argument on the topic of the Bible and the environment during the 1970s and 1980s, and this background is important because it lies behind much of the Protestant debate and has introduced many of the contested themes. Some of the most influential scholars have been Protestants, some have not been. For some, the Bible's ecological perspective is good; for others, it is disappointing.[1] But while there has been no consensus in the scholarly debate, the overall tone is critical. Many scholars portray the Bible's discussion of the Fall as a sign of God's ultimate displeasure with nature—including contempt for the whole natural world, not just humans (Romans 5:12–14). Some insist that the Bible does not see nature as sacred and are impatient with theologians who seem to obfuscate this truth and try to have it another way. Scholars point out that the Old Testament (for example, in Deuteronomy 4:16–19 or Jeremiah 2:20–23 and 3:13) repeatedly repudiates nature worship. Nature is never sacralized; only God sustains life and deserves worship; and the distinction between nature and God is absolute. By this view, the Old Testament leaves nature inferior to humans and sometimes unprotected from them.[2]

Clarence J. Glacken's classic work *Traces on the Rhodian Shore* argues that while nature in the Christian scriptures is an expression of God, the divine far transcends nature in the Bible and can in no sense be conflated with it. He reads this, for instance, in the teaching of Paul in Romans 1:20 ("Ever since the creation of the world . . . his eternal power . . . has been clearly perceived in the things that have been made") or in Job, where the mystery of nature overwhelms humans but not God.[3]

Hierarchical implications are also unmistakable here. God's rule over humanity as well as over the rest of nature is clear, and any notion of biocentrism is absent. Thus, everything about nature is ultimately God's to decide. (Psalms 29:5–9: "The voice of the Lord breaks the cedars . . . flashes forth flames of fire . . . shakes the wilderness . . . makes the oaks to whirl"). Moreover, the worst destruction of nature in the Bible comes from God (Deuteronomy 29:22: "the afflictions of that land and the sicknesses with which the Lord has made it sick").[4]

Some scholars read the Bible as testifying that the core relationship in the universe is that between people and God. The rest of nature is a secondary feature in the Old Testament and even more so in the New Testament. Other views of the Bible incorporate nature more fully but in a setting where the human being remains set apart as the "controller and modifier" of the environment under God.[5] Still others draw a two-dimensional picture: people are both in nature and, at the same time, separated from it as ethical and historical creatures.[6]

There is sometimes a recognition that the Bible occasionally depicts nature dominating human beings, though at God's command. Isaiah 34:17 presents God putting the rest of nature's creatures in the place of the faithless human. God "has cast the lot for them . . . they shall possess it for ever, from generation to generation they shall dwell in it." And there is almost no support for the idea that the Bible says nature exists for humans alone. Job 38:39 is cited as evidence that nature outside of man has considerable independent status. There God ridicules the human role in creation and in the functioning of nature: "Can you hunt the prey for the lion, or satisfy the appetite of the young lions . . . ?"

In the scholarly debate over animal rights, some interpreters of the Bible have seen that text as friendly toward other species. In this light, the Old Testament becomes something of a guidebook for a caring animal husbandry, while people, as John Passmore argues, are creatures that God restricts to protect other animals. Other interpreters are less sanguine, identifying the New Testament, for example, as a deeply anthropocentric place where there is scant sympathy for "the value of other living things."[7]

There is also much scholarly disagreement over the relationship of God to creation. Whatever the internal hierarchies present in the Bible, the question of how God views all living things is vital. It matters because it determines whether the biblical perspective envisions life as holistic and integrative, as most environmentalism currently does. Some scholars declare that the Bible portrays a God who loves all nature and that this truth was demonstrated in creation, reaffirmed after the Flood (Genesis 9:8–17), and reiterated later (Isaiah 11:6–9: "The wolf shall dwell with the lamb, and the leopard shall lie down with the kid"). Others point to New Testament Gospels such as Luke 12:6: "Are not five sparrows sold for two pennies? And not one of them forgotten before God." But in some readings such a passage in fact legitimizes treating nonhumans as mere commodities.[8]

In short, scholars present decidedly mixed reviews on what the Bible says about the environment. The best analysts do not come down rigidly on one side or another but recognize that the Bible is a tremendously complex work, authored over centuries. Its parts must be distinguished, its textured witness acknowledged, and its multitude of historical settings considered. It is a story of a people called both to resist Canaanite nature gods and to honor themselves and all of the universe as God's creation.[9]

If such scholarly reflections lie in the background, secular environmentalists' attacks on the Bible over the last twenty-five years have filled the foreground. These critics place the Bible in a storm center of controversy, portraying it as an abundant but unfortunate source of the antiecological notions in Western history. Roderick Nash, for example, is unsparing in identifying many passages in the Bible that to him confirm its pernicious antiecological doctrines.

Specifically, Nash and others of a similar mind read Genesis 1:28 ("have dominion over the fish of the sea, over the birds of the air, and over every living thing") as, at best, a justification of human governance over nature and, at worst, a license for humans to crush nature. How to read Genesis 1:28 is an important issue here. For Nash, talk of stewardship in this context rings hollow. Others agree and are indignant at the Bible's injunction to be fruitful and multiply (Genesis 1:28). That sort of advice, they complain, is exactly what human beings have followed with disastrous consequences. They urge that such dogmas be repudiated.[10]

On the whole, however, Christian views of the Bible differ from critics in the larger green movement. Wendell Berry's analysis is probably closest to the general view. Berry is bothered by the anti-Christian bias of much of the environmental movement and argues that the Bible has a good deal to inspire and sustain environmentalists. He grants that Christian practice has often been lamentable and worse, but he maintains that this fact is a commentary on Christians, not on the Bible.[11]

Liberal Protestantism

There is a vigorous and growing realm of evangelical environmentalism, and from a different direction, there is tremendous interest in this subject in fundamentalist literature, especially end times literature. Nonetheless, most of those who have attempted to define a Protestant ecological view— and have engaged the Bible in that quest—have been or are theological liberals from the mainline Protestant world. They have produced more books, theses, and arguments than any other branch of Protestantism.

The only indisputable point about liberal Protestant students of the Bible is that they have a lot to say about Scripture in relation to the environment. There is definitely no single, or perhaps even mainstream, interpretation of the Bible among the host of liberal Protestant scholars, theologians, and activists. Interpretive diversity, not to say anarchy, is the reality, and this should be a warning about simplistic assumptions regarding the meaning of such words as "liberal."

Of course, liberal Protestant theorists who bring the Bible to bear on their consideration of Christianity and ecology do so in an interpretive framework that is different from that of more fundamentalist Protestants. They do not assume that the Bible is the literal word of God or that it says all that need be said on a subject. In fact, these theologians take it for granted that one should read the Bible in light of biblical history, assorted modern or postmodern hermeneutics, and the impact of changing times and worlds.

For example, many liberal interpreters understand that reason and empirical evidence, however limited they are in a postmodern world, must play a role in assessing biblical ethical claims. A common assumption is that biblical statements on such matters must be placed in historical context, subjected to the inevitable interpretation, and tested in our time and place by our empirical understandings. What is not acceptable to such theologians, of course, are claims about the Bible's teachings on the environment derived from specific passages assumed to be self-evident in meaning. For them, there are no such passages because there is no such Bible.

The reader of such Protestant discussions, nevertheless, will be impressed by the widespread determination to take the Bible seriously. It is not abandoned by liberal Protestantism; it is not conceded to other Protestants; and there are few who argue that it does not speak to ecological concerns of the late twentieth century. As one Presbyterian document states, many innovative theologies of our age are relevant, but so is the Bible, which still has much to contribute toward comprehending nature, mankind, and God. Many major works by liberal Protestants about creation or the environment are, in fact, virtual Bible studies: citations and arguments on Scripture are frequent. Even in less biblically centered studies, there are many instances when particular biblical passages orient the discourse. Either way, the Bible is an essential liberal Protestant anchor.[12]

On the Old Testament

Most of the Scripture writings that attract the attention of liberal Protestants who address the environment come from the Old Testament, since it contains almost all of the Bible's references to nature and animals and their interrelationships with humans. Genesis provides the most significant passages. Many discussions include the now-familiar argument that Genesis has two different creation stories. There are a number of versions of where each story begins and ends, but it is common to identify one account principally in Genesis 1 and the other in Genesis 2. Genesis 2 is usually treated as the more fundamental, in part because it may be older.

The account in Genesis 2 is also a good deal more palatable to many liberal theologians, especially Genesis 2:15 ("The Lord God took the man and put him in the garden of Eden to till it and keep it" [RSV] or "work it and take care of it" [NRV]). It is frequently cited as the best guide, one that furnishes a biblical basis for human stewardship of nature, the concept at the heart of Protestant biblical ecology. Genesis 2 is also well regarded because it treats humanity as just one part of the whole of nature. There is not much stress on the centrality of the human being and no suggestion that we are called to "subdue" the earth and use it for whatever may be our human purposes. Sometimes a specific contrast is made with Genesis 1:28: "fill the earth and subdue it; and have dominion . . . over every living thing that moves upon the earth."

Many Protestant biblical scholars, however, do not understand the word "dominion" to mean "domination." This is a significant area of controversy with many secular environmentalist thinkers, who assume that Genesis 1:28 is about the hierarchy and anthropomorphism that they find repulsive. But Protestant commentators usually read the word "dominion" in a number of other ways. For example, some mainline and evangelical scholars perceive the word to suggest service, servanthood, and caring as modeled by Christ. These understandings, of course, have very different implications for the meaning of dominion.[13]

Yet liberal Protestant interpreters do not contend that Genesis 2 stands alone. Some argue that the Old Testament as a whole is replete with references to human responsibility for nature. Many passages establish that nature is God's province (e.g., Psalms 24:1); that humans have great duty to nature within that understanding, even the duty of naming the animals and birds (Genesis 2:19–20); and that we must never shirk this responsibility (Isaiah 11; Genesis 9:2).[14]

This view, though, competes with others. There is no consensus on the Bible's teachings in the Old Testament. The controversial status of human responsibility toward animals is a good example. So is the degree to which liberal Protestants assess the Old Testament as dangerously anthropocentric.[15] Commentators who incline to an anthropocentric view of the Old

Testament teachings often accent Genesis 1 and its emphasis on human rule of nature and conclude that not much can be gleaned from the Old Testament for the ecological cause. On the other hand, those who read the Old Testament to accent the theme of humans as servants in God's creation are much happier with what the Old Testament offers.

Of late there has also been a good deal of attention given to the notion that the Old Testament teaches that God loves nature and accords it great worth *independently and on its own.* This perspective links Protestant theologians with secular "deep ecologists," almost—but not quite—bringing some Protestant thinkers to deep ecology's belief that the ground of all ethics must be the sovereign, intrinsic worth of nature. Thus Protestant patrons of this interpretation insist that nature, apart from humankind, has not only an independent significance but also its own unique and important history. Implicit, and sometimes explicit, is the companion point: that humans are hardly the heart of God's creation or even integral to much of it.

Some cite as the relevant example the Bible's treatment of the land, which, after all, is basic to the Old Testament and to the history of the ancient Jewish people. It is not unusual to encounter the argument that God's covenant was with the physical land as well as the people of ancient Israel or that God intended to liberate the land as well as human beings. Psalm 107:35 states, "He turns a desert into pools of water, a parched land into springs of water." It is standard to invoke the Bible's support of stewardship of the land, and in that context Protestant environmentalists frequently declare that the land is God's and no one else's.[16]

Some stretch further, suggesting that the Bible and particularly the Old Testament cast all nature as equal to human beings. Or they argue, alternatively, that the Old Testament affirms nature through its ardent disapproval of humans' wanton destruction of creation.[17] These sorts of points illustrate again the broader case, that creation is hardly just the story of humankind and God.

Some commentators note that God's happiness in the fullness of creation is manifest in the Bible, as in Genesis 1:12 ("And God saw that it was good") and Genesis 1:31 ("And God saw everything that he had made, and behold, it was very good"). For them, these passages reveal how much God loves nature and joyously testify to the goodness, the wonder, and the beauty of nonhuman creation in and of itself, quite apart from human responsibility for nature. These interpreters cite the portrayal of nature in Job (38–39), the Psalms (e.g., 104, 40:5, 107:8), the Song of Solomon,

Leviticus (25:1), or the Noah story in Genesis as Old Testament examples that undergird this claim. Some argue further that the Old Testament shows God's continuing interest and involvement in nature after creation. God never loses interest in or gives up on nature, which has an independent existence apart from human beings.[18]

At the same time, some Protestant theologians argue that recognizing the independence of nature vis-à-vis human beings does not mean that somehow people are apart from nature. They consistently reject such an approach as erroneous dualism, a denial of creation's wholeness. What is indisputable in this perspective is that the Bible abounds with statements on the oneness of nature. Humans, animals, and all things in nature have their own uniqueness, but the standard view emphasizes that they are one in belonging to God's single creation.

Other dualisms that come under attack are those judged to have marred the Christian past. For Protestant critics, the dualism of man and nature or history and nature must disappear. A similar fate should overwhelm the traditional Christian dualism between the body and the spirit. The Bible, the argument goes, respects the wholeness of people, including the earthiness of the human being. People are creatures of and in God's created nature.[19]

Many liberal Protestant environmentalists read the Old Testament as declaring that God will provide redemption and salvation for nonhuman nature as well as for human beings. The prophets, for example, held that "nature in itself is subject to God's redemptive action. It will be remade and reordered to fulfill the divine purpose."[20] The prophets specifically assured God's redemption for animals in a peaceable kingdom where the lion and the lamb will lie down together (Isaiah 11) and announced the promise to bring God's people together with God's land in a place of milk and honey.[21]

Thus the possibilities and directions for an environmental Protestantism derived from the Old Testament are numerous. Protestant theologian and environmentalist Larry Rasmussen has argued that Christianity may deserve real blame for current environmental problems. But its history is a long and complicated one, he points out, and rests on the Bible of the ancient Jews, which contains much that is hopeful for the environmental cause. As he reads it, the Old Testament tells a story of what people assisted by God can do as a community. It is a story of hope, of the possibilities open for free humans to serve God and help free nature and humankind from oppression and mistreatment. It teaches that people are all neighbors, as Jesus reaffirmed in the New Testament. People are neighbors with great responsibility for each other and for the natural world around them, responsibility to promote freedom and justice and merciful healing of the social and the natural world.[22]

The New Testament

Unlike the Old Testament, the New Testament yields only a meager bounty for reflection on nature or on the issues of such great concern to environmentalists. Protestant commentators recognize this fact, though there is sometimes a rather embarrassing failure to face it. This conundrum deserves an explanation, in part because some critics argue that the lack of New Testament discussion means that nature apart from humankind is simply not relevant to the New Testament's presentation of Jesus' divine mission on earth or to God's new creation and new covenant. If true, this would be a major blow for the Protestant eco-agenda.

Two explanations appear. One is historical and considers the specific situation of the authors of the New Testament in the first century after Christ. It notes the obvious reality that the New Testament is much shorter than the Old and composed in a much briefer time, with the expectation that Christ's return and the end of the world were imminent. These factors, the argument goes, led away from a thorough engagement with matters of nature and creation. Thus the New Testament is not a guide to what Jesus believed about the created environment but rather concerns the preoccupations and background of a certain group of early Christians whose concerns and energies lay in other directions.

Another explanation also concedes that the New Testament is no long sourcebook for environmentalism. But its proponents argue that some crucial passages in the New Testament reaffirm the lessons of the Old Testament and are in some cases a striking restatement of the most radical of them. Thus we are repeatedly told that the New Testament speaks of the goodness of God's creation and its existence in God's grace and glory and that the "Old and New Testaments assume a unity of man and nature."[23]

In particular, a number of Protestant theologians assert that the New Testament agrees with the Old Testament that God will bring redemption to all of nature. Thus they claim that the New Testament approves of the "liberation" of nature and indeed promises it. One passage often cited in this regard is Revelation 5:13: "I heard every creature in heaven and on earth . . . saying, 'To him who sits upon the throne and to the Lamb be blessing and honor and glory and might for ever and ever!' "

St. Paul in Romans 8:21 is the key: "the creation itself will be set free from its bondage to decay and obtain the glorious liberty of the children of God." It is easy to understand why this scripture gets so much green Protestant emphasis. It is equally easy to appreciate why those who give it so great a significance invoke it so often, since there is really nothing else like it in the New Testament.[24]

The New Testament is, above all, about Jesus Christ. Thus the role of the environment in Christ's ministry is obviously crucial and can hardly be avoided. But the problem is that the Gospels picture Jesus as making only a few references to nonhuman nature. Moreover, Christ just does not seem to address environmental issues directly, including the broad range of topics explored in the Old Testament. The few references that exist are often problematic. Those cited most often are Luke 12:6–7, where Jesus declares that human beings are far more important to him than a flock of sparrows, and Matthew 6:25–34, where he applies the same ranking to all birds and flowers. About the best that can be said is that such passages are few, and their significance for Christian environmentalism is debatable.

Some thinkers are more assertive in arguing for a Jesus with an important ecological side, replacing the more usual silence. By their light, Jesus emerges as one who delighted in creation, honoring it and caring for it. This image sometimes portrays Christ as the new Creation—that is, as the embodiment of the whole of nature. This Christ self-consciously instantiated the unity of God and nature, humans and God, body and spirit, affirming at some level the oneness of the universe.[25]

Other Liberal Protestant Views

There is no tight theological consensus in the discourse on the Bible and ecology in mainline Protestant journals and books. There is no unanimity on what the Bible teaches—or on how vital its wisdom must be to a modern environmentalist Christian. W. Lee Humphreys has suggested that much of the effort to plumb the Bible for these purposes is not going to work. It is a fruitless search that is bound to come up empty because the historical context of biblical times and our own are just too distant. As Humphreys states, we need to appreciate "how much the world of ancient Israel and of its literary remains is not the world of man in this century."[26]

Moreover, he maintains, we should be honest and concede that many read the Bible and find philosophies and theologies that are not there.

Thus, he concludes that "it is difficult—and perhaps impossible . . . to find a theology of Nature in the Old Testament."[27] For him, the dialectic about nature in the Old Testament makes it a dubious source for straightforward ecological teachings. In the Old Testament, he argues, God is outside the natural order, while the world is unmistakably a testimony to God; similarly, human beings are mostly apart from the natural order, while intimately bound up with it.[28]

Thomas Derr goes in another, more controversial direction in reflecting on those within the Protestant world who try to establish tight links between their environmentalist agenda and the Bible. He has asked what motivates Protestant eco-theologians as they rummage through the Bible. He wonders how much their ecological agenda directs their search for support in the Bible. What drives the debate—God and the authors of the Bible, or the necessities of an agenda eager for biblical legitimacy?[29]

Derr reflects a skeptical wing of green Protestantism that claims to be as committed to the cause as anybody else but has reservations about some of the scriptural claims for Protestant environmentalism. Thus Derr denies that there is a textual basis for assertions that the Bible honors nature as a whole to the same extent that it honors humans. Others share this conclusion, which leads Derr to state that no amount of "selective quoting" of the Bible can make for a third great commandment: Christians are simply not commanded to love nature as they are to love God and their neighbors.[30]

Moreover, Derr and other skeptics do not agree with the standard liberal Protestant environmentalist position that there is scant validity to traditional claims that the Bible provides that mankind should govern the earth. They concede that the Bible is quite anthropocentric and that Genesis and the rest of the Scriptures provide a special leadership role for humans in creation. They insist that this biblical reality cannot be wished away even as they insist that people bear great responsibilities in exercising this God-given role.[31]

It is not obvious who is right, though it is hard to avoid the sense that some liberal Protestant environmentalists try much too hard to discern an ecological Bible. There are congenial passages in the Bible, but they are only part of a complicated and sometimes contradictory whole. Granted, it is important that Christians acknowledge and highlight the Bible's real environmental dimensions. On the other hand, faithfulness to its textured reality may be the most credible and thus beneficial strategy for defending God's creation.

Evangelicals and the Bible

A pronounced and remarkable expansion of evangelical engagement with the environment began in the 1980s. Evidence is everywhere—in books, in the North American Conference on Christianity and Ecology, and definitely in *Christianity Today*, the main periodical of evangelical Christianity. Moreover, much of the evangelical (but not fundamentalist) Protestant considerations on ecology these days are closer than one might predict to those of mainline and liberal Protestantism. Mainline Protestantism was the pioneer, and in coming later evangelical environmentalists have cut few new paths.

In *Christianity Today* Tim Stafford has persuasively argued what we already know: that pluralism abounds within Christianity on environmental issues and on how Christian faith and environmental matters connect. Yet there is no clear fault line between liberal and evangelical Protestantism. Many fewer within the evangelical world have as yet taken up cudgels for environmentalism, but those who have often sound the same themes as theological liberals.[32]

To be sure, there is a distinction, albeit one of degree, between evangelical and liberal Protestant approaches, a distinction that turns around the old battle—how deliberately and faithfully the Bible should be upheld as the literal truth. While the issue rarely comes up in this Protestant literature, green evangelicals continue to pronounce the Bible *the* guide to truth and to cite its texts more often than do many more theologically liberal Protestants. One often encounters a "Scripture index" or its equivalent in evangelical books on the environment. While this feature is useful for serious students of the Bible, it can also underline evangelical authors' conviction that the Bible must be the ultimate authority.[33]

One other modest difference between many liberal and evangelical approaches is that evangelicals often appear to write with the fundamentalists in mind, while more liberal Protestants make no discernable effort to speak to fundamentalists. The result is a gingerliness among some evangelical eco-Protestants, who know they have fundamentalist critics watching to see whether they are simply conforming to the larger, secular environment movement.

Yet most green Protestant thinkers now have reached much the same point. They agree that the faithful Christian must be ecologically aware and often proclaim that the Bible endorses this gospel. An editorial in the evangelical *Christianity Today* expressed this notion in a somewhat extravagant form: "The Bible is not an enemy of the environmental cause, but its greatest asset."[34]

Most evangelical discussion about the Bible and creation focuses on the Old Testament, as we have come to expect. Calvin DeWitt, among others, depends heavily on Genesis and the Psalms (for example, Psalm 194:10–13) to underline the special importance of God as Creator, God's provision for rest and renewal (the seventh day), and our duty to creation as God's servants. Others cite as crucial the Noachic covenant found in Genesis: God's commitment after the Flood to all life and the promise never again to threaten to destroy it before Christ's return. Some recall the many texts where God honors nature, such as God's determination to preserve fruit trees in Deuteronomy or the admiration for wild animals that God expresses in Job. Others assert in familiar terms, as does Loren Wilkinson, that the Bible demonstrates God's affection for nature on its own terms (as in Psalm 104:16–18, Job 38–39).[35]

In evangelical circles as elsewhere in Protestantism, how human beings enter into this picture is contested. There is inherent tension between "identifying with the creation and achieving mastery over it."[36] The position that the Bible teaches that God created the world and its contents for humans continues to have its recommenders, but the concept of stewardship is more popular now within evangelicalism. Some authors contend that the Bible provides room for either perspective.

While even the most ardent evangelical advocates of stewardship do not pretend that Genesis 1:28 ("have dominion . . . over every living thing that moves upon the earth") does not exist, it is common here too to interpret "dominion" to mean servanthood, with Christ as the model servant—"dominion" becomes "service," including service of all nature. Other biblical passages are sometimes offered as reinforcement, such as Ezekiel 34:2–5, where the sheep suffered because the shepherds did not care for the sheep. The message is that the Bible instructs that bad things happen if shepherds are not stewards.[37]

Humans have special responsibilities, since they are made in God's image and called by God to servanthood. Whether people can, with God's aid, overcome the practice of sin at any point short of Christ's return is not always too clear. What is apparent is the continuing appeal of the ideal of a "peaceable kingdom"—where the lion and lamb will lie down together; where nature in all its parts, including the human part, will be united with God as one. At the least this will be the reality for nature in the world to come.[38]

There are moments in these discussions when fundamentalist suspicions of evangelical environmentalists (see chapter 4) obtain reinforcement. This is particularly true of some efforts to promote human identification with nature. In critics' hands, these attempts appear to be indistinguishable from, as well as evidence of, the pernicious, corrupting influence of New Age doctrines. It is a standard fundamentalist contention that "at the heart of the New Age movement is the worship of the planet."[39] There are those, such as Loren Wilkinson, who are acutely aware of the danger here. They share the fear, too, even as they deny that it has corrupted the movement. This is why Wilkinson solemnly warns fellow evangelicals that they "must be careful" that they do not fashion biblical Christianity into worship of the earth.[40]

In these and many other evangelical writings, as in most liberal Protestant writings, the large dependence on the Old Testament scriptures can be awkward. The issue is the New Testament. To be sure, evangelicals insist that it is false to separate the Old and New Testaments, since the New Testament is the fulfillment of the Old and necessarily incorporates the Old Testament's environmental ideals. Moreover, some argue that in any case there are unmistakable signs in the New Testament of God's love for nature. Christ summons his people to love their neighbors, and that must mean serving the entire environment, not just humans.[41]

But most evangelical thinkers understand full well the New Testament's modest teaching on the environment, and they know that this awkward fact must be confronted. After all, for them the New Testament is above all about Jesus Christ, the story of Christ as Lord and Savior as well as Creator. As a result, how the New Testament fits within a green Protestantism gets more extensive discussion in evangelical writings than anywhere else in Protestantism. This focus on the New Testament—and, in part, on Jesus—has grown much stronger in recent years; in fact, it has become the most characteristic theme of evangelical explorations on the Bible and the environment.[42]

Francis Schaeffer, an evangelical pioneer in the cause, proposed some time ago that the New Testament taught that Christ would bring redemption to all nature: "creation itself will be set free from its bondage to decay and obtain the glorious liberty of the children of God" (Romans 8:21). This is now a frequent citation in green Protestant writings, advanced to emphasize God's redemptive love for nature.[43]

Wesley Granberg-Michaelson argues that Christians must conceptualize Christ as a radical who came to make dramatic change. He was by no means solely a spiritual figure concerned about the next life. Granberg-Michaelson's Christ is the Redeemer here and now and expects that Christians will follow his example, act as God's servants, and treat creation lovingly.

Granberg-Michaelson also uses standard biblical fare to remind his readers that Christ redeems all nature and thus secures the Kingdom of God over all things. Granberg-Michaelson cites central New Testament passages Colossians 1:20 ("through him to reconcile to himself all things, whether on earth or in heaven") and John 3:17 ("God sent the Son into the world . . . but that the world might be saved through him") and, again, Romans 8:19–21.[44]

Among the most recent evangelical efforts to wrestle with Christ, the New Testament, and the future of our planet are such Au Sable projects as Calvin DeWitt's *The Environment and the Christian: What Can We Learn from the New Testament?* and the papers presented at Au Sable's 1992 forum. Their theme is Jesus' sweeping redemption of all life and "the vindication of creation."[45] What their impact will be is not yet clear, but they have directed attention to the subject, and they try to speak to those who may have doubts about Christ or the new covenant regarding ecological commitment or conviction.

In some of these presentations, Christ stands for the redemption of the cosmos and the reestablishment of God's power everywhere. Such a faith implies that God is immanent in nature (if also transcendent), a contention that supporters insist finds confirmation in New Testament texts such as Hebrews 1:1–3 ("God . . . has spoken to us by a Son, whom he appointed the heir of all things, through whom also he created the world . . . [and who is] upholding the universe by his word of power") or Colossians 1:16–17 ("in him all things were created. . . . He is before all things, and in him all things hold together"). In this view, Christ reflects the glory of God and bears the very stamp of God's nature.

For evangelical writers, though, the most significant basis for the claim is the Incarnation, God's becoming human. They take Christ's appearance on earth as the supreme example of God's connecting with nature. It demonstrates the creation's goodness even as its reinforces God's commitment to the creation and the perfection of creation. It underlines as well the central importance of Jesus Christ or, in other versions, all three persons of the Trinity. Evangelical arguments claim that the New Testament provides for the Trinity and that this ancient truth cannot be jettisoned in a misunderstood rush to embrace another view of God that some believe would best promote preservation of the earth.[46]

This understanding of Christ does bring Christ, the entirety of nature, and the goal of holy renewal together. But evangelical thinkers such as

Loren Wilkinson endeavor, at the same time, to make sure that no one slips into believing that somehow we are all Christs. Evangelicals have no intention of aligning themselves with radical creation theology (see chapter 7). For them, the distinctions between human beings and God cannot and do not disappear in some mystical union. The earth is not Gaia, a divine goddess, nor is it God in any other way. The environmentalist Christ redeems and honors all of nature, just as he died for it, but that does not make nature divine or like Christ. The "transcendent God remains distinct, yet hardly aloof."[47] God is transcendent just as God is immanent, in the person of Jesus Christ.[48]

Vernon Visick has formulated a quite stimulating defense of Christ as environmentalist. To Visick, because Jesus was a Jew he was necessarily quite ecologically conscious in his outlook. Visick underlines in particular the Jewish tradition's respect for animals, its restrictions on their use and abuse, and its deep connection with the land. God's creation was not to be treated casually or cruelly. Visick argues, moreover, that Jesus followed in that path in caring about alleviating suffering in living creatures and resolutely opposing the destruction of life.

In addition, Visick argues, Jesus pursued his environmental goals in what Visick considers an admirable fashion. Visick's Jesus willingly met problems within a frankly political framework that got results. Jesus was not a dreamy theorist but a hardworking, committed, and practical person who undertook change. Visick believes that modern Christian environmentalists should follow this model. After all, Jesus created a movement of change that was practical enough to frighten the powers in his world and that, after his crucifixion, led to an even larger movement—one that transformed the world.[49]

From one perspective, the confident and increasingly widespread Protestant proclamation of the Bible as a foundation for environmentalism may leave one feeling a little dry after a time. There is a growing consensus that the Bible offers some grounds for a Christian environmentalism, but it does not point anywhere very specific. After the multitude of biblical passages have been cited and debated and the contrasting images of biblical authority receive their due reflection, one may well ask about the specific policy implications of it all.

Policy implications and proposals of green Protestants are addressed specifically in chapters 9 and 10, but here we should note that green Protestants do little "proof texting" for policy stances. That is, eco-Protestants are, as we will see, involved in policy formulation, strategies for change, and even global reform, but they rarely proceed by claiming that the Bible provides specific passages that give direct and simple policy instructions. Few are so naive. They see the Bible as a guide, or the guide, to God's will and to the principles of a godly ecology, but not as a policy handbook.

The Protestant movement toward interpreting the Bible as a legitimator of environmentalism is a step of historic importance for both Protestantism and environmentalism in the United States—quite apart from the conflicting interpretations and calls for policy specifics. But the battle is not over yet. For there are many within the Protestant tradition who reject the views of Protestant environmentalism and the claim that the Bible justifies them. To these doubters we now must turn.

DISSENT AND PROTESTANT FUNDAMENTALISM

Protestants agree, for the most part, on the importance of environmental issues. Nothing about the sometimes intense arguments over interpretation of the Bible denies that. But this fact should not mislead one into assuming that every Protestant is an ardent environmentalist, confident that true followers of the Bible should rally to the movement at once. This is hardly the case. The most assertive open dissent often comes from Protestant fundamentalists. The word "fundamentalist" here refers to the minority of evangelicals who normally defend the Bible as inerrant and advocate very high boundaries between the community of the faithful and the larger society, which they regard as corrupt. Some liberal or evangelical theologians and writers on the environment may not always take fundamentalists terribly seriously, but they are a significant part of Protestantism in the United States. They cannot be ignored for a moment if one wants to get a full picture of Protestant thought on the environment over the past quarter century. Four common attitudes toward the environment and environmentalism are present among fundamentalist writers: indifference toward environmentalism; hostility toward it; a certain sympathy for the cause; and a great obsession with what in fundamentalist language is termed the "end times"—the end of the world, a concern not so far from the sense of cataclysm that permeates environmentalist discourse.

Indifference toward the environment, or at least toward claims of environmental crisis, abounds in fundamentalist Protestant writings. Thus, while environmentalists worry over the condition of the ozone layer or about toxic waste, many fundamentalist Protestants sound other alarms, especially over end times. In fundamentalist analysis, the arrival of end times is more than a prophecy about the distant future; end times are imminent. By this view, nobody can save the earth; that is for God to do. What people *can* do is prepare for the impending apocalypse.

How to do so is the inevitable question. The fundamentalist stance has been straightforward. As Hal Lindsey has argued, the task of the true Christian is to accept Jesus now and to devote oneself to encouraging others to accept and follow Jesus as well. According to writers like Lindsey, there is nothing more important than this task; there is also no harder job or easier job. Accepting Jesus, Lindsay has insisted, really means trusting in Jesus and in whatever he has ordained for each person and for this world. It also means being willing to evangelize, to go out and share the good news that God exists and can be trusted. The Great Commission of Jesus to evangelize is more important than anything else simply because the end is so close at hand.

From this viewpoint, prayer is (as always) essential; so is pursuing the Christian life. What is not relevant is joining "doomsday ecologists" and pushing for public policies to "save" the earth. People have to understand that public policies are not the answer. God is the answer, and knowledge of God helps people appreciate that the end of the world will not be a tragedy. After all, God will bring to all creation a new order infinitely greater than the old.[1]

A second Protestant fundamentalist attitude involves unmistakable hostility toward environmentalism as a cause. Those who share this view not only agree that preparing for the end of the world is more important than the environmentalist cause but also actively go on the attack against environmentalism. Some fault the environmental movement as "the prevailing cult of our time," one that openly flirts with pantheism and is "publicized by hysteria-mongering media, bogus 'experts,' and subliterate rock stars; and enforced by arrogant bureaucrats."[2]

Others charge that Protestant environmentalism is little more than a left-wing—and secular—political movement. This sentiment came to the fore during the brief Gulf War of late 1990 and early 1991 among those who felt that the war revealed just how political many environmentalists were. Fundamentalist critics observed that while the Sierra Club's magazine and some other environmentalists raised questions regarding Iraqi actions in Kuwait that damaged the environment, the ecological movement as a whole was conspicuously silent. Strangely absent were the usual loud cries about abuse and eco-terror that are routinely hurled at U.S. oil companies at the slightest environmental misdeed. To these critics, environmentalists proved suspiciously selective in their choice of enemies.[3]

But the issue at hand is broader than fundamentalist complaints over the movement's putative errors and dubious supporters. Environmentalism is part of an overall political and moral liberalism that is far away from the world of fundamentalist Protestantism. It is about a focus on this earth rather than heaven, on the universal rather than national or individual; and about an understanding of what is important that is remote from fundamentalist readings of the Bible. The gaps are very large, and they are exaggerated by the fact that most of the public ecological movement comes dressed in secular or non-Christian clothes. No wonder that for some fundamentalist critics, modern environmentalism is really just another expression of "secular humanism." As such, for fundamentalists it has no answers but rather is very much part of the problems generated by modern liberalism.

Most famously, the tensions in this country boiled over in the James Watt controversy of the early 1980s, the most bitter public clash between end times (and other) fundamentalists and the environmental community in the years between 1970 and 1990. Once elected in 1980, President Ronald Reagan selected Watt to be his secretary of the interior, a post that Watt held until 1983. Watt was a self-declared Protestant fundamentalist, whose family and home were devoutly Christian. While Watt had long been religious, his religious commitment intensified in 1964, when he became a pentecostal and joined the Assembly of God Church.[4]

Watt considered himself an environmentalist of sorts, though definitely a critic of the environmentalist movement and "cause." That he had other priorities, however, became clear through the attention of the national media, beginning on February 5, 1981. On that date, during a discussion of the environment, Watt told a committee of the House of Representatives that "I do not know how many future generations we can count on before the Lord returns."[5]

On one level his observation merely stated what is obvious to most Christians: that the date of Christ's second coming is not known. But at another level he spoke in the special language of fundamentalists, implying that while the date of the world's end was unknown, it might be soon, and Christ's return was a fact of enormous importance that people must face up to honestly. This remark was hardly the sort of thing that one expected from any government official, of course, and particularly from a mainstream environmentalist.

Some environmentalists drew the conclusion that Watt's real message was that since the end was coming we should ignore or forget about protecting the environment. So did the cartoonist Herblock, who ran a scathing cartoon in the *Washington Post* that depicted Watt as a babbling fool and garnered widespread coverage. While Watt had regularly stated that management of the environment for future generations—however many or few there might turn out to be—was essential, his end times comment overwhelmed all else. It took on a life of its own, which he could not control. His insistence that there was no inherent conflict between his Protestant fundamentalism and a commitment to stewardship of the natural resources of the United States was not taken seriously by his critics. After all, many of them already suspected his environmentalist credentials and believed he did not care for nature except as an arena for economic developers and a playground for tourists.[6]

Watt's defenders insist that he was a victim of an elite press that mercilessly attacked him for being a fundamentalist Christian—for belonging to an unpopular branch of Protestantism, though one about which the press is largely ignorant. Some maintained, however, that a clash was inevitable for another reason. For them, the Sierra Club and others in the environmental movement have made their cause into another religion, deeply at odds with Protestant fundamentalism. This new religion crowns nature as god, and anyone of a different persuasion—one who is not an unrestrained wilderness advocate, philosophical naturalist, or pantheist— is the enemy. That was bound to include Watt, since he worshiped a Christian Creator; thus, people from this viewpoint concluded that Watt's enemies worshiped what God had created.[7]

These divisions explained a good deal of the incident, but so did less cosmic matters, such as Watt's lack of skill as a politician in what is a politician's job. As even his wife has written, Watt had a way of articulating frank opinions that grated on some people and positively angered others. He was, moreover, far from sensitive to other opinions or feelings. This tendency cost him a good deal, quite apart from his religious fundamentalism and his particular environmental policies. It allowed him to become a symbol of a side of Protestant fundamentalism that was, in truth, not entirely hostile to attention to the earthly environment.[8]

After all, as some fundamentalists stress, there is some basic agreement between fundamentalism and mainstream Protestantism regarding God's nature. In fundamentalist Protestantism as elsewhere, it is taken for granted that the earth and all that is on it is God's handiwork and creation. God is the source of the environment, according to fundamentalists, and that is the basis for what support they accord to environmental concerns.

Much more effort, however, has gone in another direction—toward reflection on the decline of creation, mostly through the agency of human sin. As people and their activities have separated the creation from God (i.e., as they have sinned), the results have been discouraging, and the possibility has increased that the death of the world will occur soon. This is the most famous side of Protestant fundamentalist thought as it applies to environmentalism—end times analysis—the idea that a terrible fate awaits the world as Christ prepares for his imminent return.

This idea strongly links both fundamentalism and environmentalism, both Protestant and secular, in an unintended embrace caused by a shared, basically apocalyptic vision of the earth's approaching dark future. This connection is perhaps the most fascinating aspect of Protestant fundamentalist thought and the environment. It deserves attention, as does the fundamentalist end times perspective in itself, since it is so central to fundamentalist Protestantism thought on the environment.

End times literature is plentiful in Protestant fundamentalist circles. It is absolutely central to their approach to Christianity and much else they place outside that realm, including environmentalism. It always faces great skepticism from others, both Christians and non-Christians, but its proponents persistently campaign for its respectability. Over and over they argue that they merely follow in the footsteps of the vigorous and legitimate tradition of prophecy found in both the Old Testament and the New Testament and the long subsequent Christian tradition of prophecy.[9]

Most end times fundamentalists are premillenialists in their focus on apocalyptic endings of the human journey on earth, and they are quite correct that the Christian tradition of apocalyptic prophecy is a long one. Its durability is one of the most noted aspects of this kind of thinking. But as an able contemporary chronicler, Paul Boyer, observes, its adaptability to different times and places represents a parallel feature that is equally remarkable and is a major factor in the tradition's robust survival.[10]

In recent decades, most contemporary end times writing has focused on Scriptures describing political events that are taken as evidence of the approaching end. Indeed, they are the main ground on which these prophesies build. Natural events, earthquakes, typhoons, and the like were often important in past prophecies, but they get much less attention in our time. Perhaps this is because while science allied with modern communications has rendered natural occurrences, however unexpected, less mysterious, politics remains as mysterious as ever.

While specific crises in nature do not seem as strange as they once did, the general evidence of degradation in nature and ecological crisis is sometimes cited as a confirming sign of the impending end. But this evidence produces no sympathy for environmentalists or environmentalism in end times literature, and one would be surprised if it did. For example, premillenialists fear that environmentalism may serve to assist the triumph of world government, which is to say, the rule of the feared Anti-Christ. Environmentalists may be aware of change, but not the types of change that Christian end times thinkers observe in the fast-lengthening shadow of the end of the world.[11]

Signs of the collapse of Western Christian culture have encouraged end times thought in recent decades, but the biggest burst of end times speculation came in the winter of 1990–1991. The stimulus was the Gulf War, set in the Middle East—the traditional location, in Christian prophecies, for the final events of world history. Book sales were brisk, which is no wonder given that even in ordinary times 15 to 20 percent of the populace believes that Armageddon is close at hand. Rarely did end times books identify the Gulf War as the last step, but the war proved to be an opportunity to remind people of the patterns that indicate the end is close. It served to educate the faithful about God's purposes and the earth's impending, inevitable fate.

The tide of interest in end times rises and falls. At the moment, such concerns are relatively quiescent. Sales of books that were tremendously popular during the Gulf War have plummeted; many are now remaindered and sold at a discount. It would be a mistake, however, to conclude that this downturn marks some kind of conclusion to this mode of thinking; far from it, for this approach is based on a reading of the Bible that is now well established and has shown great resiliency. Other ages and other events will resuscitate its broader popularity, and among many fundamentalists this version of biblical Christianity will remain strong, regardless of the tides of popular opinion.[12]

The Gulf War was only one event in a long series that make sense to end times thinkers as signs of the end. The establishment of Israel and the uneasy movement of Europe toward unity, to give two examples, are other signs that they argue cannot be ignored. In fact, environmental degradation is also compatible with the end times scenario; it dovetails well with a view that God's earth is racing toward destruction, though it is rarely mentioned in the fundamentalist literature. Thus, while it is fair to say that end times thinkers and many eco-theorists identify different signs, the signs lead both groups toward the same frightening conclusion.

The range of prophecies within Christian fundamentalism is broad. Some are modest, trying to keep within recognizable biblical texts and appreciate some of the complexity of comprehending historical and political developments. Others border on the bizarre in their reading of the Bible or contemporary history or both. Still others provide fodder for those who suspect that the prophets are frauds, aiming to make money from whatever crisis is current. Few have the backing of specific fundamentalist denominations or groups. Nor have the prophets who have taken end times the most seriously in their ministries always been the famous names within fundamentalism. Yet their appeal is significant, and their theology is widely accepted in fundamentalist Protestantism.

Protestant end times writing also comes in many genres. When it appears as fiction, it is most engaging. Fiction might seem to be too light a medium for the darkness of end times warnings, but this is not the case. Dan Betzer's *Beast* is a good example. It traces the Beast (the devil) from his past work in Nazi Germany to his contemporary reappearance through one Jacque Catroux, a figure of evil who gradually seizes control of much of the world. This story places rape, murder, and plenty of other violence in the foreground as it follows its hero, Clay Daniels, on a journey that involves his discovery of the truth and resistance to the devil.

Another example is O. R. B. Pattison's *Left Behind.* It takes its protagonist, Ken Evans, from the mysterious Rapture, which secrets away his wife, through a steady stream of events that culminate in his true spiritual enlightenment about the meaning of the world's end. A third example of the popular path of end times fiction is Salem Kirban's *666,* and there are many more as well.[13]

The recent big seller among end times books has been John F. Walvoord's revised *Armageddon, Oil, and the Middle East Crisis.* Conservative Christian bookstores promoted it prominently, and Billy Graham approved of the work so thoroughly that he bought and gave away 300,000 copies. The classic end times work of the last twenty-five years, however, was Hal Lindsey's *Late, Great Planet Earth.* It was the modern exemplar of the old outlook: prophesying, predicting, and often hinting at when the world will end.[14]

Whether preached through fiction or nonfiction, end times fundamentalism is about what its believers take to be the truth that the final days are coming. Predictions abound, and the only difference among them is the degree of boldness or caution they reveal. The current mood is unmistakably apocalyptic, though authors no longer set a definite date—a folly that is wisely out of fashion. Hal Lindsey's works, for instance, pulsate with warnings that the moment is all but at hand. "History seems to be headed for its climactic hour," he writes. A few years ago he argued that the "*decade of the 1980s could very well be the last decade of history as we know it.*" Obviously that was not the case, but Lindsey would not have been surprised had it been so. The end is just that near, in his view.[15]

John Walvoord predicts that Christ's return "may be expected momentarily," since things are rapidly falling into place for the Rapture and the rest of the end times scenario.[16] Others conclude that our world is ready for the Anti-Christ, who might be on the earth right now.[17] Even those who go out of their way to dissociate themselves from flamboyant predictions and who insist that they offer "interpretations and not prophetic revelations" expect the final era in our time. To them, indications are strong that the Rapture is "imminent" and Christ's return is close.[18]

Critics laugh at all this as silly, a hoax, or worse. Moreover, some fundamentalists draw scorn from other Christians because they seem gleeful and happy in announcing the approaching conclusion of the world. Others charge them with elitism, since the Rapture teaches that just before the end, God takes the most faithful up to heaven. The biggest complaint, however, is that end times prophets are flat wrong in their sometimes varying interpretations of both the Bible and history.[19]

Even within the contours of Protestant fundamentalism, there are plenty of critics of the end times approach. They may and usually do grant that there will be an end, and they usually share fundamentalist beliefs in premillenialism, the Rapture, and the like. Doubters insist, however, that while the world will certainly end, "We do not claim to know that the end is here."[20]

Always at issue is what skeptics take to be a miserable record of false predictions from the past. Prophecy may be a legitimate activity for some; and particularly for most evangelical Protestants, the idea that the Old Testament is a prophetic work fulfilled in Jesus and his ministry is perfectly accurate. However, that is different from granting that most Christian prophecies from the past are worth anything. Critics correctly note that history is littered with false prophets and prophecies. Final days have come and gone time and again, and attempts to identify the Anti-Christ have often absurdly misfired. Indeed, as recently as 1988, prophetic claims giving a specific date for the Rapture proved embarrassingly wrong. This, too, is an old story.[21]

Naturally, such skepticism does not sit well with end times fundamentalists. Some defend the record of prophecy over time as "to the letter" and "amazingly accurate." To be sure, what counts as a legitimate prophecy varies from thinker to thinker, and nobody claims that every prophecy made in Christianity's name has come true. But within their range of acceptable biblical prophecies, end times fundamentalists insist that prophecies have come true—or are coming true. Thus, they argue, skeptics dare not ignore them by taking refuge in cheap scoffing.

Others contend that people have gained in discernment and wisdom about prophecies over time. Contemporary prophets can and do prophesy better because they have learned to be more careful and more tough-minded. This position is something of a middle way. Its proponents understand that past prophets have made misjudgments—errors of understanding, though, and nothing else—but insist that contemporary prophets are refining those problems. To them, it would be silly to give up "simply out of disappointment with the mistakes of past commentators."[22]

From another angle, prophecy (even prophecy that resembles end times thinking) plays a considerable role in Protestantism. Frankly, it pervades all of Protestant environmentalism. Ecologically minded Christians repeatedly speak in this language, declaring their "growing apocalyptic mood."[23] Indeed, end times thinking is in many ways a staple of all current ecological movements, whether they are connected with Christianity or not.[24]

Michael Barkun has developed this claim in an acute and controversial analysis that notes how greatly dramatic prophecies and intimations of apocalypse have dominated such environmental classics as Barry Commoner's *Closing Circle* and Jonathan Schell's now-dated *Fate of the Earth*. Like many other works in the environmental canon, these are decidedly secular, so their prophecies are not about God. It is the crisis of the ecosphere that fills their pages, but parallels with Christian apocalyptic thought are impossible to ignore.[25]

Thus, according to Hans Schwarz, our "present environmental crisis has taken on apocalyptic dimensions and many predict a doomsday for mankind in the near future."[26] Indeed, such claims are routine. So is the widespread affinity for worst-case scenarios, characteristic of pessimistic prophets of all genres. Also present is a familiar undertone of smugness or satisfaction on the part of some secular environmental prophets, just as there is among some of the fundamentalist Christian ones, as if the realization of their prophecies affirms the wisdom of the prophet.[27]

For some observers, the dramatic difference between the two types of prophecies is that modern ecological prophecies aim to spur on action, while end times apocalyptic belief is apparently quiescent.[28] This conclusion does not make sense to end times thinkers, since they judge themselves deeply committed to action. For them, the real issue is what kind of action people should undertake in the face of the crises of this apocalyptic age. They insist that the answer is evangelism and waiting on Christ, not the futile effort to save nature.

The End Times System

End times fundamentalism is no simple thing. Those who might be tempted to assume that it is a series of mindless assertions have not delved into its books of prophecy. Many end times prophets build a complex, intricate system, complete with an elaborate set of historical charts and computations and seemingly plausible arguments to support their understanding of the past and the future. Again and again they legitimate their view by citing passages from the Bible that indicate to them the unmistakable intimations of the coming end of the world.

End times biblical analysis rarely mentions Genesis, or the Psalms, or the particular New Testament passages that Protestant environmentalists so often invoke. This is no surprise, of course, since it is not the Bible's commentary on nature that interests them. What *is* surprising, perhaps, is that despite some variation, there is little controversy over what the Bible teaches about crucial stages and events within the process. Nor is there much debate that the human fate will be grim until Christ's triumphal return. This is why end times fundamentalists believe that environmentalists who hope that we can master our global problems are not only wrong but also out of touch with the Bible. Moreover, for end times thinkers, such hopes are also sad, for they represent powerful snares that lead away from preparation for the difficult days that lie ahead.

End times Protestant writings invariably identify the re-creation of Israel as a nation in 1948 as the most significant modern sign of the coming end (Amos 9:11: "In that day I will raise up the booth of David that is fallen . . . and rebuild it as in the days of old"). They also predict other geopolitical events that will follow, according to their understanding of the Bible. Russia (and sometimes China) will grow stronger and become aggressive. Arab nations will come closer together, and Europe will unify (the modern interpretation of Revelation's prediction of the rebirth of the Roman Empire).

According to the most popular of several versions, the Rapture will inaugurate the final seven years before Christ's return. It will be the sudden and unexplained ascension of Christians to Heaven. Whether or not the Scriptures explicitly detail the Rapture is controversial even among end times authors. At the least, they agree that it is implied in such verses as 1 Thessalonians 4:17 ("then we who are alive . . . shall be caught up together . . . in the clouds to meet the Lord in the air"), Matthew 24:37, 40–41 ("So will be the coming of the Son of man. . . . Then two men will be in the field; one is taken and one is left. Two women will be grinding at the mill; one is taken and one is left"), and 1 Corinthians 15:52 ("in a moment, in the twinkling of an eye"). Of these, the most-cited passage is the one in 1 Thessalonians.

The Great Tribulation will occur after the Rapture, though there is some debate on the exact order of events. It will be the seven terrible years directly before Christ's Second Coming. Some accounts describe the last three and a half years of the Great Tribulation as a special catastrophe. Russia will attack Israel and be defeated. A reunited Europe will mercilessly assault Israel, Jews, and Christians wherever possible. Natural disasters will multiply, and a world war will explode all over the globe, with its bloody epicenter located in the Middle East.

Obviously, Russia's role in this scenario currently poses a problem, and it will be more than interesting to see how future prophets wrestle with the disappearance of the Soviet Union, which has been so important to end times analysis in this century. In the last few decades or so, Russia's expected prominence in the final struggle was repeatedly and perhaps lovingly detailed. The tumultuous and particularly obscure events of Ezekiel 38 and 39 and Daniel 11:40–45 have been the main biblical sources for its major role, while the great, famous last contest—the Battle of Armageddon—has its source in an interpretation of the Book of Revelation that is now almost two thousand years old.

The devil, of course, is integral to the full end times scenario. He is a clever and manipulative leader who, as the Anti-Christ, acts to control the world. First John 2:18 ("you have heard that antichrist is coming, so now many antichrists have come; therefore we know that it is the last hour") and Revelation 13:1 ("And I saw a beast rising out of the sea") are two of the chief verses detailing Satan's appearance and deeds.

According to final days fundamentalists, in the midst of the attendant horrors, Christ will return (Zechariah 14:1: "Behold, a day of the Lord is coming"; and Revelation 19:11, 15: "Then I saw heaven opened, and behold ... He who ... is called Faithful and True ... From his mouth issues a sharp sword with which to smite the nations, and he will rule them with a rod of iron") and the world will end with the defeat of the Anti-Christ. This will be a moment of unspeakable glory and grandeur, but it will not involve the salvation of plants or animals, much less the earth itself. The end times prophets interpret the Bible to say that the final days are concerned with human beings and God and that Christians not already in Heaven will go to their eternal life with Christ.[29]

Everywhere end times fundamentalists have looked they have seen confirmation of their prophecies. Over the last twenty-plus years, the power and activity of communism, especially in the Soviet Union, was uncomfortable confirmation. While such signs are hardly clear now, the continuing Arab-Israeli conflict still attracts a great deal of attention. Also noted is the advent of an increasingly pluralistic religious world in the United States and elsewhere. The flourishing of religions such as witchcraft confirms to end times fundamentalists the brazen presence of the devil. By this view, as false faiths grow and the true faith stumbles, we are witnessing the West's drift toward death.[30]

The outbreak of war in the Middle East in late 1990 and early 1991 posed no challenge to the basics of the prophecies. Indeed, end times fundamentalists saw the Gulf War as a confirmation of the Bible. The rise of Saddam Hussein—and of Iraq, whose capital is the biblical Babylon—was a mark of such potent significance that it could hardly be ignored. That Iraq lost the war was also no surprise. The Bible predicted the destruction of Babylon as part of the end times (Jeremiah 50:9: "I am . . . bringing against Babylon a company of great nations . . . she shall be taken").[31]

Social theorist Christopher Lasch was no Christian and no admirer of either Christian optimism regarding the outcome of history or of secular confidence in "progress." At the same time, Lasch expressed distaste for our age's taste for pessimism and disaster, which in a curious but real way end times fundamentalism also reflects: "As a corrective to the idea of progress, the 'imagination of disaster' . . . leaves a good deal to be desired. All too obviously it simply inverts the idea of progress, substituting irresistible disintegration for irresistible advance. The dystopian view of the world to come, now so firmly established in the Western imagination, holds out such an abundance of unavoidable calamities that it becomes all the more necessary for people to cling to the idea of progress for emotional support." No wonder, Lasch writes, that "horrifying images of the future, even when they are invoked not just to titillate . . . but to shock people into constructive action, foster a curious state of mind that simultaneously believes and refuses to believe in the likelihood of some terminal catastrophe for the human race."[32]

Rarely is end times literature completely pessimistic, but it sometimes serves as an example of what Lasch bemoans. It can lead to the kind of half-denial that hardly encourages action. So can some of the secular eco-catastrophe literature. Yet there is a major distinction between the apocalyptic views of end times fundamentalists and those of radical eco-thinkers: the latter maintain that the future of the planet may still lie in human hands even at this late date. Such a conviction may or may not be a great strength, though those within the movement assume that it is a great strength. It does contrast sharply with end times convictions that there is nothing that humans can do to retard the looming prospect of the end of the world. Yet given their interpretation of things, end times fundamentalists are hardly pessimists. After all, for them the end of the world is nothing to lament. It marks a new beginning for human beings and the arrival—at last—of the Kingdom of God.

Not all fundamentalists are end times thinkers. There are other attitudes regarding the environment and God's creation among fundamentalist Christians. Some are concerned, others concentrate on attacking the environmentalist movement, and more grapple with the coming end times. What they all have in common is a resistance to the dominant outlook of Protestant environmentalism. For them, the Bible is not about biocentrism; nor is it even about stewardship in a traditional sense, if that implies that the human is equal with all other parts of nature. God rules nature; God gave nature to humans for their use under the care of the divine rule; and God now calls people to prepare for the end of the world as we know it.

From this perspective, God does not call on us to reinterpret the Bible as a modern environmentalist manifesto in which service of nature takes precedent over all else. In fundamentalist Protestant analysis, the crisis in creation today is not about the mistreatment of nature so much as it is about human sin in all its forms. By this view, the answer lies not in an environmental movement but in preparation for the return of Jesus Christ.

THE ARGUMENT OVER CHRISTIANITY

The Bible is the foundation of the Protestant Christian faith, and arguments among Protestants over its environmental teachings are guaranteed to continue for a long time. This fact reflects not only Protestant thinkers' sincere desire to be faithful to the Bible's witness but also the contest over who may legitimately claim that authority. Yet Christianity is much more than the Bible. It is a belief system and a historical religion. Over the last quarter century, its doctrines as well as its history have faced intense scrutiny within Protestantism—and outside of it—in terms of their relationship to environmentalism.

There have been two basic issues. First, how does Christianity stand on the environment? Quite apart from the Bible, is it a friend or an enemy of the ecological cause? Second, what is the record of Christianity in practice? What in its history inspires hope or induces pessimism for a faith of continued or renewed service for salvation of the earth? Moreover, these issues lead to others, including the important question of green Protestant attitudes toward science.

Current Protestant considerations of environmental matters reflect the stern criticisms that in modern times have been inflicted on Christianity as a faith and as a religion with a history with regard to the environment. Sometimes the Protestant response to such criticism has been defensive, but not always. Ironically, perhaps, one reason why a defensive spirit has not always been typical is that many Protestant authors are at the front of this critical wave—and sometimes their work has an unforgiving edge. Many Protestant voices have joined secular critics to single out the whole of Christianity—not just the Bible—as inhospitable soil for cultivating an ecological ethic or, worse, as a major culprit in the destruction of planet earth.

Lynn White's critique sparked the first major debate about the Christian record. We know White had less than glowing things to say about the environmental teachings of the Christian Bible. He was equally critical of the Christian legacy, quite apart from the Bible. His assessment was that as a religion and a historical tradition, Christianity failed to help preserve the environment. It was this contention several decades ago that set off the fight over the Christian tradition and the ecological crisis.

To be sure, White appreciated that "no sensible person could maintain that all ecologic damage is, or has been, rooted in religious attitudes." After all, Christianity did not kill the dinosaurs.[1] Nevertheless, White saw a Christianity that had been consistently anthropomorphic. He contended that this attitude inevitably led to negative consequences for our planet, among them a raw exploitation of nature. Christianity permitted this since it rejected animist thought and thereby granted its followers "a license to exploit" nature.

White also introduced the common and controversial topic of the role of Christianity and science. He argued that Christianity in the West had nourished a modern science and technology that in turn had helped ravish the earth. For him, the Protestant Reformation in particular legitimated a ruthless technology that Eastern Orthodox Christianity had wisely avoided. As a result, White maintains, Western "Christianity bears a huge burden of guilt."[2]

White's original charges have achieved great resonance within Protestant environmentalism. Some of his later writings—such as his argument for the undifferentiated equality of all things in nature, which led him to question the moral correctness of combating such things as the smallpox virus—have had less appeal. But his naming of St. Francis of Assisi (1182–1226) as the model Christian environmentalist has garnered the most praise. In praising St. Francis, White and other Christian critics make the point that Christianity has a history that is not totally dismal. Christianity must be drastically revamped, even revolutionized, and much of its history repudiated, but its story contains a few good moments.

St. Francis is by far the most popular Christian hero to green Protestants. This has been true since White resurrected him as the Christian ecologist par excellence. White's St. Francis was totally devoted to nature as God's creation but deftly avoided pantheism. St. Francis upheld the equality of all creatures and practiced an impressive humility before nature in its splendid variety. He denied anthropomorphism and hierarchy in nature and thus was "the greatest radical in Christian history"—indeed, the "greatest revolutionary in Western history."[3]

Secular Critics

White is not an apologist for what he identifies as Christianity's faults. Yet his critique is tame in comparison to the charges hurled against Christianity from outside the gates of the faith. The mood of these non-Christian critics is often unremittingly hostile. Many secular environmentalists insist that the Christian and Jewish religions are a (or the) major enemy to the environment and have been so for thousands of years.[4]

Objections to Christianity and Christian practice in the West are fairly straightforward. Many concern the familiar accusation that an anthropocentric orientation within Christianity has fostered ugly hierarchies and tragic dualisms that in practice have crushed much of nature. For example, Roderick Nash contends that as Christianity arose in the West, the status of nature declined because of Christianity's anthropocentrism. Specifically, Nash faults the traditional Christian tenet that only humans have souls. To him, such a doctrine is anthropocentric and dualistic, leaving the rest of nature as "other" and thus "fully exposed to human greed."[5] He also attacks the idea of heaven as the final resting place for saved humans. This notion too is human-centered and dualistic. Nash laments as well the "pervasive otherworldliness" he discerns in Christianity; it is an attitude that he contends leads to both the neglect and abuse of nature.[6]

For harsher critics, such as Nash, the idea that St. Francis represents an alternative Christian tradition merits no interest. St. Francis may stand for all that White and others attribute to him, but this one figure does not rescue a Christianity that Nash believes deserves censure and rejection. St. Francis "was the exception that proves the rule of Christian anthropocentrism," nothing more.[7]

Philosopher John Passmore, who is widely read in the United States, has also faulted Christianity to some extent for what he takes to be its unfortunate attitudes toward the environment. To be sure, his most prominent point is that Christianity's limitations, especially its dualism between God and nature, derives mostly from classical Greek influences on Christianity rather than from the heart of the religion itself. But he disapprovingly notes that, like Judaism before it, Christianity has a long and determined tradition of seeking to distinguish Christianity from nature worship; and the implicit effect of these efforts, he points out, is denigration of nature.[8]

Other secular critics make the familiar point that traditional Christianity is a religion wedded to a hierarchical conception of the universe, and they declare that this reality has hurt nature, which has always ended up at the bottom of the Christian hierarchy. The fact is, Passmore complains, that "Christianity has encouraged man to think of himself as nature's absolute master, for whom everything that exists was designed."[9] It is no wonder, Passmore concludes, that "for centuries it came to be standard Christian teaching that men could do what they liked with animals, that their behavior toward them need not be governed by any moral considerations whatsoever."[10]

Critics do not agree on any single aspect of what they take to be the Christian model—one that some call a "conquest" model—as the basis for their conclusion that Christianity has waged war on nature. Emphases differ with individual critics. The overall portrait that critics paint, though, is consistent and predictable. For them, Christianity has historically been hostile to nature.[11]

These analysts have not necessarily claimed that Christianity has been worse for nature than have other causes of environmental degradation—or even that it has been one of the principal causes. Secular critics list a number of competitors to Christianity in terms of what has had the greatest negative impact on nature. For example, some contend that capitalism, more than anything else, has produced our environmental situation. Today this argument is increasingly thin from a global perspective, in the wake of the environmental mess left in Russia and Eastern Europe, but it still attracts stalwarts. Many versions link capitalism with Christianity, identifying the religion as a major, or *the* major, force behind capitalism. One account of Max Weber's classic analysis of the relationship between Christianity and capitalism makes the accusation that Christianity has encouraged capitalism, which in turn has exploited nature.[12]

The Critical Mood inside Protestant Christianity

Secular environmentalists who fault Christianity are far from alone. They have many eager allies within Protestantism itself. Indeed, some Protestants are scathing in their judgments of the Christian environmentalist record. Most agree with White that Christian failures regarding nature "can be generally substantiated"[13] and complain that Christianity "has allied itself to an anthropocentrism and the neglect of nature."[14] Evangelical Francis Schaeffer summed the story up as one of "Christian arrogance toward nature."[15]

Loren Wilkinson makes a crucial distinction between Christianity itself and what he calls "Christendom." For Wilkinson and some others, often evangelicals, the problem is not Christianity, even a recognizable, fairly conventional Christianity. Instead, the problem lies in the question of how Christians have lived their lives. Too often Christendom has been a tale of abuse of God's creation. This distinction, however, does not work for many Protestant theologians, for whom the problem goes well beyond the lives of Christians in the past.[16]

Eco-theologians and others from within Protestantism have three main complaints about Christianity, which overlap with a freedom that is understandable, given their sweeping character. Some lament particular Christian doctrines—charges that are hardly new or startling. They assert that Christianity gives too much sanctity and attention to the relationship between God and humans at the expense of the rest of creation. They think God's creation included all nature but believe that Christianity has regarded the crux of creation as God's formation of men and women. They complain that this mistake has been an integral part of Christian doctrine from the beginning and that the Protestant Reformation accented it even more. As John B. Cobb Jr. puts it, we must acknowledge the painful truth of "the Christian centering of all intrinsic value in man."[17]

Of course, green Protestant critics join to scourge what they perceive as the dualisms rife in Christianity. They agree that Christianity has long incorporated dualisms between spirit and body, this world and the next, and humanity and nature at immense cost to nature. To be sure, some understand that this kind of thinking is not unique to Christianity and that Christianity has not been the only force infecting the Western tradition with such notions. But they believe these dualisms have simply been too prominent in Christianity. And, as Paul Santmire remarks, Protestantism has made no progress in eliminating them.[18]

These two complaints in the eco-Protestant literature are joined by a third accusation: that Christianity justifies the domination of nature by humans. Some choose to analyze this tendency as a product of a given period of historical Christianity, usually the Middle Ages, while others see it as inherent in the religion in every age. Standard accounts judge the consequent suffering of nature at human hands to have been enormous. Christianity has left us with a terribly diminished natural realm and a "predatory legacy."[19]

Some Protestant critics do attempt to determine where Christianity went off the true path. Thus, while this enterprise is a critique of Christianity, it is also, often, an effort to exonerate Christianity as a religious faith. By this approach—gentler than some—the problem is not so much the religion as what humans have done with it.

Paul Santmire, for example, singles out the record of the Christian

Fathers in the second through the fifth centuries. For him, they were too absorbed with spiritual matters and slighted the material and natural realms, which they perceived to be distinctly inferior. Others share this analysis and identify particular agents of this early misdirection. Origen of Alexandria (c. 185–254) is a favorite target for criticism, because he imported into Christianity neo-Platonist abstractions that helped direct Christianity into a spirituality antagonistic to nature. He denigrated the earth and implicitly justified its terrible mistreatment.[20]

St. Augustine (354–430) ordinarily receives somewhat better reviews from green Protestant writers. Few offer him warm praise, but even the most disenchanted cannot ignore Augustine's celebration of the beauty of God's creation. On the other hand, Augustine unmistakably embraced an interpretation of Genesis that set mankind over nature. This position, of course, wins no plaudits, though his Protestant defenders note that for Augustine, man's role as ruler of nature came only after the Fall; it was neither natural nor intrinsic to creation. Others object to Augustine's affinity for an asceticism that they suggest discloses a disturbing ambivalence about human beings.[21]

Compared to the earlier Fathers, St. Thomas (1225–74) receives kinder treatment from Protestant environmentalists, who discuss him because he was a Christian who honored and respected nature. He is far from another bad chapter in the Christian story. Protestant eco-theologians appreciate that his meld of Aristotelian and Christian ideas involved love for God's creation. Thomas had no contempt for the earth or what dwelled there, including humans. At the same time, though, St. Thomas earns no hero status. He is identified as another Christian who visualized the world from an "ascent" framework. For him, people and all nature are far below God and should aspire to ascend toward God. To his critics, such beliefs legitimate devaluation—and misuse—of nature.[22]

Overall, however, green Protestantism accords little sympathy to medieval Christianity. It simply did not display adequate concern for nature. Neither did the Renaissance or the Reformation. They may have been the seedbeds of Protestantism, but they were not fertile soil for an environmental Protestantism. From critics' perspectives, this is true partly because the Renaissance and the Reformation created no profound reformulation of Christian doctrine regarding nature. Moreover, the secular offshoots of these great periods, such as modern science and technology, have too often proven pernicious. Some critics link the beginnings of modern science in the seventeenth century with the Christian tradition's habit of treating nature as primarily for human benefit. By this view, modern attitudes justifying scientific and technological power over nature for the "benefit of mankind" represent the old Christian dominion attitude metamorphosed into secular, modern language.[23]

Alternatives to Christian Approaches

The environmental critique from outside Christianity mostly translates into an explicit rejection of the religion. Even among Protestant defenders there is a clear rejection of a certain Christianity, one that was and is false to green values. At the same time, there is increased consideration of alternatives. One alternative is, of course, the fashioning of a green Protestantism. Now, however, there is also a major industry that is busy fashioning grounds for environmentalism that leave all forms of Christianity far behind. This study is not the place for a full-scale exploration of that fascinating enterprise, but some reflection on it is necessary, since it is an integral expression of the critical mood we are examining.[24]

There has been interest in developing an "ecological humanism," a belief system balancing humans and the rest of nature in a nonreligious community of concern.[25] Some environmentalists have also proposed the idea of rights as the proper ground for an environmental ethic. One aspect of the discussion has been an argument over animal rights, and a good deal of the debate is over when such rights exist. Must a creature have self-consciousness to have rights? Is having some level of feeling enough? Is having any sense of identity sufficient? The issue of how to reconcile human rights with other possible rights is also frequently on the agenda. Can a flower, or a rock, or a cancer cell have rights? If so, which ones, and why, and how do they affect human rights?[26]

Roderick Nash has led the way in defending a rights view regarding nature as a whole and in its various parts. His *Rights of Nature* has had great exposure and consistently argues for a rights approach. Everything in nature has rights, he argues, and these rights must be respected before all else, including human society. He contends that his approach is in the American liberal tradition of natural rights and is simply (but radically) an extension of the idea of natural rights expounded so memorably in the Declaration of Independence. Thus, for him, environmentalism is another step in the American story of the expanding concept of rights. For Nash, it is time to recall the struggle to recognize the natural rights of blacks and the consequent death of slavery. We are engaged in exactly the same struggle regarding the rest of nature. According to Nash, the human being's enslavement of nature will also have to die.[27]

Nash does not really defend the existence of natural rights—a task that is necessary, of course, if such claims are to be taken seriously. What is clear is that a good deal of their appeal for him is pragmatic. He knows full well that they are intrinsic to American history and culture, and that makes them effective as a vocabulary in his cause. Ironically, perhaps, such an approach is quite far away from the drift of much contemporary American intellectual opinion. Talk of natural rights fits poorly with postmodern intellectual skepticism about absolute claims and with suspicions that claims on moral foundations such as natural rights are just social constructions founded on air.

Bob Pepperman Taylor has argued that most environmental ethical outlooks from within the larger environmentalist movement have fallen into two traditions in American thought. One is linked with Gifford Pinchot and has often been sympathetic to rationality and pragmatic awareness. The other is connected with Henry David Thoreau and has involved a much more intuitive approach, stressing nature's intrinsic worth and focusing on experiential and spiritual aspects of environmentalism. This distinction is explored at some length in chapter 6.[28]

But the distinction is also valuable here in looking at some of the alternative ideas proposed. Nash's views and those of others who argue for natural rights as a basis for preserving nature are in the Pinchot tradition. The intuitionist perspective of J. Baird Callicott is closer to the tradition of Thoreau, though the lines between one view or another are not rigid. Perhaps the most interesting direction today is biocentrism, an approach that can involve affirmation of the rights of nature within the biocentric community or can be based on the intuition (or science) of the biocentric world. Among the crucial biocentric works are Bill Devall and George Sessions' *Deep Ecology: Living as if Nature Mattered*, Christopher Manes's *Green Rage: The Unmaking of Civilization*, and Dave Foreman's *Confessions of an Eco-Warrior*.[29]

Of the many alternative approaches, perhaps it is Aldo Leopold's that has attracted the greatest attention. Leopold (1887–1948) was a pioneering environmentalist whose extensive writings were capped by the widely read and praised *Sand County Almanac* (1949). As Rene Dubos correctly observes, *A Sand County Almanac* has become something of a Holy Writ in environmental movement circles due to its powerful evocation of the glories of nature and their ebb and flow.

Leopold wrote a good deal else, but his body of work does not constitute, nor was it intended to constitute, a full-scale, systematically argued ethical philosophy. Leopold's views, however, are not mysterious. He was no Christian; indeed, he was not conventionally religious at all. Instead, Leopold argued that nature itself, or the overall community of life, is the appropriate standard for values. What this means, he explained, is that the integrity, stability, and beauty of nature and biotic communities in nature is good and that whatever does not promote these values is bad.[30]

Leopold's work has influenced many environmental ethicists, including J. Baird Callicott, Holmes Rolston III, and Paul Taylor, though each has a distinct perspective.[31] Consider Callicott, a professional philosopher, who places himself in the tradition of Aldo Leopold and is a leader in the quest to preserve Leopold's legacy for the future. In crafting what he calls an "environmental ethic based upon Aldo Leopold's land ethic," Callicott adds his own contributions to Leopold's basic argument, not least through his systematization of Leopold's ecological outlook.

Callicott belongs to what is often called the intrinsic school of morality. For him, nature has worth on its own, and that people understand this intuitively is an excellent justification for its truth. Paul Taylor, whose book *Respect for Nature* has drawn considerable praise, is another thinker in somewhat the same mold. Taylor does not try to make a case for nature's value on the basis of scientific facts but defends its worth on an essentially intuitive basis.[32]

Callicott rejects the thinking of those who derive their morality from nature either through claims that it confers rights or through the invocation of a romantic union with nature and its beauties. Callicott maintains that nature's intrinsic worth counts pragmatically in this world only when humans self-consciously honor nature's inherent value. Thus, for Callicott, ecological education is the best means to moral awareness and a moral life.[33]

Callicott's resistance to natural rights as the appropriate outlook stems from his sense that it is too often anthropocentric. The rights of nature have almost always referred to the rights of human beings, and it is just this kind of human focus that Callicott wants to escape. Callicott, however, is like a number of other non-Christian biocentric thinkers who are open to a rights approach that is holistic from a biocentric perspective. That is, there may be equal rights in nature, but they exist for all natural beings as part of (and limited by) the whole. They are not just the rights of people against society and the rest of nature.

Callicott also acknowledges that humans have other values and norms besides those rooted in nature, and he does not propose to dismiss them. Yet he is fairly confident that few value conflicts are likely to occur, believing that in a holistic world all true values will work in concert. Obviously, this is a significant assumption, one that is necessarily grounded more in faith than anything else.

Callicott is well aware that nature's existence as a complex interactive community does not unequivocally establish its legitimacy as a foundation for morality. Skeptics insist, following the classic formulation of David Hume, that just because something exists does not mean it has moral worth; in other words, "is" does not necessarily equal "ought." While Callicott does not accept this distinction, he knows that he must engage it. In an analogy to quantum physics, he proposes an understanding of the world which holds that there is a complex interconnection between the self and the surrounding world. It is thus impossible to separate human beings, their subjectivity, and the larger world outside of them. Since people do not normally doubt their own worth, it does not make sense to doubt the world's worth either. People are inseparable from the world and know that they and the world are of value. Thus, at this level there really is no difference between what is and what is morally right.[34]

Callicott consciously endeavors to fashion an ethic that is soberly rational and philosophical, even though at times he is open to other approaches. He argues for his holistic vision, but he affirms it in a mystical and personal fashion as well. He recounts that he discovered holism not in a philosophy classroom but at the Mississippi River. There he came to understand that "the river is part of me."[35] In truth, Callicott has his doubts about philosophy and even about reason and is confident that "the appeal to sentiment is more promising and appropriate than a reasonably defended view."[36]

Religion was not important for Leopold, and Callicott follows in his footsteps. Callicott is unsympathetic to Christianity in particular. He appreciates that the faith has its good sides, but he rejects it firmly because he believes it sanctions human control and abuse of nature. Callicott much prefers Native American perspectives, and he has written more than one paean to them. He thinks many tribes practiced a true land ethic, one that embraced a holistic worldview and appreciated nature's beauty and stability. For them, "is" and "ought" were unified in the oneness of life and earth. Yet Callicott is careful to explain that his approval of a Native American land ethic does not imply support for any Native American religious or spiritual views. Spirituality and religion even among Native Americans have to do with transcendence and otherworldliness, just the sort of thing from which Callicott urges us to escape.[37]

Callicott has complained vocally that his profession, the field of philosophy, has been slow to warm to the land ethic of Aldo Leopold, let alone to accept Callicott's own formulation of that ethic. He is certainly correct.[38] Part of the difficulty continues to be the is/ought problem. Callicott (and others) are repeatedly forced to deal with the charge that they unacceptably slip from fact to value, that they take the fact that the world is in some sense holistic and conclude that we are morally obligated to that world or that the natural world (land) has intrinsic value. Callicott's responses to this objection have not impressed his critics; for that matter, neither did the arguments of Callicott's mentor, Aldo Leopold. To a rigorous analytical philosopher such as Keith Yandell, Leopold's "reflections" are "unsystematic and undeveloped" and cannot be taken seriously as philosophy. To do otherwise is to place "on them a burden they just will not bear."[39]

Callicott's enthusiasm for Native American attitudes toward the environment exceeds even his hostility toward analytic philosophy. But his interest in Native American conceptions of the environment is standard both among those pursuing an alternative to the Christian tradition and to many who want to refurbish the Christian tradition. But Callicott's work stands out because he makes distinctions that some neglect. He appreciates that Native Americans were not self-conscious ecologists or conservationists; he suspects that their motivations were complex and included fear of punishment by the spirits if they abused the environment. Furthermore, he knows that, in practice, they did not have a blemish-free environmental record.

Yet he believes the truth is that Native Americans deserve our admiration. American Indian cultures had an instinctive environmentalist ethic which they often lived and which Callicott wishes we would equal, or even begin to equal; and this judgment is often echoed by other environmentalists.[40] The constant theme is that Native Americans were respectful of nature and in harmony with it. This conclusion is currently taken for granted in Protestant eco-writings as much as in secular, alternative ones. Few, though, replicate Callicott's nuanced discussion.

One writer who does is Adolf Gundersen. In his intriguing reflections Gundersen agrees that people have much to learn from Native American life and practices but stresses that we must recognize that there is no way we can re-create that lost world or carry over to our world some abstract part of it. For Gundersen, what we can use is the broader, overall reality of how Native Americans lived together—what Gundersen calls their "embedded membranes," especially their village life, not the abstract idea represented by the Native Americans' environmental ethic. Only by studying that reality can people appreciate, and learn from, Native Americans' ecologically conscious way of life.[41]

Another popular alternative to Christian thinking about the environment continues to be the Eastern religions. Taoism in particular receives numerous and highly laudatory discussions in green literature, especially for its celebration of nature. Sometimes Taoism is mentioned largely to attack Christianity, but there is also genuine interest in it as a perspective oriented toward the natural environment.[42] This is true also regarding Zen Buddhism. To its devotees it is superior to Christianity as a path for those committed to our ecosystem. For them, the Buddhist approach genuinely reveres nature, acknowledging nature's holism and seeking human integration with it.[43]

However, Zen, Taoism, and other Eastern religions have not had entirely smooth sailing in environmentalist seas. The pantheism that suffuses Eastern religions poses a major problem for traditional Christians. Some non-Christian critics, such as John Passmore, fear that Eastern religions prescribe an ethic of personal passivity as well as a weak role for the state and that these tendencies pose unsuspected difficulties for change-oriented environmentalists. Skeptics also ask whether Eastern religions have, in practice, made a difference in people's treatment of the ecosystem. They ask, Where are the signs that Eastern people spurn the Western values of economic growth and favor the tough environmentalism that stimulates Western interest in Eastern religions in the first place? They note that in Asia, development and growth are eagerly embraced, often at the expense of the environment.[44]

In Defense of Christianity

Reading Protestant literature on Christianity and the environment as well as green opinions from outside the Christian tradition can be depressing. They generally have a bleak tone, since the image of Christianity toward the environment they portray is rarely very positive.

There is another side, however. Some writers defend Christianity and its historical record on the environment. Few do so without reservations, and few fail to give attention to what they judge to be balance. Yet many analyses of the history of Christian thought and practice are not unreservedly negative and do not concede that an honest interpretation must be negative. Defenders complain that in this instance "conventional ecological wisdom . . . is just too facile; indeed dangerously facile."[45]

Defenders point out that when generalizations take over, a faith articulated in myriad theologies and lived over several thousand years often becomes reduced to a few unflattering negatives. In fact, some environmentalist opponents of Christianity and Judaism make no effort to speak to these religious traditions' richness. Defenders protest such casual arraignment of their religions before the court of modern environmentalist opinion and the guilty verdicts they summarily receive. The good disappears into the bad, and the subject is closed.

Often enough, the case against Christianity takes an astonishingly ahistorical direction, sometimes through the reduction of Christian history and ideas to a few damning items. This also happens when critics fail to consider Christianity or Christian civilization in comparison with other religions or cultures as they actually exist or have existed. To explore whether Christianity has been a greater offender than other religions and cultures will require hard work, tough analysis, and a rein on a desire to romanticize the unfamiliar. Casual assertions are not acceptable, especially those that manifestly lack cultural perspective.[46]

Consider, first, the Christian tradition's attitudes toward nature over the past two millennia. Almost all nonpolemical commentators observe that the situation is complex. John Passmore, an analyst who is no apologist for Christianity, argues that the Western tradition is indeed complicated and that many of the West's objectionable ideas regarding nature derive from classical Greek intellectual life. This tradition, he contends, played a greater role in Christian development than did Jewish ideas. Thus Greek thought is a more appropriate source for our attention, if we are seeking to point the finger of blame.[47]

In his massive treatment of the Western tradition, Clarence Glacken is as impatient as John Passmore with glib but uninformed generalizations. For Glacken, it is simply wrong to assert that the Western tradition is all about humanity ruling over nature. While that is part of the story, he argues that the tradition has also regularly acknowledged the "union" of humankind and the rest of nature. Another dimension of the tradition has cast humanity in the role of the finisher or polisher of God's creation. Each formulation includes God in the picture, but what humankind is expected to do varies dramatically in each instance.[48]

Thinkers from other perspectives agree that Christian thinking has gone in diverse directions over time and emphasize that many of them conflict with each other. Thus Christianity has simultaneously envisioned humans as stewards and as exploiters; it has posited redemption for humans only and held that all nature may be redeemed; and it has understood nature as a revelation and as a denial of God.[49]

On the Historical Record

Two questions receive serious attention in explorations of the history of Christianity and the environment. One is whether the treatment of the environment in the West, or the Christian West, has been uniquely bad compared to other times and places on earth. Is there really any evidence that Christianity has had an especially pernicious effect on the planet's ecology? Many within Protestant environmental circles believe the answer is yes, but others have searched in vain for supporting evidence. They note that Japan's poor environmental history is hardly the product of Christian ideas or culture. The same applies to Africa's record.[50]

Yi-Fu Tuan and Rene Dubos both attack the implicit view, common in this literature, that the rest of the world is in much better ecological shape than the West or than Christendom in particular. To them, this idea is as silly as it is false. And the same applies to romantics who indulge in finely spun illusions about prehistoric peoples. They were no great respecters of their environment, either.[51]

A second question asks what the substance of Christian teaching regarding the environment has been in Western history. "Teaching" is the important word here, because in this literature there is modest evidence at best about Christian practice, and there is even less discussion of its practice. Commentary on Christian ideas often substitutes for information about practices, which may have been very different. As Yi-Fu Tuan argues, there are relevant cases here. In China, Taoism and Buddhism are profoundly sympathetic to the ideal of ecological wholeness. Yet China's natural environment has suffered greatly over the centuries. The country was systematically deforested, and the land was devastated by distinctly nongreen farming practices. The teachings of a religious faith is no sure guide to human practice anywhere.[52]

In any case, in the fifteen hundred years before the Reformation, the Christian tradition's teachings regarding nature were, as we already know, highly controversial. No one disputes the existence of the view that nature was created solely for human use or the fact that this view sometimes involved approval of what today we would call abuse. However, the pre-

Reformation Christian tradition also included a stewardship tradition, though its depth is uncertain.

References to St. Francis of Assisi (1182–1226) are frequent in defenses of Christianity in history, echoing Lynn White's sentiments. Francis Schaeffer spoke for many when he declared, "I propose Francis as a patron saint for ecologists."[53] In some analyses, St. Francis embodies a long, robust Christian tradition of a love for animals and a yearning for a holistic peace between humanity and all creation. He illustrates, in other words, that some aspects of Christianity have a high view of creation: it should be honored because God made it or because God will redeem it fully.[54]

Not surprisingly, more than a few Protestant writers on the environment praise the Protestant Reformation highly. While Calvin and Luther were overwhelmingly Christ-centered, their interest in God's creation often receives special welcome. A number of Protestant commentators associate stewardship with the Reformation tradition. For some, the Reformation led back to the Bible and thus to the Bible's stewardship principles. For others, the Reformation principle of the unity of humankind and the rest of creation mandates stewardship. Most often, these analysts point out that the Protestant Reformation emphasized the creation and expected humans to care for it as part of their responsibilities to God's world.[55]

Opinions are divided over the role of the eighteenth century, the Age of Enlightenment, in our present environmental situation. Many defenders of the Christian tradition are sharply critical, because they conclude it was in the eighteenth century that the modern fallacy of the human as all-powerful governor of the earth gained sway. The Enlightenment made mankind king and the rest of the natural world subject without much of a God to restrain or direct humanity. For others, the Enlightenment separated nature from God and often from philosophy itself; its eventual influence on Western thought was both baleful and powerful. For still others, the problem came from what is perceived to be the Enlightenment's unreflective embrace of the scientific revolution. Those who promoted that movement did not ask or even care about its consequences.[56]

Other Causes of Our Environmental Decline

The truth is that much of the green Protestant literature that investigates the past interprets ideas as the central energy fueling human history. This explains in good measure why so much time is spent arguing over Christian history—which is understood as the history of Christian doctrine and thought. The clear assumption is that ideas matter tremendously, often more than anything else. This assumption affects all of the Protestant writing on the environment: its proposals for changing the future just as much as its grasp of the past.

Few analysts fail to comprehend that there are many intertwined causes in history; but for many eco-Protestants, ideas are what matter most in history. The ancient and fascinating question of whether this is so cannot be resolved here, but its implications for green Protestant analysis merit attention. Some Protestant environmentalists, however, want us to investigate other putative causes of the present ecological crisis, and, in fact, Protestant writers on the environment have put forward a good many other hypotheses. Each raises the question as to whether blaming Christianity or Protestantism may be mostly beside the point.[57]

From this angle, the search for alternative explanations becomes a kind of backhanded defense of Christianity. In some instances, this result is unintentional. In others, however, as in *Christianity Today*'s argument that the industrial revolution and science have done far more environmental damage than Christianity, it is quite intentional. The thesis redirects critical energy away from Christianity. Among the alternative targets in Protestant arguments are capitalism, urbanization, expanding wealth, a rising population, consumerism, and especially science and technology.[58] Capitalism is one target in the search for blame. In Protestant environmentalist thought today there is considerable hostility toward capitalism, hostility that is sometimes overt but often lurks just below the surface. Usually the word "capitalism" is not mentioned. The softer phrase "market economy" is the term of preference, but the message is the same: capitalism causes, encourages, and justifies using and abusing the environment for human purposes.

From this perspective, capitalism as a force has been far more influential than chatter about the Bible or Christian doctrines in the age of Augustine or Luther. For proponents of this analysis, capitalism has left—and continues to leave—a tragic mess in its wake; people therefore must grapple with the possibility that market capitalism requires serious structural change before humanity can address ecological problems.[59]

Another analysis concentrates on the fact of human sin, something a good deal older than capitalism or science as we know them. By this analysis, it is sin—not one or another set of thinkers or ideas, nor capitalist or socialist institutions—that is to blame for environmental abuse. Some evangelical Protestants in particular make this argument, though they are not alone. Their specific language may speak of sin since the Fall, or it may speak of human selfishness. The surprise, perhaps, is that this analysis rarely appears as the central Protestant Christian explanation of our environmental situation.[60] Part of the reason lies in mainline Protestant discomfort with the concept of sin. Many feel that the concept is unnecessarily negative and derives from notions such as the Fall whose value, if it exists, is at best mythic.

Moreover, sin is a problematic concept for reformers, much less for radicals. It is not clear that it is likely to inspire people to transform the planet, nor to suggest that they can do so in the first place. It may lead humanity toward repentance, which is something that more than a few Protestant environmentalists urge. But repentance and regeneration, not to mention rebirth, are different things. Few green Protestants deny some notion of sin altogether, but explaining environmental degradation in terms of the Fall or permanent selfishness is often too pessimistic for them. For all their talk of a desperate situation, Protestant greens are rarely pessimists.

Science and Technology

It is over science and technology that Protestant environmentalism has protested the most. Criticisms of science and technology overflowed in Protestant literature from 1970 on and regularly implicated Christianity. There has been widespread acceptance of Lynn White's thesis that Christianity's tendency to legitimate exploitation of nature encouraged the development of Western science and technology, which in turn accelerated exploitation of nature. Insofar as Christianity did not conceive of nature as sacred, it pried open the door for modern science and technology and what many Protestant environmentalists see as their predatory attitudes toward nature.[61]

Within Protestantism, however, there is some dissent to this analysis. Some skeptical Protestants ask, How it could be that Christianity was so integral to the growth of science and technology in our civilization when it took more than fifteen hundred years after Christ for science and technology even to begin to move toward the center of Western civilization?

Thomas Derr contends that the historical perspective supports such skepticism. After all, there have been remarkable developments in science and technology at various junctures in the histories of China, ancient Greece, and Islamic civilization, to give three examples. Christianity has hardly been the only chapter in the growth of science and technology and their possible consequences.[62]

Ian Barbour agrees that Christianity and science and technology cannot be glibly tied together, nor should they be condemned together. Moreover, Barbour insists that Christianity should be neither hostile nor necessarily sympathetic to science and technology. According to Barbour, the reflective Christian must examine each use of science and technology closely, and such analyses should be guides to their value.[63]

In fact, some Protestant environmentalists are scientists themselves and understandably argue that sweeping criticism of science and technology is unwarranted. Calvin DeWitt, for example, states that the goal must be a science and technology guided by a proper ethics, not a science and technology that are ends in themselves.[64]

In fact, we have good reason to recognize the consistent ambivalence regarding science in Protestant environmentalism—the ambivalence that, according to Joe Bowersox, applies to the entire green movement's attitude. Attacks on science are as frequent as attempts to use findings of science to buttress green agendas. Indeed, most Protestant images of nature and its moral mandates (such as holism) depend on the truth (one version or another) of scientific findings about nature and the universe. These scientific understandings are rarely probed conceptually or empirically. That is why the relationship between green Protestantism and science deserves and receives so much attention in this study.[65]

STEWARDSHIP

Since 1970, stewardship has been the environmentalist path most often proposed by Protestant Christians seeking to serve God and God's creation. A good many dissenters have offered other routes—and their numbers grow—but the call to stewardship remains the leading note sounded within green Protestantism. Stewardship is encountered repeatedly in such liberal Protestant publications as the *United Methodist Reporter* or the *Presbyterian Survey,* but it has also been endorsed by the conservative General Council of the Assemblies of God, the Evangelical Lutherans, and the Episcopal Church, among many others.[1]

Many Stewardships

While stewardship is the most common concept of Protestant environmentalism, its meaning is often contested.[2] At one level, that meaning is quite straightforward. It is the idea that God has designated human beings as "stewards, or guardians, over creation."[3] As we would expect, the foundation or at least part of the justification for Protestant stewardship rests in the Bible, particularly in Genesis. Several passages are crucial, but perhaps the most cited today is Genesis 2:15: "The Lord God took the man and put him in the garden of Eden to till it and keep it" (NRS) or "The Lord God took the man and put him in the Garden of Eden to work it and take care of it" (NIV).

Yet the idea of stewardship comes in many versions. It is a concept that spans a commodious universe whose residents are not all perfectly compatible. Thus, the extensive Protestant discussions of ecological stewardship often involve much more than simple hortatory proclamations and affirmations—though the number of these is not small. There are also many reflections on alternative understandings of stewardship, because stewardship implies significantly different things to different thinkers.

But some common themes percolate among stewardship advocates. One is an image of God as the sacred Creator and of all nature—all the material world—as God's creation. This relationship makes nature special and all life sacred and establishes that no one should dare to destroy what God has created. This link with God through creation is absolutely central for religious environmentalists and forms the moral ground for the care of nature, quite apart from particular biblical verses. It forms the basis for the idea of the environmentalist Eleventh Commandment—"Thou shalt cherish and care for the earth and all within it." While not every green Protestant supports such an addition to the Ten Commandments, there is consensus that God's creation deserves the treatment such an Eleventh Commandment suggests.[4]

The place of Christ in Christian stewardship thought is more problematic. Occasionally Jesus is simply missing. More often, stewardship thinkers invoke a Jesus who teaches stewardship, as in his parable of the talents (Matthew 25:14–30). Others cite Jesus' Incarnation and Resurrection as indicators of God's love for his treasured creation. The Incarnation, they argue, shows that God sought the deepest possible connection with nature and human nature, so both must be honored and loved. From this perspective, the Incarnation is God's dramatic statement that creation is good.

Green Protestants also use the Second Coming to illustrate that God cares about creation and will redeem it all in its fullness. Here Romans 8:21 receives the major emphasis: "The creation itself will be set free from its bondage to decay and obtain the glorious freedom of the children of God."[5]

Most Protestant environmentalists insist that all of creation is a holistic unity. Created as one by God, it must be approached holistically. Reverence for life includes honoring life as part of the full community that is God's creation and, of course, acting to preserve it. God and all parts of the universe are about "being together" in relationship—horizontal relationships as distinguished from hierarchical ones. In such a vision, the Creator/Redeemer as a relational being expects us to relate equally to God and to the rest of God's creation.[6]

Thus people cannot be understood apart from the rest of nature any more than they are logically, apart from God. We are members of God's community and should never put ourselves outside of, or above, nature or God's complete community. Thus, human "embeddedness in nature" is a defining truth about ourselves. No one can grasp any portion of the human story, including human redemption, without appreciating how much human beings are connected with the natural world.[7]

While such an analysis is currently attractive to many eco-Protestants, there is no unity among them on what constitutes its implicit view of the human. Some stress community and holism to the extent that men and women almost disappear into the whole of creation, or at least become no more than one part among infinite equal parts. Others, Protestant evangelicals especially, reject such a view, contending that it conflicts with the Genesis account of the specialness of human creation. Loren Wilkinson argues that any proper understanding of Christian stewardship necessarily implies that humans are different from the rest of creation. While they may be the source of our ecological problems, they are also special creations of God and have distinct stewardship responsibilities. By no means should we think they may be conflated with the rest of nature.

Some secular animal liberationists and deep ecologists are particularly upset with this conclusion. They complain about any biblical Christianity which holds that the human is unique and not just another animal or that God sanctioned the sacrificing of animals for human benefit but rejected the killing of humans. Secular environmentalists have complained about the leading evangelical preacher, Billy Graham, in exactly these terms and judged his environmental record very mixed. After all, he concentrates on people, their lives, and their salvation. The larger community of nature is not Graham's normal subject, a fact that disturbs those within and without Protestantism who have invested in the holistic metaphor for nature.[8]

Many of this critique's implications disturb evangelical environmentalists. As they interpret this viewpoint, it flatly rejects God and a divine creation and substitutes a random, accidental universe as the alternative. They also ask, How can humans have a solemn duty to do something about the ecological crisis from an understanding of the universe as accidental? What is the source for such a moral imperative in a morally empty universe? And why should we think people could do anything in a universe where accident is the rule?[9]

Overall, in Protestant visions of creation there is little contention over the model of community and the close relationship with God implied by it—as long as the terms remain general. There is much disagreement, however, on where the human being fits into that picture. To put it another way, the issue is what role God intends for us to play in creation, not whether we are an integral part of God's larger community.

The arguments over this issue take place within a shared conviction that people are to act as God's agents in the community of creation. God must matter. All creation is of God—"Lock stock and barrel it is his and his alone"[10]—and it exists for God. All humans are of God and in covenant with God. In that role, we are to be servants, or caretakers, or stewards of creation, or stewards of dominion. The models differ, but the fierce insistence that humans must be God's agents does not vary.[11]

Of course, this agreement gets the green Protestant only so far. If one is wondering what practical action to take, the step toward stewardship is less helpful than at first glance. Perhaps the companion consensus on the failure of humans as stewards helps some. While this belief does not tell people how to change, it can spur them to act. But here, too, there is an impediment. The conviction that human beings have been bad stewards is so axiomatic within environmental Protestantism that there is rarely enough analysis of what such an assumption means or implies.

According to some narratives, human sin has caused failed stewardship. Sometimes this sin is understood as the result of individual choices that led to alienation from God. It is often also described as "structural" sin, the result of social and institutional factors. Either way there is rarely a suggestion that the sin of failed stewardship is somehow a permanent or inevitable sin. In this world of Protestant thought, sin may be real, but in most accounts it is needless and redressable. Some believe that only in recent decades, or at most, centuries, have we moved away from stewardship. Others think the problem is age-old. But the assumption is the same: humans have terribly abused creation and must—and can—stop.[12]

Behind this assessment of human behavior there often lies a warning. Stewardship advocates agree in emphasizing human responsibility for creation. Stewardship is "the awesome responsibility of preserving its inherent value and worth."[13] It follows that the failures carry consequences. "We are accountable . . . for the polluted air we breathe, mercury in the water . . . the DDT in the land we spade."[14] Thus there is often more than a little aura of guilt in the air of Protestant environmentalism. Such sentiments come expectedly from those evangelical Protestants for whom guilt—and hell—are real. Yet they do not sound this theme alone. Even in mainline Protestant writings that stress love and universal salvation, the attitude can shift when abuse of the environment comes up. Then the tone can grow stern, and themes of guilt and punishment appear.[15]

Roderick Nash has noted this and has concluded that in "large part" the concept of stewardship is founded in guilt, which has "figured as a mainstay of the appeal."[16] Assertions about motivation, however, are tricky things; whether or not they are plausible, they are beyond substantiation. But Nash's claim that guilt is an integral element for many Protestant (and other Christian) thinkers recognizes how important the green Protestant belief is in human responsibility for the eco-crises of our time. Things are going badly; humans are responsible; therefore, we must shoulder great guilt. Such is the analysis—one based on classic assumptions about human agency both for good and for evil.

Contrasts within Stewardship

Stewardship as an approach to the environment is, of course, not the only path the green Protestant movement has taken. In the larger environmental movement, in fact, stewardship met increasing criticism, beginning in the 1980s. We have already noted the critique of much of Christian environmentalism—including its stewardship doctrine—from those environmentalists who are determinedly secular and especially those who are biocentric. For many of them, Protestant stewardship, no matter how touched up, involves a divinely created universe they deny and an anthropomorphic orientation toward nature that they despise. Thus green critics of stewardship are impressed primarily with the distance between their vision and that of Protestant stewardship.

On the other hand, the contrast can be exaggerated. The anthropomorphic understanding of stewardship, even when stewardship is defined conventionally, is only partly plausible. After all, stewardship does not crown human beings as the rulers of nature—far from it. In a stewardship view, God commands the universe, and human beings are God's servants. Stewardship is not biocentric in most of its Protestant versions, but it should not be characterized as anthropocentric either. Theocentric is the more accurate description.

Moreover, Protestant stewardship is like secular environmentalism in that it, too, has gone in several directions. Each of its branches is recognizably parallel to those in the larger environmental movement. Bob Pepperman Taylor's analysis of environmental thought in the American experience also makes sense when applied to Protestant stewardship thinking. Taylor argues that American environmentalism has viewed its relation to nature in two ways: as a tradition of stern duty and service, and as a tradition of mystical and aesthetic celebration. In fact, both of these traditions have long been visible in Protestant stewardship.

Stern Duty

The main road of stewardship has been stern duty, and many assumptions have been shared by those who travel it. This common core is shared by the

National Council of Churches as well as *Christianity Today*. Its essence is an emphasis on God's making humans responsible for the protection and care of nature. This approach has several forms, however, and the differences among them matter.

Consider, first, the dominion thesis on God, man, and nature. Derived, as we know, from Genesis 1:28, it has sparked controversy for a very long time. According to one of the oldest Christian understandings, the verse teaches that the universe is a hierarchy under God and that God gave humankind the animals, plants, and the land and its resources to use for their benefit. Within that context—human dominion, established by God's sovereign rule of the universe—people are to exercise stewardship.

In the 1970s, America's main evangelical publication, *Christianity Today*, was sympathetic to this analysis, especially when some writers carefully underlined that mankind was at the crux of God's creation. As a result, in both editorials and essays, the magazine cast a somewhat skeptical eye on what it perceived as too much enthusiasm for stewardship. It feared any interpretation that made stewardship into an outsized principle that somehow was more important than anything else, including God's affirmation of human dominion over the rest of nature. Such skepticism did not mean that the publication rejected stewardship or refused to support environmental reform. There was some support for environmental change, but with a caution and skepticism not found in more contemporary stewardship advocates. One editorial called for realism and noted that "to live is to pollute." Another essay complained that perspective was badly needed, since a far more important and more pressing problem than environmental pollution was society's denial of the truth of God's holy word.[17]

Today, Protestant theologians more often understand dominion in quite a different way. Now it concerns stewardship, not domination in any fashion. The argument comes in many forms but makes the single point that dominion properly understood is about the duty of serving nature. Thus some interpreters translate dominion as service or even love, love in the service of others.[18] The idea is that a true participation in God's universe requires stewardship by people as our part in the universe. In this translation, dominion does not deny stewardship but requires it.

Perhaps this is the best way to understand *Christianity Today*'s current position. The evangelical publication now maintains that a "human-centered view is not the problem, as long as it is understood in a God-centered context. Only by recognizing humanity's exalted status as God's stewards on earth will we find the motivation and energy to enact the necessary changes."[19] In other words, stewardship is a duty that makes sense in God's world.

This enterprise predictably and perhaps necessarily involves an effort to read troublesome biblical passages in relation to the green cause. But, after all, reinterpreting biblical passages for new times is a hallowed Christian tradition that goes back to Origen and Augustine and others in early Christianity. To be sure, Protestant fundamentalists such as Pat Robertson defend past meanings of dominion; they maintain that Genesis 1:26–28 ordained the right of human beings to have nature serve human interests. For Robertson and those of similar disposition, this understanding of dominion remains the answer. It is the word of God; it accords with the historic practice of Christianity; and it means that human use of nature is legitimate, no matter how much stewardship is also lauded.[20]

Defining stewardship as the call (or duty) to "earthkeeping" or "caring" is a position that has also been popular in recent years. These analyses agree that caring is the proper human attitude toward the natural universe, and they explicitly reject any dominion approaches that define dominion as human supremacy over the rest of nature. For them, the concept of caring necessarily involves renunciation of human rule over nature.[21]

What are the implications of caring or earthkeeping for stewardship? One is that caring is a moral imperative—a duty and an obligation. Another is the importance of intense, interactive love relationships. Caring takes stewardship another step—and a much larger step—toward closeness of humankind and nature. The major component is love, and in this outlook, love leads to caring, which is what God expects of us regarding creation. In more dramatic versions, love of creation is not just *one* goal of humans, but the *only* goal. The universe becomes more than a community or even an especially caring community. The idea is that the universe is about love and that we are God's special lovers of nature.

To advocates of this perspective, what love means in practice is the call to be a caretaker and a healer. Such an understanding, however, does not get one as far as some adherents might wish—or expect. The problem is that "caretaking" or "healing" can and does mean almost anything when put in concrete policy terms. Rather like the casual, if earnest, use of the word "compassion," exhortations to become a caretaker or healer often arrive unaccompanied by tough, clear specifics.

And this is not the only baffling feature sometimes encountered in the caretaker view. While its adherents visibly grow, the norm of caretaking cannot be taken for granted.[22] Serious arguments that touch its deeper resonances and implications could strengthen the case for this view. Energy spent on reinterpreting dominion or stewardship to encourage a more positive vision of God, human beings, and nature is energy well spent; more attention to the case for caretaking would be too.

Large realms of ambiguity remain after the grand affirmations are over. Choices have to be made, and no amount of enthusiasm about "caring" can eliminate them. Thus it is fortunate that some thinkers do struggle with the dilemmas that lie beyond incantations of caring. For example, some have recognized that one cannot achieve a reconciliation of humans and the rest of nature simply by defining stewardship as caring. How does one care for humans and the polio virus and the tsetse fly all together?[23]

A significant element of the movement to interpret stewardship in terms of earthkeeping or caring is the work of the Au Sable Institute, of Mancelona, Michigan, and especially that of Calvin DeWitt. During the 1980s, the Au Sable Institute and DeWitt became increasingly prominent in the debate over religion and the environment and the matter of how to bring the two together in a fruitful manner. What is particularly interesting is that they operated within an evangelical Protestant perspective. As such, they represent more evidence of the gathering interest in and attention to religion and the environment within evangelicalism, as in other areas of American Protestantism.

The Au Sable Institute was self-consciously designed to assist in the development of stewardship among Christians and the larger public. In Au Sable's lexicon, stewardship means "to bring healing and wholeness to the biosphere and the whole of Creation."[24] Practically, this familiar language of the earthkeeping paradigm translates to spreading knowledge of ecology and of the means to preserve, enhance—and heal—nature. But these tasks are set in a recognizably evangelical Protestant context. The world is God's and the Bible is the "sole authority." Environmental and evangelical preferences come together in the provision that those who visit Au Sable are not to smoke, use drugs, or drink alcohol.[25]

Since 1990 DeWitt and his analyses have appeared to be everywhere, reflecting his active involvement in the green religious movement. From one angle, DeWitt is simply another, if unusually prominent, Protestant advocate of earthkeeping, operating from evangelicalism with a strong accent on the Bible as the proper source for authority. From another, DeWitt has moved beyond the conventional evangelical position in arguing the value of other sources of truth. He has begun to claim that we can learn from the cosmos and from our own spiritual journeys as well as from the Bible.[26]

Perhaps this expansive view partly explains DeWitt's notable emphasis on creation. For him, God is above all the Creator; at least, there can be no doubt that DeWitt employs this image of God far more than any other. Such a judgment does not automatically sit well with all evangelicals. Their emphasis falls more often on the Incarnation—God as manifested in Jesus Christ, not God as the Creator. Failure to underline this priority by DeWitt has necessarily caused some uneasiness.[27]

Part of the same creation mode—and perhaps equally controversial—is DeWitt's recommendation that churches turn into "creation-awareness centers," systematically striving to respect and preserve the environment. He suggests a multitude of actions for churches, from prayer to buying the next-door lot and saving it as a natural park.[28] More broadly, DeWitt advocates a life philosophy that rejects any "abuse of God's creatures, the abuse of life." Such abuses include abortion, pornography, and economic exploitation. His explicit criticism of abortion in particular is rare among Protestant environmentalists. A few come close to favoring it to facilitate population control. Others finesse the issue, aware that it always brings conflict and bitterness in its wake.[29]

DeWitt comes back again and again to the creation as the key metaphor for Christian environmentalism, a perspective I discuss in its fullest expression in chapter 8. The most devoted adherents of creation theology rarely come from the evangelical tradition; in fact, many are not Christians at all. But in the larger Christian world there is nothing unusual about DeWitt's highlighting the creation side of God, and in this regard he is joined by many others.[30]

It is possible to cross into a world where all other sides of God disappear and humans become co-equal creators with God. DeWitt knows this, of course, and stays well to this side of such a line. Thus, controversy has sometimes broken out that has pitted DeWitt and his compatriots against far more committed creation environmentalists within the movement.

DeWitt does not relish this kind of division. He is of interest in this study in good part because he is such an energetic activist for his cause, an intellectual who has made the commitment to act in specific ways, to which the programs of the Au Sable Institute testify. He is very much the stern moralist, driven by his idea of human duty to nature, but he is prepared to do what he judges has to be done, including being flexible politically. He insists that no one should be sectarian in the realm of practical action. He draws no litmus test for political coalitions and gladly accepts any help he can get. He argues that debates over the allies one attracts do nothing but get one off the track. DeWitt is an unusual political "realist" in a move-ment uncomfortable with the demands of ordinary politics.[31]

Wesley Granberg-Michaelson represents another important variation on the stewardship theme. Granberg-Michaelson was for some time asso-ciated with the Christian publication *Sojourners* and eventually became its managing editor. He has also been associated with the World Council of Churches, working to advance its environmental agenda. Granberg-Michaelson has received support from evangelical senator Mark Hatfield of Oregon, and gained experience at the Au Sable Institute.[32]

In contemporary terms, Granberg-Michaelson is a radical Christian environmentalist who is distinctly ambivalent about the concept of stew-ardship. He says he does not belong to this tradition if it defines steward-ship in an ordinary way. For Granberg-Michaelson, the Bible stresses God's care for the earth and our duty to nurture creation at God's wish. Thus, for him, stewardship makes sense only in the metaphor of deep, complete caring. It has nothing to do with human authority in a hierarchi-cal universe, including the authority to protect the rest of nature, since humanity is somehow both separated from it and superior to it.

While Granberg-Michaelson carefully distances himself from panthe-ism, he contends that God is intimately involved in creation and that nature, in turn, profoundly reflects God. Thus creation is not something that happened once in the past; it is an ongoing process. God, nature, and human beings create together, and all have a duty to ensure the life of this new and ever-holistic creation.[33]

Granberg-Michaelson is equally impatient with much of the routine Christian endorsement of stewardship. As far as he is concerned, it often amounts to little more than verbal pleasantries or Sunday morning pieties. Like DeWitt, he is very much a proponent of stern duty and complains of others' lack of dedication. Stewardship must cut against the immoral mod-ern culture. It requires serious commitment and demands real costs from its adherents. It must respond with disgust to the "reckless, wasteful, or selfish exploitation of the environment" that surrounds people everywhere in the contemporary age. As a result, for Granberg-Michaelson, serious followers of stewardship must have a burning determination to change things, far beyond an effort to recycle and the like. They must engage structural realities such as the current economic systems and the world of nation-states, both of which he rejects as sources of evil.[34]

For Granberg-Michaelson, a green Christianity that is not action-oriented inevitably bears false witness to God. Yet he is sensitive as well to the danger of "worldliness" without "piety." He proposes to slay any such dualisms and replace them with a unified Christian witness toward a holistic world. He realizes that this step will be radical in its economic, political, and cultural consequences. What is not so clear, however, is exactly what that world will look like or how such a Christian environmentalism will work toward it in a world of many faiths, and many divisions, that are not likely to disappear.[35]

In Celebration (But Not Worship) of Nature

The duty model of stewardship is the usual theme of green Protestantism, but it is not the only one. The celebration theme constitutes another and increasingly frequent disposition. Its diverse exponents are alike in their emphasis on great enthusiasm for God's nature as something wonderful, a matter of godly beauty. From this focus, they derive their version of stewardship—that is, of what one must do. We are to celebrate nature and its glories and to care for them in their beauty so that they endure.

The word "enthusiasm" is crucial in understanding this widespread attitude among Protestant environmentalists. Its advocates speak more in terms of joy and happiness, which inspire care for nature, and less in terms of duty or responsibility. They beg us to accent the positive and accept nature's "invitation to wonder" and to glory in the amazing beauty of God's creation.[36]

At its most celebratory, this perspective skates close to pantheism, although its enthusiasts invariably deny any imputation of pantheism. Their overarching theme is the oneness of humans with nature: the human as part of a single community in which praying with nature makes great spiritual sense and gives great joy. While those who relate to nature in this fashion provoke scorn from critics, their numbers should not be underestimated.[37]

Richard Cartwright Austin has thoroughly developed the themes of beauty and the beauteous unity in nature. For Austin, the usual concepts of stewardship or earthkeeping are rather lame. We must learn a new and more grand concept. We could learn from environmentalist John Muir and understand nature as "a lush garden with us in the midst of all life." Its great and godly beauty can be "healing,"[38] and we are called to engage nature with the joy and enthusiasm that comes from "sensuous contact with all living things."[39]

An expressive celebrant of nature, Austin is unusual in that he is equally expressive in discussing his personal life, his loves, or his therapists. But he is not unusual in arguing within Protestantism for an approach that involves more than routine stewardship. Among many green Protestants there is a great enthusiasm about nature that is hardly characteristic of much of the Christian tradition—though it seems related to past forms of Christian mysticism and even ecstasy. The hymns to nature's beauty that are so often a part of Protestant considerations on nature and the environment best illustrate the spirit.

Green Protestants who concentrate on beauty as a theme often cite the Psalms. For example, Psalm 27:4 ("that I may dwell in the house of the Lord all the days of my life, to behold the beauty of the Lord") and Psalm 19:1 ("The heavens are telling the glory of God; and the firmament proclaims his handiwork") sing of God's beauty and the beauty of God's creation. But many also invoke their own prayers to accompany those of the Psalms. Mainline denominational periodicals in particular have given voice to such expressions of joy and awe at nature's beauty as a gift of God.[40]

Some, moreover, go quite a bit further; for them the beauty of nature is about more than glorious summer afternoons, beautiful flowers, and awesome snowstorms. It is about human beings and about how God's beauty creates human beauty and leads us on toward beauty everywhere, and thus toward God. In this vision, people who discover the sensual in themselves and in their surroundings can awaken to the beauty of God. Such an awakening to sensual beauty can teach us life's worth and facilitate human interaction and love. Thus beauty can be in each of our lives and in the relationships we treasure. The more this beauty is present, the more people will spread beauty into the world, for themselves and for others. Beauty can make us live and live fully with God. Indeed, beauty is the way to live a full and true life with our sensuous selves, with others, and with our God.[41]

Of course, for some green Protestants, all this provokes suspicion and fairly cries out to be criticized. Some complain that it is all insubstantial, a bit like a brief camping trip in which city folk safely "experience nature." Such campers know well that escape is available anytime and that the beauty and other attractions of nature matter only within a restricted and tame context.[42]

Another critique focuses on pantheism. Critics warn that intermingling nature and God too closely can lead into dubious territory. They remind their fellows of Christianity's age-old belief that God created nature but is not to be conflated with nature, nor vice versa. Christianity was founded on this doctrine, first established by the ancient Jews when they chose Yahweh over the numerous nature cults of their time and place.

As a result, some fault Protestant "nature romantics" when they appear to veer toward nature worship.[43] Evangelical Francis Schaeffer argues that the human being is denigrated by such a view; through pantheism the human "becomes no more than the grass."[44] Others charge that uncritical nature-admirers outside the Christian tradition have sometimes been profoundly evil. The most sensational example offered is that of the Nazis.[45]

At times there is some confusion between two related but distinct concepts—pantheism and panentheism. Pantheism holds that the world as a whole is divine, while panentheism is the idea that the world is part of but not all of God. It is not always clear that those who do indeed worship nature in principle or in practice are really the pantheists that critics sometimes suggest. Some are—as were Henry David Thoreau and, perhaps, John Muir. But such people within green Protestantism are much more often panentheists—worshipers of nature who understand that nature does not comprise all of God.

There remains, however, the more general complaint that among nature celebrants there is considerable confusion of nature with part or all of God. This is never meant as an objection to celebrations of nature. Many green Protestants brim with enthusiasm about the glories of nature, but that joy need not and does not imply pantheism—or panentheism. Yet sensitivity to the limits here is partly why green Protestants are cautious about rushing back to prescientific nature cultures, proposing to junk all science and technology, or endorsing a simple hunter-gatherer life.

Recently some Protestant environmentalists have undertaken to distinguish their regard for God's creation from so-called Gaia spirituality. The Gaia hypothesis in its several forms transforms the material world (nature) into the divine and repudiates stewardship as anthropomorphic arrogance. But to Loren Wilkinson, honoring and caring for nature must not lead the Christian to deny "the shepherdly rule of God," God's separation from and yet concern for creation. God's stewardship in turn establishes and justifies human stewardship of the rest of nature.[46] Others argue that the Fall separates human beings from God and that humans can thus in no way be equated with the Creator.[47] This is, in fact, an interesting point. It is not clear how a full telling of the biblical creation story could avoid grappling with the Fall and its consequences in terms of human relations with God.

Sterner critics assert their belief that excessive celebration of nature clouds over the dark sides of nature, including human disease and natural disasters. Thomas Derr decries nature romanticism among environmentalists when it leads to avoiding such evil in nature. For him, nature is at best neutral once one takes into account the suffering, predations, and death that abound there. The best that can be said is that it is "half friend, half enemy," and we should not deceive ourselves otherwise.[48]

This balance is far too pessimistic for most, but some analysts share his uneasiness about uncritical enthusiasm for nature if it leads to an unthinking passivity that Protestant environmentalists also reject. They insist that sentimentalism is no substitute either for hard thinking or for concentrating on action. In this day and age, they say, we need activists and reformers to tackle the problems of creation.[49] In this judgment we can hear once again the call of stern duty, the dominant language of Protestant stewardship. Passivity is never a good state in this very Protestant and very American outlook.

Study of green Protestantism confirms that Bob Pepperman Taylor's analysis applies beyond the realm of the secular environmental movement. Here, too, are two approaches, one grounded in what I have called stern duty and another more inclined to celebration of nature. Both attitudes are integral to green Protestant thought.

Stewardship discussions normally take place in the mode of stern duty and at one level represent a widespread unity on the content of Christian responsibility. But beneath this consensus—not very far beneath it, in fact—is a great deal of disagreement over what stewardship should mean. Such disagreement is not necessarily a sign of failure. Instead, it signals just how important stewardship is as the religious foundation stone for a green Protestant politics. Stewardship is, as a result, something worth contesting.

Those who wish to redefine stewardship as "earthkeeping," for example, may not go far toward dramatically new concepts to describe divinely sanctioned relations between humans and the rest of nature. But they are struggling to get Protestants to inch away from the established notion of stewardship, about which there was once a consensus within green Protestantism. And their impact is becoming more and more noticeable.

The more celebratory and sometimes mystical approach points more toward the development of radical eco-theologies than toward stewardship. This mystical approach does not necessarily offer any profound insight beyond its enthusiasm for both nature and the self as experience. But it definitely challenges conventional views of stewardship—in its focus, its holism, and its very belief in experience. It was the first alternative to traditional stewardship views (though perhaps not always perceived as such). It may not have won many theological adherents, but other Protestant thinkers have joined with its enthusiasts to argue that our dangerous age demands the formulation of new eco-theologies. To that expanding enterprise this book must now turn.

TOWARD ECO-THEOLOGY

This chapter and those that follow explore the determined efforts within Protestantism (and Christianity in general) to craft new eco-theologies. The several examples to be considered include the work of H. Paul Santmire, creation and process theologies, and ecofeminism. In each instance, Protestants who have struggled to create these new eco-theologies have taken as their starting premise "the ambiguous ecological promise of Christian theology,"[1] as Santmire gently puts it.

At one level, the motivation for the contemporary eco-theology enterprise is the desire to fashion a Christianity that offers a greater promise for the survival of creation than most past Christian theologies have provided. That desire in turn derives from the conviction that creation is in crisis—the universal constant of religious environmentalism. The result has been a fascinating, diverse, and fiercely controversial proliferation of eco-theologies.[2]

Philosopher and environmentalist John Passmore recognizes that the West, including religions of the West, have had complex attitudes toward nature. These attitudes reflect multiple traditions, and we should be careful to avoid simplistic generalizations about "Western attitudes." Passmore also notes that "Christian theology has in the past proved itself to be remarkably flexible," and he understands that it is in fealty to that tradition that contemporary "theologians are now busily attempting to work out new attitudes to nature . . . denying that men have a 'sacredness' which animals do not possess." Passmore has expressed skepticism, however, about the new eco-theological efforts within the Christian tradition, concluding that the extent of change that would be needed within Christianity is enormous. He has written, "I more than doubt Christian theology can thus reshape itself without ceasing to be distinctly Christian."[3]

Despite his skeptical prediction, Passmore's perception of the theologians' efforts twenty years ago is still more accurate today. The process of designing eco-theologies for the contemporary era is booming in the world of Christian, including Protestant, theology. As Roderick Nash reported, "by the 1980s . . . 'Ecotheology' had not only become a new word but a compelling world view."[4]

The Example of H. Paul Santmire

Paul Santmire has played a significant and influential role in the development of renewed Protestant eco-theology. He is not the sole figure of importance in this enterprise, but he has been a major one. For this study, his thought serves as a valuable example of the movement. A Lutheran minister and writer, Santmire has long argued that Christians have insufficiently engaged the environmental cause.[5] He has undertaken to help change the situation by promoting a reexamination of Christian thinking about the environment, arguing not for a new Christianity but for a new, eco-theological vision of the old Christianity.[6]

Santmire has skirted the more radical eco-theologians and creation and process theologians, though he has much in common with each. His support for eco-feminist theology, too, has not been uncritical. He has welcomed that school of thought insofar as it raises critical issues regarding patriarchal theologies and patriarchal societies and represents a standing judgment on the failures of much of traditional Christianity—and if such failures had not existed, he argues, ecofeminism would not have been necessary. But Santmire explicitly rejects non-Christian ecofeminism, and he has doubts about the legitimacy of Christian ecofeminist arguments that the world is best understood as God's body.[7]

Yet Santmire always returns to agree with ecofeminism and the other radical expressions of eco-theology that something must be done to enliven current theology as it encounters (or fails to encounter) what he believes is our serious environmental situation. Thus he bemoans "how static, not to say dead in the water, the current theological discussion about the environmental crisis actually is." For him, the time for creative rethinking is past due.[8]

Santmire has defined his part of the project in this way: "I just look at myself as one little Protestant boy over in the corner trying to do his thing and to see what can be done with the Reformation tradition."[9] This description is, to put it mildly, somewhat modest; actually, Santmire has sought to do much more. He wants to construct an ecological theology true to a revamped Christianity, or, as he puts it, to provide "an ecological reading of biblical faith."[10]

Santmire has argued that in pursuing this mission, strong internal integrity is essential. One must derive insights from within, not copy current cultural fashions. For him, this means in part that Protestant thinkers should not permit secular environmentalist critics to stampede them into scrapping Christianity in the rush to construct a more adequate eco-theology. On the other hand, Santmire does not intend to be trapped into conservative intransigence just because Christianity is under fire in some secular environmental circles. He is not interested in the slightest in giving up the search for a green Christianity and retreating to what he thinks is an unsatisfactory, traditionalist, anthropocentric Christianity.

The answer, for Santmire, is to be captive to neither approach. He moves along in his own path, one that respects both broader environmental concerns and conventional Christianity.[11] He also insists that those fashioning eco-theologies must make a commitment to rigorous thinking. He knows that emotional and impulsive declarations simply will not do. The usual explanation—that time is short as the planet hurtles "toward an ecological catastrophe"—does not move him.[12] He agrees that the threat of impending doom is real; all the more reason, he argues, for a disciplined, thoughtful response. In such a situation there is no room for sloppy and undisciplined thinking. It is necessary to look below the surface of things and not repeat "the dangerous tendency on the part of the conventional ecological wisdom to by-pass any thoroughgoing kind of social analysis and criticism."[13] Moreover, in Santmire's hands, serious thought has to come to grips with a world that is not simple-minded. History is not a straight line, he argues, and human thought and experience are full of difficult ambiguities, mixed patterns, and inescapable complexities.[14]

Santmire begins his own environmental argument with the contention that at its core Christianity is ecological. The challenge is to get people to appreciate this neglected truth. This Protestant believes that if people examine the Bible, they can discover its many ecological themes, demonstrated especially in God's gift of the land (and its fecundity) to the ancient Jews and in their involvement with it. For Santmire this story illustrates how integral nature is to God and has been to God's people. The Bible also shows how wonderfully inclusive God's kingdom is. All of nature belongs because God created it, and all creatures have their home within it.

Thus, Santmire contends, the ancient Jews did not need to escape nature to find God or to watch God at work. They simply had to encounter nature and its workings on the land. Their God was not remote, nor was the human being a kind of anthropomorphic island. God, people, and nature were inextricably involved with each other. This was the historic Jewish ecological legacy to Christianity.[15]

Of course Santmire appreciates that the Christian legacy is complicated and that not all of it can inspire green Christians. One dimension of that legacy has focused too exclusively on spiritual concerns, especially the relationship between God and human beings. While Santmire acknowledges this dimension, he points out that the environmental tradition that began with the ancient Jews is also part of the Christian story that is far from "ecologically bankrupt."[16]

Santmire also wants to persuade his readers that evidence of green thinking in the history of Christianity has been plentiful. He cites, for instance, the teaching of Irenaeus and other early Christians against Gnosticism. As Santmire understands it, Gnostic spirituality urged people to shake off the evil, material world and reach toward the transcendent with all their energy and purpose. Santmire's Irenaeus rejected such a view; defended creation as good, albeit marred by human sin; and declared that creation was not exclusively for humans.[17]

Other early Fathers defended or cared for nature also. As an important example Santmire identifies St. Augustine, who lavishly lauded the beauties of God's creation. But Santmire particularly identifies with the witness of St. Francis of Assisi, whom he considers a far more plausible Christian environmentalist hero than St. Augustine. St. Francis's legacy to Christian environmentalism was a profound yet childlike love and affirmation of God's creatures. Moreover, St. Francis had faith that when the world ended, God would bring all together into a new creation of peace—a perfection of harmony among God, humankind, and nature.[18]

It is perhaps not surprising that Paul Santmire speaks on behalf of the environmental side he finds in the Protestant Reformation. While he grants that the Reformation largely dwelt on the God-man relationship, he believes it also included God's whole creation. Moreover, the Reformation's attention to humankind existed within a context which assumed that men and women were intimately intertwined with nature. References to God and nature, nature's wonders, and the human relationship with nature abound, particularly in the writings of Martin Luther.

In that sense, the Reformation that Paul Santmire discerns was true to the Old Testament and, in his judgment, something of a return to the traditions of the Old Testament. The sad thing, he argues, is that the Reformation's legacy was lost due to a host of factors, including the Industrial Revolution and capitalism; a science that permitted human misuse of nature; and liberal philosophers, such as Immanuel Kant, who tore nature (and most everything else) from the protective mooring of God.[19]

For Santmire, these factors, especially ideas that legitimate exploitation of nature, deserve much more of our attention. They have had a devastating impact in the ravishing of the earth. Unfortunately, they have crept into Christian thought and the practice of the Christian church, or at least the part of the church which has continued to believe that nature is primarily for human use. But they have reigned most exuberantly in the production-oriented ideologies of the nineteenth and twentieth centuries—both capitalism and communism.[20]

To Santmire the modern Christian church continues to have an ambiguous record on the environment. It cannot easily escape either its past or the corrupting influences currently around it. Such influences have, however, been exacerbated by the dubious limitations of this century's Protestant theology, much of which Santmire considers pernicious in the extreme. For him, too much of it has centered on God and humans and has been utterly anthropocentric. Karl Barth is his favorite exemplar of this tragic error, but he proffers a full list. Modern theology, Santmire charges, has often relegated nature to a sidetrack, held it to be of little significance, and laid it open to rapacious exploitation.[21]

Moreover, according to Santmire's analysis, it has not helped that the culture of the United States has been beguiled by an "ecological schizophrenia." U.S. culture has experienced a deep fissure between nature and society and has seen a sharp chasm cut between lovers of nature and abusers. Santmire argues that one side of our tradition has adopted what he terms the "Ethic of Adoration" of nature. Its practitioners, of course, include Henry David Thoreau, John Muir, and a host of present-day figures. For some, the attraction of nature has been in its beauty; for others, nature has provided a religion. Often nature has served, as it did in ancient Israel, as an alternative society to a perceived corrupt social order where people can dwell (largely in their minds) free from the disappointing world in which they actually live. In each case it is a refuge, a safe harbor.[22]

But Santmire has no use for such an approach, whatever its origin. He is hard on those who make a cult of the simple, rural life in headlong flight from modern urban conditions. Nor does he join those who reify intuitive spiritualities among Native Americans or Zen Buddhists or those swept away by that "enchanting thinker," Henry David Thoreau. To him, they are all fleeing rationality and the gritty world of today, and they are therefore unlikely to help the environmentalist cause.

To be sure, Santmire has his moments of appreciation of the romantic inclination and indulges in it himself. From Cape Cod he once wrote, "under my prostate body lying face down with no blanket and no bathing suit to separate me anywhere from a million variegated granules of warming sand, my brother the earth was full of caresses"; and, while swimming, "I floated on my back in another world, looking up at the stars with blinded joyful eyes. That is what the Christian's ritual is like, when it is right . . . childlike trust and play and sensuous joy."[23]

Yet for Santmire, most romantics are addicted to an "opiate" that does not help people formulate a practical theology or address real ecological problems. He suggests that many such individuals are products of the 1960s. This generation fails to thrill him, because he thinks its members often lack realism. Santmire wants to address environmental problems as a Christian; he is not interested in issuing grand statements or making romantic gestures.[24]

Santmire also holds that a destructive "ethic of exploitation" has found a too-comfortable home in the United States. He argues that ever since the Puritans reigned, Americans have demonstrated a uniformly unfortunate mixture of behaviors toward nature: enthusiastic destruction, mindless exploitation, and simple carelessness. In his view, part of becoming environmentally responsible is to grapple with this appalling record and not pretend it did not happen.

Santmire argues that an acceptable eco-theology must also recognize the fissures in American and Christian thought and history and try to mend them. To advance this formidable goal, he has crafted a "theology of complementarity." His point is that the American tradition is valuable in its richness but that some of its tensions must be brought together in a kind of harmony if we are to address the environmental challenges of our time. We cannot, for example, just abandon our tradition of liberty because it permits damage to our environment. That would be neither possible nor desirable. At the same time, we must strengthen our failing traditions of community and thus moderate unchecked individualism and freedom. The aim is to achieve as much as possible of both goals.

An air of vagueness, however, not to say wishful thinking, surrounds this proposal. The idea is attractive, but questions arise. Exactly how much of which freedoms should we preserve? How much of which freedoms need to be reduced—and for precisely what kind of community? Moreover, his idea sounds more than a little like trying to have it both ways—again and again. Santmire, though, intends just the opposite. To him, it makes no sense to hunt for new values or to try to make definitive choices for one part of our tradition over another. People can only proceed from where they are to develop a wholeness that will be realistic *and* preserve the earth.[25]

For Santmire, perhaps the fullest success will come when people grasp a "vision of wholeness and renewal for all things." If they do, they will experience ecstasy, while retaining their rational selves as well. This process will unite individual souls just as all nature should be united.[26] How all these positive things can be achieved is hardly clear, though. There is a fine line between Santmire's rich appreciation of the diverse goods in the world and an affirmation of everything, without enough sense of the demands of priorities.

Santmire has summed up his outlook by recommending to his readers the Old Testament prophet Isaiah. In Santmire's reading, Isaiah had zeal for social justice on earth and for the redemption of his people in God's universe. He cared about both human civilization and the glory of nature. He also thought holistically and wanted to bind up the conflicts of his time and place. In Santmire's view, Isaiah had it right: resolving the old divisions (such as those between human beings and the rest of nature) is an essential mission as one proceeds toward a new order with God. Locked in old conflicts, one is unlikely to discover new ground.[27]

The community Santmire wants us to discover is, of course, natural in all its fullness, which he interprets as a joyous creation of God, created for humans and for God: "So God created the great sea monsters and every living creature that moves, with which the waters swarm, according to their kinds, and every winged bird according to its kind. And God saw that it was good" (Genesis 1:21).

While Santmire grants that there is much in nature that we cannot understand or accept—especially death—he is sure God rules nature and has always done so wisely: "O Lord, how manifold are thy works! In wisdom hast thou made them all; the earth is full of thy creatures" (Psalms 104:24). Indeed, God's presence in nature goes even further, much further. Nature is "an immense constellation of God's activity, an ocean of Divine power and wisdom, constantly in flux under his guidance."[28]

Santmire is especially earnest in his effort to establish firmly the proposition that nature has its own integrity. He insists that while God is inextricably involved in nature and created nature in part for humans, nature has its own integrity and independence. To deny that, he asserts, is to deny God's creative power that gave nature "a life of its own, its own citizenship."[29]

Others deny that God gave nature this liberty, as Santmire well recognizes. That is why by the mid-1980s he had become something of a radical Christian environmentalist. Lynn White was a model for him, as one who believed that all creatures lay within God's possible grace and who identified St. Francis as the exemplar of this truth in Christian history. Santmire now argued that there was an urgent need for Christians to rally to the liberation of nature, a call that earned him praise from Roderick Nash, among other secular environmentalists.

Santmire finds in the Bible a universe where God and nature exist quite apart from the human and where God established nature with its own independence, a position that one critic has charged is a plausible reading of the Bible only if one employs some hardworking "principles of selectivity and emphasis."[30] As evidence for his view Santmire cites Romans 8:21 ("the creation itself will be set free from its bondage to decay and obtain the glorious liberty of the children of God") and 1 Corinthians 15:28 ("When all things are subjected to him, then the Son himself will also be subjected to him who put all things under him, that God may be everything to every one").

But this picture is not as clear as it might be. For example, the sympathetic critic may ask, what does the independence of nature mean, given Santmire's parallel claim that nature is ineluctably a product of God's creative power? What do Santmire and those who agree with him mean by "integrity" in the context of nature? The answer is not obvious, and the claim appears abstract—not a good illustration of Santmire's commitment to practicality. Moreover, what does it mean to speak of nature's freedom and nature's liberation? What is nature to be freed from—or freed for? Indeed, where nature is concerned, what sense does it make to talk about liberation at all?

Throughout his analysis Santmire brings Christ into the picture, and he is obviously comfortable with Christ as the center of Christianity. Santmire asserts that when Christ returns, Christ will reach out to humankind *and* to nature. Christ will usher in a new heaven and a new earth. People will see God's creation in its fullness, and there will be peace between people and all nature at last. He cites Colossians 1:16, 20: "for in him all things were created, in heaven and on earth . . . and through him to reconcile to himself all things, whether on earth or in heaven, making peace by the blood of his cross."[31]

In a recent formulation, Santmire has once again described Christ (the Incarnation) as central, the sign of God's determination to act for "the perfecting and the restoring of the creation."[32] However he puts it, though, Christ is integral to Santmire's Protestant environmentalism. In his case, "Christology thus embraces theology. . . . Christology and 'loving nature' are inseparable."[33]

In the face of all this enthusiasm for a new age, one may ask, how does Santmire explain what has gone so wrong that a new order is urgently needed? For some Protestants, sin would arise in this context. While Santmire gave the concept of sin barely a page in his *Brother Earth*, the book he characterizes as his major theological statement, more recently he has had more to say on the subject. Perhaps he decided our problems were so bad that the concept of sin was needed after all. He declares, "The human creature has sinfully turned away from God, wreaking untold miseries within human history in the process, and indeed upon the whole earth, more so in our time than any other. This is the curse of human sin upon the world."[34]

While the rest of nature may suffer or even be cursed because of its inevitable association with humans, though, Santmire concludes that this larger nature is free from sin. Thus when Christ returns, he will not usher in a new nature, for no new nature is needed. In this green version of Christianity most of creation is too good to require saving. Rather, Christ will come to transform human beings, who do need saving, and as a consequence all nature will flourish.[35]

Santmire reads the Bible as speaking of human responsibilities and possibilities as well as human failures. God has specific expectations of humans that we must answer and—here is the basis for hope—that we *can* answer. Santmire's God expects people to celebrate the beauty of nature, to acknowledge its wonders and glories with great awe, and to honor its independence as our "brother earth." God also expects people to serve as "caretakers" of nature.

Santmire distinguishes such a duty from ordinary stewardship. For him, the usual meditations on "responsible stewardship" are "fundamentally uninspiring."[36] His concept of caretaking is grounded in his theology of the universe and Christ and his conviction that human beings must be "servants and celebrants of the whole creation, for Christ's sake." He argues that such an outlook cannot possibly be confused with the normal concept of stewardship. As he sees it, stewardship is thin in its passion, modest in its commitment, and elitist in its attitude toward nature. He understands his caretaking, on the other hand, as passionate for the cause, strong in its commitment, and devoted to the servant model of care.[37]

In policy terms, however, Santmire does not pretend to offer anything special or unique. His policy program coincides recognizably with the standard agenda of green Protestantism (see chapter 10). He advocates population control, curbing economic growth, recycling, and greater "social justice"—all predictable fare.[38]

One may ask why Santmire finds it important to develop his distinctive eco-theology if it results in such a predictable set of policy objectives.

Perhaps such a question does not take Christian theology and, in a sense, the Christian faith seriously. The answer is that Santmire considers it his goal to understand and proclaim as much of God's truth as possible. That *might* include fashioning a unique political program, but in his case it does not.

Santmire finds a "gracious" God of many parts—creative, inclusive, living, and holy. He finds a God who intends to bring people together with themselves and with the entirety of nature.[39] Yet Santmire does not claim to have a neat or unchanging set of answers. His work just does not stride down a single, uncluttered path (or, at least, it does not do so for long). Santmire has traveled in several directions, and perhaps it is this theological journey that has honed his sense of history and perspective so well. He has been among the best searchers for a new, or renewed, Christian ecological vision.

Paul Santmire has been a major voice within Protestant Christianity in the struggle to reconceptualize Christian theology for our ecological times. He is not alone, however, and is now by no means a remarkably radical voice. A chorus now calls for radical eco-theology and the forging of a common cause "to rebuild the Christian creation tradition."[40]

This movement has great faith in the possibility of a world where the gap between people and the rest of nature is closed and where there is a nonpantheistic but intimate union of deity and planet. A contemporary Presbyterian document declares that the Bible and Christianity understand "the impossibility of separating the human creature from the rest of creation."[41] Lynn White argues that we can and must "sense our comradeship with a glacier, a subatomic particle or a spiral nebula."[42] The goal here is to see all nature as part of one creation and to recognize that God's redemption exists for all equally.[43]

Creation Theology

Eco-theology has gone in two directions over the past several decades—toward process theology (see chapter 8) and creation theology—though neither of these perspectives falls into or respects neat categories or predictable bounds. Underlying each is a mood, a sense that Christianity must reorient itself to reflect a better appreciation of God's world than the old theologies did. Creation theology's strength is in challenging believers to rethink their basic Christianity in the light of the environmental crisis. Its weakness is an abstractness that too often leaves eco-theology remote from practical environmentalism.[44]

Proponents of creation theology celebrate what they see as a glorious and unending creation (or evolution) that they perceive to be the central reality in the universe. They laud holism and deny dualism on any level. Though they normally acknowledge Christ, the Christ in creation theology often metamorphoses into the "cosmic" Christ, a figure who summons all life to divinity and represents the interrelatedness of everything. Creation theology's framework is often intentionally more mystical than analytical; proponents frequently insist that the mystical affirms community, while the analytical divides creation.[45]

Among Protestant eco-theorists, there are many who have been attracted to creation theology. Signs of its impact can even been seen within evangelical Protestantism, where admonitions about the importance of creation and praise for "the gospel of creation" abound.[46] While creation theology is no longer a strange or occult perspective in Protestantism, Matthew Fox, an eclectic thinker, is perhaps the best-known contemporary advocate.

Fox is a clever and skillful essayist, gifted in presenting his views in a palatable style, one that makes what he has to say far more appealing than some numbing theological reflections on nature and the environment would be. His books often have colorful designs and spirited prose and include interesting quotations from others. For better or for worse, they have titles such as *Whee! We, Wee All the Way Home: A Guide to a Sensual, Prophetic Spirituality.*[47]

Fox's books are available everywhere today and have sold widely. His influence among diverse spiritual publics is considerable. He had not had the same influence on leading eco-theologians, however. In these circles, Fox has a reputation as a popularizer, not as an original thinker.

Creation theology describes an ongoing process of spiritual development and general evolution. There may have been a first creation—what Matthew Fox calls the "Original Blessing"—but the process of creation has continued steadily, since it is an unending process. Wesley Granberg-Michaelson agrees, arguing that "God's presence as sustainer of the creation comes before God's mighty acts in history," and he insists that God's true covenant is with all nature, not just with people. For him, the key covenant experience came with Noah after the Flood, when God promised never to destroy nature again. It was not the covenant with Abraham, because that was between God and man alone.[48]

For proponents of creation theology, evolution is integral to the story of the earth and the universe, and they identify similarities between creation theology and scientific evolution. They define the process as a creative evolution that all creatures can and should participate in as partners in the one universe. While critics contend that this model conflicts with Genesis, creation theologians dispute the claim. For them, Genesis describes one point of creation, but not the only one in what they perceive as an ongoing process. What creation theology does challenge, however, is the concept of an autonomous creator.[49]

Matthew Fox has been more in the public eye than other creation theologians, and critics have sternly attacked him. The magisterium of the Roman Catholic Church led the charge, maintaining that Dominican priest Fox's creation theology was a syncretic, New Age religion that was unacceptable. The Church sought to uproot Fox from his California Institute for Cultural and Creative Spirituality and eventually terminated his membership in the Dominican order when he resisted. Most recently, Fox has joined the Episcopal Church.[50]

The influential Thomas Berry, on the other hand, has had a greater impact than Fox among eco-theologians. In his call for a "sweeping synthesis, imaginative insights and courage in confronting the narrowness of traditional theology,"[51] Berry asserts that "Nature is both benign and terrible, but consistently creative,"[52] and in that creative reality we encounter the "primary revelation of the divine."[53] Fox labels the same encounter the "Via Creativa" and fairly bubbles with excitement over the creative possibilities within nature. People can and should be "co-creators" with the divine.[54]

This analysis implies that for creation theologians, the proper focus must be on optimism, potential, and the future. As good evolutionists, they admire "creation processes" and often regret what they judge to be the gloomy dimensions of much of Christianity. They do not want to hear much about sin, or about Christ understood as a desperately needed Redeemer. They argue that what we need are creators, not redeemers; affirmers and doers, not savers or confessors.[55]

Yet there is some agreement that creativity is not always good, since it can lead in disastrous directions. After all, some results of human "creativity" have damaged nature, or part of nature. Thus people must ensure that creativity serves to stimulate positive activities, ones that affirm divinity in the world and in human beings.

What creation theologians expect in such a world is sometimes clear and often quite predictable in terms of political agendas. Third World liberation, radical feminism, economic equality, and, of course, radical environmentalism are the usual objectives.[56] What is less predictable is why science or philosophy or literature are not associated with creation and creativity here. One could argue that science, for example, has been the outstanding realm of creation and creativity in our century, but that, of course, would require a more favorable view of the accomplishments of science than creation theorists usually hold.

Creation eco-theologians hold that the realization of creative possibilities will depend on a suitable understanding of nature—a task that immediately leads to the most controversial dimension of full-scale creation theology. While many Protestant thinkers share the vague creation consciousness now routine in Protestant environmentalism, self-conscious creation thinkers are distinguished by their determination to eliminate virtually any distinction between human beings and the rest of nature. The goal is both to humble the human and to exalt the rest of nature. In its most unhesitating form, the result would be the abolition of any special or unique aspect for or about the human species in creation, in nature, and with God. In the larger environmental movement, this is the position of radical biocentrism.[57]

In some religious versions, notably those of Thomas Berry, this perspective is no doubt something beyond an intellectual construct or creed. Ultimately, it is a mystical feeling. For Berry, it involves a profoundly spiritual sense of oneness between humans and nature, "an intense sharing with the natural world."[58] It includes a commitment to the continuing evolutionary journey and a "returning to our native place after a long absence, meeting our kin in the earth community."[59] For Fox, this mystical journey is essential for creation. It requires breaking the established shell of our lives, leading to a descent into nothingness that in turn helps us pass to a realm of inner meaning without which the promise of creativity will be empty. The importance of this journey explains why Fox has spent a good deal of effort recounting the history of mysticism within Western spirituality. People need to appreciate mysticism's worth and history.[60]

The somewhat free-form result of Fox's mystical journey is a collection of fragments of personal spiritualities that he finds congenial. Fox is quite taken with the 1960s religion of sensitivity—the glory of self-affirmation, "letting go and letting be"—and he warns his readers to avoid the "Via Negativa," the unwillingness to surrender the wisdom of the rational ego.[61]

To Christian critics, this syncretism is disturbing. Wayne Boulton, for example, has attacked Fox in *Christian Century* for falling captive to the modern era and a syncretic religion of self-affirmation and self-indulgence. To critics, creation theologians do not appear to have any other foundation for their view than a diffuse optimism and faith in individuals' "creativity." Indeed, creation thinkers do often renounce such traditional anchors as a transcendent God.

They do the same regarding sin. For creation thinkers, the concept of sin is a negative concept that impedes human creativity, emphasizing what we do wrong and promoting pessimism. Those creation theologians who are willing to acknowledge that there is such a thing as sin believe that it involves damaging the present creation or the unfolding creation. Sin need not occur, it is not determined, and it is not at the root of things, contrary to St. Augustine and the tradition of Christian thought based on his genius. Creation theology wants to be upbeat and hopeful regarding the human experiment, and those who talk merely of holding on before the onslaught of human sin win few plaudits.[62]

The toughest and most controversial charge about Christian creation theology, though, is that it is not Christian. Some creation theologians do slide over into pantheism and break with traditional Christianity, which takes pantheism as a denial of God's transcendence. Matthew Fox is perhaps the boldest here. He goes far beyond suggestive complaints about the dualism of God and nature in conventional Christianity; in fact, he celebrates pantheism and praises such pantheists as the witch Starhawk.[63]

The status of Christ in creation theologies is equally controversial. In some of these works, Christ is mentioned only vaguely as the very model of the good creator and thus "the image of God par excellence."[64] But in others there is hardly a mention of Christ, except in warnings against those who are labeled "Christolotrous." After all, people are not to worship Christ but to be co-creators with Christ.[65]

Other Protestant creation thinkers make more of Jesus, though generally they make sure to fold him into the creation process. One describes Jesus' Incarnation as an example of God's "vulnerable embrace" of creation; another characterizes Jesus as a moment in which the future is shown to us. There are also other versions, occasionally murky, so that what they mean or are intended to mean is translucent at best. Rarely is Christ at the core of committed creation theology.[66]

It is clear that more than a few creation theologians are ready to break from what they recognize as traditional Christianity. For example, in a book published in 1990, Douglas Bowman works hard to develop a contextual ethics for an environmental life, assuring his readers that Scripture provides support for such a morality and thus also allows him to make his break: "We are now beginning to understand that the wisdom of human-kind . . . can and often does transcend the wisdom of Christianity."[67]

Thomas Berry pushes on in the same mold, but he is a good deal more explicit. We are now in a new age, he declares, a time in which we must lay aside the past and such works of the past as the Bible. The same applies to Christianity itself in all but name: "My own view is that . . . the existing religious traditions are too distant from our new sense of the universe to be adequate to the task that is before us."[68] Creation theologians conclude that we must be open to fashioning new theological ideas in a new time, espe-cially one of crisis, in the life of the world. Through such creativity we will encounter our salvation.

A sympathetic account of these theologians, from Santmire to Berry, must praise them for their effort to bring a religion alive and make it congruent with environmental demands. It is wrong to suggest that most participants in this journey are merely crass manipulators grasping for the Christian label, with its cover and potential power to advance their project. Their effort is both more sincere and more complicated than that.

There are many images of Christianity, and as many dreams about what it could become. Most contemporary eco-theologies do not echo tradi-tional Christianity, but that is not to say that eco-theologies and Chris-tianity are not compatible or cannot be more compatible. Like Christianity, current eco-theology is remarkably pluralistic; hence, there are several visions of how Christianity and eco-theology might be one.

Perhaps Paul Santmire is the most wide-ranging eco-theologian of the last several decades. His analysis and argument is diverse and textured. He has no neat or tight eco-philosophy, easy to grasp but thin to study. He definitely does not present a fresh program of action. Yet in his rich reflec-tions over more than twenty years, he has been deservedly influential.

Creation theology is a more focused eco-theology than what Santmire offers. It is also, in its way, a less complicated approach, though a decidedly more radical one. It radicalness is political as well as theological, for many creation theorists have in mind dramatic changes toward human equality and community—changes that go quite beyond the more sober and mea-sured proposals of Santmire. They appear frequently to favor such radical changes with little concern for means of change—a spirit that also differs from Santmire's, for better or worse.

Some proponents are as creative as their theology. Yet the question of how thoroughgoing creation theology accords with a recognizable Chris-tianity remains an important issue for many green Protestant thinkers. The question is neither absurd nor illegitimate. Direct and searching discussion of the relationship between Christianity and radical creation theology can benefit both faiths and is much better than the coyness that has been known to substitute.

There is also a need for more development of creation theology, especially in philosophical terms; this call for clarification respects creation theology and does not denigrate it. For example, it would be worthwhile to explore creation theology's claims about the "intrinsic value" of a co-created universe. How something acquires value except through the judgment of a transcendent God or through some kind of human practice or system merits more discussion. So do conceptions of a God who is supreme and yet part of an evolutionary process.

The relationship between creation theology and process eco-theology (see chapter 8) is another area worth exploring rigorously. Most creation theologians clearly have a distinctly process side (most obvious in their evolutionary mode). At times, creation theology and process theology seem to meld into each other, a phenomenon that also merits exploration, though it is not necessarily a problem.

The connections between creation theology and science also demand considerable reflection. Creation theology is not friendly toward science, on the whole, despite its affinity to evolutionary theory. Yet one puzzle here is that much of modern creativity has taken place in the realms of science and technology. This aspect of Protestant environmentalism is postmodern in its suspicions of science, but "antimodern" might be as accurate a description. In any case, the issues of science and creativity need study in terms of creation theology.

One irony is that despite the tension between creation theology and science, a great deal about both creation and process theologies fits with some dimensions of modern science, especially complexity theory. After all, creation theology is sensitive to a universe of change, where creative emerging and reemerging are the order of the day in a complicated, interactive universe. Unlike much of environmental theory, creation theology sees a great sense of change, spontaneity, and dynamism in the universe and is completely comfortable with them and with the idea that the universe's order is ever-changing. In just these aspects it seems to parallel complexity theories within the scientific community. It also shares a frequent disdain for the traditional, analytical, dissecting methodologies of science.[69]

The goal of a more rigorous and developed articulation of creation theology, including serious engagement with its puzzles and problems, is a worthy one and no doubt will be achieved. While some creation theologians may resist such a direction on the grounds that it might sacrifice creation theology's mystical side, they will need to discuss why mysticism and creation theology go together.

Perhaps the larger story, however, is that as the engagement with the crisis of the earth generates eco-theologies, much of the discourse undertakes to build from and on Christianity, including Protestant Christianity. This discourse goes on, and it will go on, as part of the age-old search for and struggle over God's teaching.

PROCESS ENVIRONMENTALISM

The most-discussed radical eco-theology from the 1970s to the 1990s has been process theory. While process theology annoys both analytic philosophers, who think it distinctly imprecise, and some Christians, who question its legitimacy as Christianity, it now has affected many thinkers both within and without Christianity. To more than a few theologians, process theology is the answer to the search for a serious spiritual basis for an ecological ethic. This topic is a sensitive one, as we will see. A lot is at stake, and battle lines have been drawn.

While there are many versions of process theology, the most important for our purposes flourish in Christian and especially Protestant circles. The basic idea of process theology is that the universe is always developing and always in process, an always-changing whole in which each part includes all others. In this conception of reality, dualisms, hierarchies, and fixed truths make no sense. What matters is the development and flow that infuse all aspects of the universe.

Process theology is not always neatly separable from creation theology, but there are differences. Process and creation theologies are descended from different forebears and thus have varying histories. Process theology tends to be more focused on the *idea* of continuing development in the universe, creation theology on the *reality* of continuing creation in the universe—a subtle but definite distinction. Moreover, process theology is usually self-consciously philosophical and determined to connect with scientific understandings of the modern era. Creation theology tends much more to the mystical, is sometime suspicious of the philosophical, and is often highly unsympathetic to modern science.

Three major figures have influenced the emergence of process theology within Protestant environmentalism in the past twenty-five years: Teilhard de Chardin, a Roman Catholic theologian; Alfred North Whitehead, an Anglo-American philosopher; and Charles Hartshorne, a longtime University of Chicago theologian. The impact of their visions has been substantial, and their thought has touched many who would not describe themselves as process thinkers. In order to appreciate contemporary process theology and its role in green Protestantism, we must examine the ideas of these twentieth-century founders.

The Precursors of Process Theologians

Many of the pioneers for a new Christian eco-theology cite Teilhard de Chardin (1881–1955) as a significant influence on them, even though he died before the birth of the contemporary ecological movement.[1] Teilhard was a French-born Jesuit priest who lived and worked in several parts of the world; he spent most of the years from 1951 until his death in the United States. He worked primarily as a scientist, exploring the paleontology of mammals, and his master work is the reflective and philosophical *Phenomenon of Man*, published in English forty years ago. He described his now-classic work as "a scientific treatise." In fact, it has had no impact on modern science but has played a decided role in religious and environmental thought, though Teilhard's ideas did not actually contradict all aspects of modern science.[2]

Teilhard perceived the universe and the life within it as evolutionary. There is a process under way, he maintained, in which humans are moving, *"all together,* in a direction in which *all together* can join and find completion."[3] This evolution brought humanity closer to a higher order, Teilhard devoutly believed, and he was buoyed by that belief. He contended that however discouraged people sometimes got over the human condition, they should keep in mind that the evolutionary process upward was unmistakably in motion.

Teilhard called the final destination the "Omega point." It was the already existent place where all converged and would converge, the perfect and realized unity in the universe, the "spiritual and transcendent pole of universal convergence."[4] In more traditional Christian language, it was the second coming, or the full realization of Christ and of the universe. On the way to this end, God was always present in every part of the journey over infinite time. The entire process was a remarkably creative one, and thus, to Teilhard, God was the great Creator and re-creator. God as Christ was the energy and the unity of the process.[5]

Teilhard consistently emphasized that the universe was a unity and that evolution was a real process toward greater unity. His goal was, above all, to gain recognition for this unity in the universe and an appreciation for the fact that higher development and greater unity went together. For

Teilhard, focusing on individuals clashed with the findings of modern science and was a spiritual blind alley. It led to isolation and a kind of death—a sad state, given the dramatic alternate reality. The truth was that no one was alone and the world was one. This celebration of a unified creation and resistance to a divided one has been one of his strongest contemporary appeals to Christian ecologists uncomfortable with seemingly dualistic Christian understandings of God, humankind, and nature.[6]

One may wonder if Teilhard should be aligned with the mystical tradition. Teilhard's vision is mystical, and some might applaud him for this tendency, not because his vision is somehow true but rather because it is useful. Teilhard fashioned a practical myth that understands the universe ecologically as a single entity, unfolding with God.

Teilhard was determined, however, that people not get lost in the process. Indeed, it was Teilhard's conviction that as evolution went forward, the importance of the human being would remain great. He maintained that evolution contained a law of "complexity-consciousness" that affirmed the superiority of humans within the whole. As evolution, complexity, and consciousness expanded, those beings with greatest capacity for consciousness would respond most. Evolution for Teilhard was above all a rise in consciousness, especially a rise in human consciousness.[7]

Religious environmentalists' admiration for Teilhard is naturally related to how much process theology appeals to them. If they like it, they salute Teilhard as a pioneer. They often have reservations, however, since Teilhard was not an environmentalist. Moreover, he was anthropomorphic, quite focused on the human being, and he downplayed the importance of other forms of life. The entirety of nature did not really concern him, but rather the unity of humankind with its end, with the Omega point or God.[8]

From another perspective, perhaps the most pressing question about Teilhard is the place of evil in his thought. Skeptics have routinely asked whether there is a role for evil in any version of process thinking, a question to which this chapter will return. Teilhard was quick to assert that he did accept evil. He did not visualize the evolutionary process as one where the road would always be smooth, because life—evolutionary life— just was not like that. The confusions, incompleteness, and failures in the process were Teilhard's evil or what he chose to call evil. This perspective was far from a traditional Christian conception of sin, but in Teilhard's vision there was no place for a tougher doctrine of human sin nor for the pessimism he feared such an idea implied.[9]

While Teilhard de Chardin explicitly identified himself as a Christian, Alfred North Whitehead (1861–1947) did not. Yet Whitehead even more than Teilhard influenced Christian process theology, especially as it is applied to ecology. John B. Cobb Jr., perhaps the most important religious process environmentalist, acknowledges Whitehead's influence in his own case, and he is by no means alone in his enthusiasm for Whitehead's contributions.[10]

Like Teilhard, Whitehead sought to construct a metaphysics that would comprehend and incorporate modern science. Indeed, this aspiration underlies much of process theory. As a mathematician, physicist, and philosopher, Whitehead's reach as a thinker was broad enough for him to undertake such a daunting task. He spent most of his career in England, but like Teilhard, Whitehead spent years in the United States; he came to Harvard University in 1924. From there his influence began to spread within the United States at exactly the same time that he moved away from physics toward humanistic concerns. His most important book is the formidable *Process and Reality: An Essay in Cosmology* (1929).

Whitehead's philosophy is speculative (as he freely admits), complex, and technical enough in its arcane vocabulary to satisfy anyone for whom no theorist can be great without a highly elaborate and semimysterious language. Yet that does not appear to have diminished its appeal for thinkers who seek to build a process environmentalism and who anoint Whitehead "the ecological philosopher par excellence"—although he was not self-consciously an environmentalist at all.[11]

In Whitehead's universe, everything is perpetually in process, or change. Everything has its own goal and proceeds toward that goal's realization. Thus the world is an incredible multiplicity of entities, each creating and re-creating itself, combining and recombining, in a fluid process where individual elements last only briefly. As basic entities combine, the process as a whole edges toward a greater unity. As Whitehead conceptualized it, this process was to a large extent a movement of mind, but its participants had properties, relations, and patterns that actually existed.[12]

Thus Whitehead was a deeply organic thinker in the approved environmentalist mode. He saw everything as interconnected, a part of evolving patterns and processes. Indeed, each entity had the whole within itself from the beginning. He insisted, moreover, that all things, including human beings, had intrinsic value, while at the same time they were inextricably interdependent. Meanwhile, Whitehead dismissed dualism and anthropomorphism as hopelessly out of touch with the reality of the universe.[13]

Whitehead held that God is the ultimate point toward which the process moves, though Whitehead's God is not a creator of the universe.

Instead, his God is another way of describing that element within every thing that both preserves its uniqueness and speeds it toward combination and unity. Each entity, small or large, creates itself, but God works as, in Whitehead's words, a "lure" that pulls the universe's elements along. To put it another way, Whitehead's God is about potentiality and the realization of every entity's inner self. God lures each thing to realize itself, and the ultimate goal is the realization of all potential.[14]

The basis for values in Whitehead's universe is the cosmos, the purpose of which (or, God's purpose) is to enrich experience to its maximum. Each cell experiences feeling, though not necessarily consciousness. How they combine, and into what, greatly affects their capacity for feeling. The value of each part of the universe is assessed within that framework, establishing a hierarchy, but a hierarchy within the organic whole. Whitehead judged, just as Teilhard did, that in that world the human being had the greatest capacity to feel or to experience.[15]

Whitehead's ranking of the human being within the organic whole—indeed, his willingness to rank at all—poses problems for egalitarian environmentalists. Yet Whitehead was no triumphalist about humanity. People might have the greatest capacity for conscious experience, but they could and did go astray. They could forget their connections with the physical universe, including the animal world, with tragic consequences.[16]

Overall, the basis of Whitehead's appeal is clear. It comes from his sense of wholeness, his respect for the value of each individual thing, and his combination of a modern, scientific (if distinctly nonempirical), evolutionary model of the universe with a spiritual vision of oneness. Fortunately, it has little to do with his artificial vocabulary or turgid prose.

Whitehead's thought has played a real part in the entry of process ideas into Protestant theology and its environmentalist offshoots. At the same time, Whitehead's thought presents barriers to any traditional Christian. After all, Christ is conspicuously absent in Whitehead's account—a crucial difference between Whitehead and Teilhard. Moreover, Whitehead provides no role for God as Creator. With that stance, Whitehead separates himself not only from Christian thought but also, more particularly, from that branch of Christian thought that has proven most fruitful for Protestant and other Christian environmentalists: the image of the universe as God's creation and hence sacred.

The process theorist Charles Hartshorne may well have exercised the greatest direct influence on Protestant environmentalism. Hartshorne was a longtime professor of theology at the University of Chicago Divinity

School who boldly created a process theology in what was—in the 1950s and 1960s—a distinctly Protestant setting. He took the process concept and cast it in a "religious, or at least philosophy-of-religion, direction."[17]

Hartshorne's background, as he tells his story, was distinctly liberal in terms of religion. Perhaps that made him open to the ideas of Alfred North Whitehead when he was Whitehead's assistant at Harvard University. Whitehead's influence on Hartshorne is obvious in everything from Hartshorne's technical writing style to the substance of his ideas; but Hartshorne was not simply a modern-day Whitehead, although he freely admitted how much Whitehead had affected his own theology.[18]

Hartshorne did not apply his own thought to environmentalism any more than Whitehead did, but he did apply process theology to religion. His central claim is that "reality is a social process,"[19] which was his way of enunciating the familiar process claim that everything in the universe is connected with everything else. For Hartshorne, the feeling of sympathy is the principal instrument by which this interconnection is accomplished. All creatures, he contended, are social and all have feeling, even if one could not locate a specific feeling organ in them. These feelings, especially sympathy, are at the heart of the social life that is reality. How advanced or elementary feeling, especially sympathy, is in different creatures varies enormously, but it is basic to all life.[20]

Hartshorne brought in religion through an extensive theology of a process God. He argued that as each person changes and develops in life, so does God. As each person feels sympathy, so does God. As each tries to create, so does God. Thus for Hartshorne, God was much like humans and not independent, abstract, and removed from all else. God was with people and in them, and humans were with God in a living and creating universe of sympathies.[21]

There is little doubt that Hartshorne was wedded to the idea that the world and God are deeply interdependent. He was also, at the least, something of a panentheist, accepting that God includes the world as part of God's being. Or perhaps it would be more accurate, if more controversial, to suggest that Hartshorne leaned to pantheism, for he spurned the notion that dichotomies could exist between God and nature or any parts of nature. According to Hartshorne, those who envisioned such a divided world had left us a sad legacy: "metaphysics was sidetracked for two millennia" by that mistake.[22]

Christ did not really seem to fit in this system. Hartshorne's Christology is vague, in fact, and amounts to little more than mentioning Jesus as the supreme example of living sympathy. In his writings there is no declaration that Christ was God, much less the Son of God. What Hartshorne offered instead was a reassurance that he accepted "the Spirit of the Gospels."[23]

Contemporary Process Theology

There have been a number of active contributors to the construction of a process theology of the environment in recent decades. Not all of them claim to be Christians, but this viewpoint "is being developed predominantly, though not exclusively, in Christian circles."[24] Of those in Christian circles, most are Protestant in background. It is in ecumenical and/or liberal Protestant theological schools that process theology has arisen and attained respectability.

While there is no specific doctrinal position that unites process theologians as they consider the environment, they agree that they must encourage humans to realize that the universe is alive and energized, ambiguous and free-flowing, holistic and harmonious.[25] As Jay McDaniel observes, such a perspective takes for granted a "postanthropocentric" analysis, one where the human being is not the only or even the major focus in the world.[26]

Some process thinkers contend that there is nothing new about such a conception of the universe. They call attention to a tradition dating from the ancient Greeks that perceived what we may call a living universe—an entity full of change, life, and feeling. While in the West this tradition eventually lost out to what they believe is a dead, mechanical conception of the universe, they take comfort in their ancient roots. Many process thinkers bemoan the sixteenth and seventeenth centuries as particularly fatal times. They argue that philosophers of science made a tragic detour then and began to think about the universe in a recognizably modern, mechanical fashion, worshiping materialism and rejecting the living vitality of the cosmos.[27] This partly explains why a common thread in current Christian process theory is an attempt to honor science while resisting any scientific findings that describe the universe as a cold, godless place. Versions of modern biology—those that emphasize wholeness and the life of the world—constitute the science of choice.[28]

Despite process theology's deserved reputation for often being "inaccessible and abstract,"[29] in this branch of American thought, as in others, there is an inclination to be practical. Convinced that reality demands "a fresh vision of the universe of God,"[30] Christian process theologians argue that Christianity must be revised—and can be revised—to tackle the crisis of the earth. Process theology's great attraction is that it points out how God and nature, humans and nature, and the entire universe can come together in a necessary interdependence.[31] At the same time, process theology exhibits a great sensitivity toward the living and respects "the new sensibility in Western culture."[32] Religion, science, and modern sensitivity come together in process theology as it engages the environment.

A leading Protestant eco-process theologian of recent times is John B. Cobb Jr., who has long been associated with Claremont College and its Center for Process Studies. On his own and in association with such colleagues as Herman Daly and Charles Birch, Cobb has directed a host of publications that define process theology from a Christian outlook. "I am speaking as a Christian . . . [one of] those who have been shaped in their perception of meaning and importance and in the very structure of their existence by Jesus."[33] But Whitehead has also had an influence on Cobb, as has Charles Hartshorne. Indeed, Cobb dedicated one of his books to Hartshorne, who respected Cobb's understanding of his work.[34]

Cobb believes that Christianity is compatible with the demands of a process conception of the universe, and this belief reinforces his commitment to Christianity. Together, he maintains, Christianity and process theology will yield the new "vision the world so urgently needs,"[35] if religion, like everything else, makes the commitment to change that is Cobb's true "faith in life."[36] As Cobb is well aware, process theology does not always receive assent; even those who recite the key words are not necessarily true allies. But Cobb contends that the need to stop "the mad rush to destruction" requires a willingness to form temporary alliances wherever possible.[37] For many others, Cobb recognizes, process theology is a bold view. Cobb is comfortable with that fact, and he knows that process theology's vision of the universe is not easily proven or "shown." That does not intimidate Cobb, however, who confidently defends "responsible speculation."[38]

What is the goal of Cobb's process theology? The goal is explicating what he sometimes calls the ecological model and at other times the biospheric vision—that is, a vision of God and nature together and unfolding. Such an understanding, Cobb says, brings him close to the land ethic of such secular environmentalists as Aldo Leopold and Baird Callicott, and to those interested in deep ecology as well. But Cobb, like others in this study, does not desire a secular ethic. For him, something much larger than the secular goal of survival must drive ecological thought, and with the Christian tradition he accepts that people are more important than "a mosquito or a virus."[39]

The process conception of the universe stresses that it is about a "continuous series of events or interactions," not inert matter or a fixed universe.[40] Since the universe is a whole, it contains no dualisms, though the universe is composed of actual entities. As each part moves within the larger process, each is connected with the others. In this sense all entities are one, and the parts that comprise any individual entity are one. Interrelatedness, understood as an interrelatedness in continuous motion and flow, is the overwhelming fact of the universe. Process discussions often revolve around the image of a web, an image that fits well with ecological conceptions of nature. This inclusive web encompasses the physical and the mental, the human and the rest of nature, and the subjective and the objective.[41]

This understanding is set against the traditional Christian view, in which many theologians conceptualized God as the creator of a largely fixed universe. There is no such universe, process theologians argue, nor any such God. The universe and God together are involved in evolution and are moving toward a teleological fulfillment of the goal of ever greater understanding and connection with each other. This objective, they agree, is not by any means guaranteed or determined. There is no fixed nature either, only evolving and adapting relationships in nature. Boundaries are neither firm nor clear. One does not know where the mind ends or the body begins, for example, in a situation where matter itself is really process. Yet at each stage, each part is valuable and complete in itself, and we should celebrate each as a member of the whole.[42]

Process thinkers emphasize the goal of "self-realization in community" in a cosmic sense. This perspective forges a link between them and an ecological understanding of the universe but also reminds readers that process thinking clearly participates in current American thought, where "community" is the watchword of the hour. The revolt against liberal individualism is standard today in American thought, both among Protestant process theologians and most everywhere else.[43]

Process theology conceptualizes each object in terms of its relationship to its environment. Thus some process theorists resist a traditional and exclusive "rights" approach to protection of animals or humans. Some versions of "rights" can legitimate an individualistic or group outlook that to process thinkers denies the communal and interactive basis for life—and may in fact be mostly anthropomorphic. On the other hand, biotic rights—

such as those discerned by John Cobb and Jay McDaniel—are to be understood within the holistic world of nature. They stand not against the rest of nature but as an integrated part of the full ecological community.[44]

This point cannot be made too firmly, from the process perspective. But at the same time, process theory insists that each part of the universe deserves great respect and has intrinsic value. Proponents' vision of the universe as community does not and, they urge, should not involve dissolving individuals into an amorphous whole. The universe's richness includes all its parts (variously defined), and there is no room for the possibility that the suffering of any portion may be ignored as insignificant in light of the whole.[45]

One way to grasp the process model is to visualize the universe as a series of communities, united in a large community, each part interwoven with the others. Individualism and community are both central and intrinsic to the overall process. Every thing belongs, while every thing also retains its own self and experience. Every thing is itself yet simultaneously exists in relation to the larger community. Every thing has its relations and its surroundings, though it is never reducible to them.[46]

McDaniel and other process thinkers insist that "the entire cosmos is alive with subjectivity, with aims and interests, and hence with intrinsic value."[47] For them, every creature has some sense of feeling for itself, for others, and for the whole. McDaniel believes that this feeling is intuitive and spiritual and that it mirrors God's feeling for us. It forms a deep bond within the overall community of life and provides the caring and integration vital to the enduring universe.[48]

Others apply the view to the plant world, arguing that its members' sense of relationship to others is real. Indeed, process theologians maintain that their belief in interconnective feelings in the universe is scientific. They are convinced that science produces more and more evidence that emotions similar to human ones are found throughout the living world—in animals and plants, even in the simplest cells.[49]

People often assume that capacity for feeling or experience of feeling is reality and that all else constitutes a kind of shadowy neo-Platonic realm. Therefore, richness of experience frequently becomes the measure for life. Some process thinkers follow Whitehead in arguing that capacity for experience or feeling is not equal among all life forms. The argument is that differences in capacity for experience allow for distinctions among the varieties of life forms around us. All life has worth, but the life that has more potential in terms of experience may also have greater worth. This position rests uncomfortably between those for whom little besides the human being has worth and those who would conflate human worth with that of a mosquito.[50]

One may ask at this point, if not well before, what about God, not to speak of Christianity or Protestantism? Where are they in the process universe? In many versions of process theology, God is central. Indeed, not a few process theorists contend that they bring God much closer to people than do traditional conceptions of God. They describe their God as warm, open, receptive, and changing, like everything else in the process universe, and they understand traditional views as positing a cold, remote, and fixed God.

A favorite image describes God in terms of feeling. God feels (i.e., has sympathy with) each part of the universe in its uniqueness and thus graces each with inherent value. God also has feeling for the universe as an evolving whole, and for both the parts and the whole, in terms of their potential—which is neither guaranteed nor fixed and will alter over time.

Process thinkers believe that all of us, as followers of God, must try to live a spiritual existence, and that means identifying with everything in the universe—with each entity's sacred particularity (and potentiality) as well as with the universe as a whole. This attitude is, process advocates insist, the only proper basis for a spiritual environmental ethic that honors God, humans, and the entire universe.[51]

God is immanent in the process view, which rejects theologies that accent God's transcendence. Since God is so overwhelmingly present in real lives and actual experiences, God affects and is affected by everything. But determinism is not the reality of the universe. God and the world are to some degree different from and independent of each other, though to what degree is never clear and perhaps cannot be clear. While "the world is not God" and neither determinism nor full pantheism captures reality, God still is in all things and represents a bridge between all things.[52] Since process thought discerns God as open, developing, and "in process" as well, its proponents laud a God who is a center of creativity, creating and re-creating, just as people can and do. Such a God respects all and does not try to impose or force.[53]

One may wonder whether there is evil in such a universe. Evil, not to mention sin, is rarely admitted into the process universe. There are Christian process thinkers, such as Jay McDaniel, who do acknowledge evil, though they are exceptions. For McDaniel, evil is symbolized "in the fatal experience of the youngest in pelican broods"—that is, in their inevitable destruction by other pelicans. Yet though he sees evil as inescapable,

McDaniel argues that it has nothing to do with God. After all, nature has its own creativity, and God is not accountable for all that happens in nature. In the process universe God can only "lure" nature or human beings to a world that accords with God. In the process universe, in fact, God's limitations free God from responsibility for evil.[54]

Some other process analyses also acknowledge evil and thus a "fall" in human experience, but they argue that such a fall must be understood in terms of evolution. Evil is the "fall upward," the cost of overall progress in life. Mostly, though, there is silence about evil, a concept whose very existence is problematic in a universe in which a good God is so overwhelmingly immanent.[55]

The process vision does, however, include consideration of human beings, especially in contemporary versions, which pay so much attention to ecological matters. Process theologians describe humans as centrally involved with God, but with a God that is also intimately associated with all of nature—as is humanity. People are part of nature and thus part of God or, to put it another way, part of God and thus part of nature.

For most (if not all) process thinkers, a proper understanding of the human-nature-God relationship casts doubt on the appropriateness of the stewardship model of the environment. Stewardship may be popular among mainstream Christians, but it is commonly repudiated by process theoreticians. To them, stewardship Christianity suggests a hierarchical universe, which is far away from the process model. In the process reality, humans and God are intricately intertwined with nature, and there are no hierarchies and inferiors in traditional senses. There are only participants, mutual healers and creators, and fellow lovers.[56]

Christian versions of process theology place a consistent stress on hope for the future. This optimism derives from the belief that everything in the universe has value and the capacity to fulfill itself and that God will not fail anything. Such a view is profoundly redemptive, and Christian process theology understands it as such. The future is hope, even though it also is a mystery.[57]

Whether the process of development and fulfillment will ever reach an end or whether it is, instead, a perpetual, ongoing system varies from thinker to thinker. What does not vary is their confidence in the inclusiveness of the process. Christian process thinkers repeatedly cite Romans 8:19–21 as their guide: "For the creation waits with eager longing for the revealing of the children of God," when the time will come "that the creation itself will be set free from its bondage to decay and will obtain the freedom of the glory of the children of God" (NRS).[58]

While many of process theory's advocates neither claim to be nor want to be Christian, this chapter has largely concentrated on those such as Jay McDaniel and John B. Cobb Jr., who explicitly identify with the Christian tradition.[59] They do not pretend that their understanding of Christianity is particularly conventional or familiar. Their argument is that Christianity, like everything else in the universe, must be seen as in process. The way it is, or has been, is not normative for the future. The same applies to the Bible. After all, the argument goes, the Bible is also of the past. Christianity must be renewed by continued creativity that taps into other traditions and new insights as it moves onward.[60]

It is hardly a surprise that this Christianity has met with a sometimes fierce challenge, particularly from within the evangelical Protestant tradition. Critics ask whether Christian process theology is anything but sentimentalism posing as serious theology. Or they suggest that it is a kind of nineteenth-century evolutionary optimism that "succeeds" only at the cost of abandoning Christianity.[61]

The most frequent complaint is that the Incarnation, the central event of Christianity, is either missing or severely discounted in process theology. For that matter, so is Jesus Christ. So is the Trinity. So is God as Creator, and so is the Creation itself, replaced by process and movement, which are something else. Much of historical Christianity disappears in process thought, and critics insist that this loss is not justified by earnestly announcing that Christianity must evolve. For them, the Christian faith can never evolve from the bedrock of the Incarnate Christ as God.[62]

Some other conception of God than the Christian one is at work here, critics charge—a non-Christian God, limited and somehow dependent on nature and creation, with which it is frequently conflated. This is a God without authority, cut loose from its Protestant biblical foundations and disconnected from what has always been the final authority in Christianity, Jesus Christ. Critics complain as well that process theory conceives of a world where evil fades away and nature somehow acquires self-awareness and its own purposes, contrary to traditional Christian doctrine. Protestant critics are less agreed, however, on process theory's implications regarding the human being. Some maintain that process theory enhances humanity at the expense of God's rule; others suggest that humankind disappears into the web of process theory's evolutionary universe.[63]

Some skeptics find implausible process theology's claims for its scientific grounding, and they note the virtual absence of support in the scientific community for process assertions about the presence of universal feeling or sympathy.[64] Yet there is no doubt that proponents of process theology are sincere in making links with modern science. Proponents of this perspective, from Teilhard on, have insisted that process theology is the truth about the universe and have often described it as the scientific truth. Some contemporary process thinkers make a more serious effort than others to draw on scientific evidence, but most put science and process theology together in their arguments. This linkage is very different from most of creation theology.

The fact is, though, that in many ways process theology clashes with much in the reigning models of science. It is, for example, far more intrigued with neo-organic metaphors for the universe (such as feeling and breathing) than ordinary science. Nor is there much process effort overall to test and substantiate their conception of the universe by the empirical methods of ordinary science. Process theory concerns grand conceptions of cosmology and metaphors for the universe and life. Such speculation has been the beginning of much great science, of course, but only modest efforts have been made to join process thinking to the world of ordinary science. Exceptions, such as the work of John Cobb, stand out.

On the other hand, a good deal of "complexity" science might provide a fertile basis for many of the claims of process theology—as for creation theology—though there is little sign that process thinkers make use of it. While complexity theory offers no scientific grounding for any particular version of process theology—and, indeed, encounters the same charge, that it is mostly untested speculation—the theory supports the idea that the universe does grow steadily more complex and interdependent over time. Indeed, this is the universe's fundamental process. Complexity theory also argues that self-organization, adaptation, and the experience of novelty are constants. Meanwhile, there is no single controlling force (in process theory terms, no God the Father); rather, control is highly dispersed, with many levels and many changes.

The parallels with process theology are apparent, though complexity science does not speak in religious metaphors. But perhaps this distinction is not important. What one view—process theology—terms religious, another may call scientific. The fact is that boundaries between these two realms have never been clear or significant to many process thinkers, at least since Teilhard de Chardin.[65]

Regardless of where process theology might find help in modern science, it is dubiously scientific in conventional terms; and, as we have seen, it faces charges that it is dubiously Christian as well. These represent serious points of conflict, but they are not the only ones. The often relentless abstraction of process theology can bother and even confound the environmentalist who wants much more practical advice than sometimes comes from this source. What are the connections between process theology and practical environmental policy?

Of course, there are also questions from a more philosophical outlook, and none are more important than questions about process theology's conception of God: exactly what makes this God divine, as distinguished from anything or everything else? The most basic question is, from a process perspective does it makes sense to speak of God at all? Moreover, process theology is often not clear enough about the source of value in its universe. It is not a transcendent God, but what *is* it? What does it mean to say the universe is subjective and yet also yields intrinsic values? What is the relationship between "feelings," consciousness, and morality? There are also problems regarding the status of humanity. If human beings have the greatest "potential" for experience in the universe, why is process theology not just another human-centered theology?

Despite such inevitable queries about process theology, its appeal within green Protestantism is significant. At this point, it would appear to hold sway mostly among some quite liberal Protestant theologians. But its influence has spread beyond that world into broader precincts of Protestant environmentalism. The basis of its appeal in that context is the idea that it has potential to recast Christianity for the present, environmental age, aiding it to become evolutionary, holistic, interactive, and committed to the goodness of nature and the universe.

THE ECOFEMINIST CHALLENGE

The ferment generated by ecofeminists—particularly spiritual ecofeminists, whom some have termed "the chaplains of the environmental movement"—has constituted another route toward a radical rethinking of the relationship between Protestantism and environmentalism.[1] Irene Diamond and Gloria Feman Orenstein celebrate ecofeminism, which they call "this tapestry in green," as life-affirming in its diversity, a movement that cannot be reduced to a single ideology.[2] What ecofeminists do share, though, is an assertive affinity with nature, an identification of women in particular with nature, and an analysis that describes women and all nonhuman nature as victims of male domination. Some thinkers stress the nature connection more than others and have come to ecofeminism from environmentalism. Others concentrate more on a feminist perspective and have come to ecofeminism from feminism. Many have a spiritual dimension and have become involved with ecofeminism through conventional or goddess religions.[3]

Much of the environmental debate within Protestantism bypasses ecofeminism, sometimes gingerly, sometimes brusquely. Some debate that does engage ecofeminism, moreover, is distinctly critical of it. One need not be a soothsayer to speculate that controversy and ecofeminism will continue to travel together—in Protestantism and elsewhere. But the fact is that ecofeminism is a part of Protestant thought today. There is a distinct drive toward ecofeminist spirituality that challenges old boundaries and divisions and at times make some people uncomfortable, as an expanding critical literature testifies. What is unclear is its future in Protestantism. It may depend on the larger fate of feminism and environmentalism and how ecofeminism addresses its growing number of critics.[4]

The ecofeminist outlook is old, though the term "ecofeminism" dates only from 1974.[5] Since 1970, however, a dramatic change has occurred in ecofeminism's currency and influence. Just twenty or twenty-five years ago, this perspective received almost no mention, but today ecofeminism is a topic frequently discussed by feminist intellectuals, both secular and religious. This is especially obvious in many writings by feminist environmentalists, including their liberal Protestant representatives.

To understand ecofeminism's directions and impact in Protestant environmentalism, we (once again) have to burst conventional bounds: Rosemary Radford Ruether, the leading Christian ecofeminist, is a declared Roman Catholic. We must also go outside Christianity and sometimes outside all conventional religion. While key theorists and defenders of ecofeminism are religious, many others are distinctly non-Christian, and some are not religious at all.

Thus any treatment of the movement of ecofeminism and its spiritual dimensions necessarily sometimes ranges far from Protestantism. But the phenomenon is very much alive within Protestantism, attracting attention and controversy. It enters the Protestant realm through prominent theologians such as Sallie McFague, and it also attracts a host of Protestant critics, especially evangelical Protestants.

Ecofeminism is a "postpatriarchal" intellectual stance. Its basic position is that throughout history, the practice of human cultures has been equally oppressive to women and to nature. Ecofeminists argue that a hierarchical view of the world—that some are superior and others inferior—has been the principal cause of these twin oppressions. Through time, male dominance over women came to determine human life and thinking about all kinds of relationships, including those of people with the rest of nature.

According to ecofeminism, nature has suffered horribly as a result of this domination. It has been damaged over and over, because in a hierarchy, the dominant force inevitably crushes whatever is nondominant, such as women and nature. As Elizabeth Gray puts it, nature has been treated as the "green nigger."[6] Ecofeminists often go on to argue that it is no surprise that males have been the specific agents of the destruction of women and the rest of nature. They argue that males live as they think: in a dangerous and tragically hierarchical framework.

For some ecofeminists, nature is the source of value, and that is enough to establish the moral rightness of the ecofeminist cause. For others, nature is not the foundation for values; indeed, such foundations may not necessarily exist. But ecofeminists do agree that whatever the source of value, humans are dependent on the earth and, in practical terms, must care for it. The more common position is the first—the affirmation of nature as the good and women as the (or a) paradigmatic expression of nature's good.[7]

The central goals of ecofeminism are the liberation of women and of nature. The consistent assumption of its advocates is that the achievement of both goals is deeply interconnected because women and nature are intimately intertwined. To accomplish the liberation of women and nature, Rosemary Ruether argues, women must come together and work to make sure both causes are one, thereby prompting a transformation of society's thinking, structures, and ordinary practices. The basic change must be a shift from hierarchy to equality. Ecofeminists insist that in the process, religion must demonstrate nonpatriarchal egalitarianism, though they routinely express doubts about whether traditional religions can meet this standard.[8] Wary Christian ecofeminists share this skepticism as they evaluate the possibility of Christianity's adapting to a more inclusive and egalitarian worldview.[9]

But this goal is hardly the sole theme of ecofeminists. Another is overcoming the dualisms that they believe are fostered by such hierarchies. For example, ecofeminists frequently describe a mind/body split as endemic to the West. They exhort people to overcome this split and replace it with a holistic attitude, supporting a world properly understood as one wherein boundaries between people and the rest of nature disappear.

A fair amount of ecofeminist historical commentary already has cited several of the causes of this split. Some blame Greek thought, others Christian belief and theology, others Greek influences on Christianity; and some blame early modern thinkers such as Descartes and Newton for the rational mode of analysis by which they distanced themselves from the world of flesh and nature they studied.[10]

Carolyn Merchant's work has undoubtedly been the most influential, especially her classic 1980 study, *The Death of Nature*, recently supplemented by *Radical Ecology: The Search for a Livable World*. In *The Death of Nature*, as in many ecofeminist works, the larger part of the author's efforts consists of her explanation for why she believes the West went wrong: how it came to promote what Merchant dramatically terms "the death of nature." What she means to indicate by this phrase is her analysis that over the course of Western history a sharp dualism between nature and culture was established. This dualism led to the surrender of a natural wholeness that was instantiated in many traditional societies: the "world we have lost was organic."[11]

Perhaps surprisingly, Merchant is not especially interested in religion. She does fault Western religions, however, including ancient Judaism and Christianity, for their roles in what she takes to be a long record of Western denigration of nature. In her opinion, both Judaism and Christianity failed to acknowledge "the benevolence of nature" and have been too committed to separating, isolating, and then ruling nature.[12]

Her principal focus falls on sixteenth- and seventeenth-century Europe. She argues that the development of early capitalism, the emergence of scientific thought, and the arrival in that era of "a new metaphor—the machine"—destroyed the cohesive and integrated human existence that had long characterized the West. Mechanistic science recast knowledge as a thing that could be understood abstractly and in analytic parts. Abstraction and analysis replaced organic unity at the same time that capitalism began to overwhelm workers and peasants' integrated lives, which had been rooted in forest, field, and home.

This process swiftly crushed any forces that stood in the way. Women, in particular, were treated just as nature was. Both were seen as things that needed to be subdued and alienated from a holistic life so that man and the capitalist machine could work their will. Women who were associated with an untamable nature were dealt with severely. They were labeled witches and sent to their death, just as any parts of nature that were wild had to be destroyed.[13]

Thus, for some ecofeminist voices, the dualism between mind and body is just one significant expression of far too many dualisms, including those between man and woman and the human being and nature. While ecofeminism roundly condemns each of these dualisms, there are competing emphases on who or what is primarily responsible: the Greeks, Judaism, or Christianity; the rise of modern reason; capitalism or socialism; or, most frequently, several of these elements combined.[14] The search for explanation never rests, in part because ecofeminists believe that in order to make change we must understand the origins of our problems.

Ecofeminists insist that Western dualisms can be overcome. People can achieve unity—in religious terms, a unity where the world is understood as "the Body of God."[15] There is little pessimism among ecofeminists, in part because of their widespread belief that once there was a nondualistic life; sometimes they trace this life to a prebiblical world of goddesses and matriarchy. Images of such worlds are standard today in ecofeminist writings.

Also important is the ideal of community. In fact, ecofeminist literature is suffused with the exaltation of community as a goal. This ideal is usually conceived of as an egalitarian community, sometimes defined as women united with the rest of nature, sometimes as women and men and the rest of nature. A good portion of the praise for holism and community appears in self-consciously mystical and romantic metaphors. Paula Gunn Allen titles an essay, "The Woman I Love Is a Planet; The Planet I Love Is a Tree." Susan Griffin writes, "The earth is my sister, I love her daily grace, her silent daring and how loved I am."[16] Judith Plant speaks in similar terms when she lauds "our sisters and brothers who are the forests."[17]

There are other vocabularies as well. Some ecofeminists proceed in a more "scientific" mode, drawing on empirical evidence that leads them to conclude that nature is best understood as interconnected, or relational, or a kind of "web of energy." Some speak in the language of health, a characteristic vocabulary of the twentieth century. For them, the relevant goal is that of *healing* the dualisms between man and nature and man and woman. The metaphors vary, but the theme of holism is persistent.

Less clear is what role women are to play in the process. For many ecofeminists, gender is rooted in nature. Others describe it as socially constructed. Either way, though, the standard and crucial assumption in the ecofeminist literature is that, in practice, women today are closer to nature than men are and thus should lead the journey to community. Thus Rosemary Radford Ruether argues that women must first take control over their womb, then abolish economic injustices, and finally end the abuse of nature; each of these acts represents another step toward holism. Always, women are heralded as the appropriate leaders in this movement.[18]

More controversial are those ecofeminists who contend that holism requires mostly the transformation of men into creatures that are, in general, more like women and nature. Such an analysis proves an easy target for those who are suspicious that feminist triumphalism is at work and that the real goal is less an egalitarian community than the creation of new hierarchies of gender and nonanthropomorphic nature. Most ecofeminists, however, as advocates of community, deny such suspicions and insist that they want no dualisms of any sort.[19]

But one cannot avoid the tension that sometimes hovers in the air around those ecofeminists who persistently argue that nature is especially feminine and that on this belief ecofeminism must rest. "It is out of women's unique, felt sense of connection to the natural world that an ecofeminist philosophy must be forged," according to one such writer.[20]

While its origins are in dispute, there is no doubt that in this literature the link between women and nature is widespread and intentional. Ecofeminists often claim that women are fuller representations of nature. This belief has ancient historical roots and rests on women's menstruation and childbearing as well as on a perception that their gender is naturally caring. For many ecofeminists, some or all of these factors establish that women as a group are far more deeply intertwined with nature, while men have "a much diminished experience of body, of natural processes."[21]

However, ecofeminists do not all agree on this point. Sara Shute argues in *Environmental Ethics* that such a perspective is an outright embrace of dualism and hardly an embrace of holism. She also doubts that "nature" is any more fully expressed through childbirth or menstruation than through eating, sleeping, sexual intercourse, and other things men and women share together. Sally Binford also complains about this ecofeminist analysis, because in a haunting way, it echoes the age-old prejudice of women's oppressors. It seems to her that the "natural" roles ecofeminism establishes for women are both fixed and normative. This scares her, she says, and she insists that feminism must be about overcoming just such stereotypes about women—as natural creatures or anything else. Such stereotypes, she argues, are false anyway, and women are inevitably imprisoned within them.[22]

We should not assume that ecofeminists have an uncritical acceptance of current environmentalism. In fact, some have considerable reservations about much of environmentalist thought. Too many environmentalists, they maintain, are far from the ecofeminist worldview. By no means does mainstream environmentalism automatically perceive the hierarchy of man over nature and women that is the crux of ecofeminist thought.

Moreover, many environmentalists argue for the rights of animals, trees, and the like—a stance that rubs against the grain of ecofeminists who reject a rights analysis. Ecofeminist critics of "rights talk" wish to avoid slipping into the individualistic mode of thinking. Their goal is community and holism, not individualism and individual rights. Nor does the deep-ecology strain of environmentalism win unreserved plaudits from ecofeminists. Determination by deep ecologists to abolish all hierarchies and respect natural interrelatedness is one thing; but at the same time, this philosophy neglects problems of gender relations, which ecofeminists argue must hold center stage.[23]

Ecofeminism and Feminism

The uneasy connection between feminism and conventional forms of environmentalism is one that many feminists, secular as well as religious, stress a great deal. Mary Daly, Judy Chicago, and Rosemary Radford Ruether are three major examples of this wide-ranging group. However, relations with mainstream feminism are not perfectly smooth either. Ecofeminists have little enthusiasm for feminist thought that bypasses or barely touches environmentalism. Just as ecofeminist thought does not routinely support standard environmentalism, so it does not rally to all aspects of feminism.

Much feminist thought just does not see women as a part of nature or especially in tune with nature, and from an ecofeminist outlook, this kind of feminism fails before it even starts. Liberal feminism also runs into trouble for being too oriented toward the individual and the human species as an undifferentiated whole. Liberal feminism is not really committed to a holistic and nonhierarchical universe. Ecofeminists are rarely enthusiastic about Marxist feminism either. Marxism hardly abolishes the conflict between humanity and nature or the hierarchy of man and nature, and it is far more obsessed with capitalism than with gender relations.

Radical feminists such as Susan Griffin or Mary Daly do bask in eco-feminist approval, but they do not garner unqualified approval. Critics lament that they are hardly free from the curse of dualism. They too perceive a universe sharply divided between nature and culture and man and woman, with little sense of positive resolution. Ecofeminism, on the other hand, supports a sweeping reformulation of all such traditional categories, a revolution its advocates believe to be both much-needed and distinctly possible.[24]

Ecofeminism and Religion

Spirituality is not part and parcel of ecofeminism, but it is something that a number of ecofeminists favor. There are many who consider themselves Christian ecofeminists, as well as many who look elsewhere for their spiritual grounding. Wherever they turn and whatever they conclude, almost all ecofeminists engage religion in one way or another. Of course, for some of them this step includes coming to terms with Christianity.

Many ecofeminists are intensely critical of Christianity. One example is Charlene Spretnak, a major chronicler of ecofeminist spirituality. She accuses Christianity of failing to work with nature, of standing over and often in opposition to nature, and she maintains that it thus deserves repudiation as a false religion. Susan Griffin is contemptuous of Christianity, which she describes as hostile to nature in general and especially to women as part of nature. Elizabeth Gray, who places herself in the Christian tradition, does not have more any favorable things to say. For her, the story of Christianity has mostly been a sad story of hierarchy. As expressed in the Bible's account of creation and in much subsequent Christian history, God the Father and then man have been superior over all else, including women, animals, and the rest of nature.[25]

By no means are all ecofeminists prepared to give up on Christianity, however. Although there is frequently a spirit of frustration with Christianity, there is sometimes an equal dissatisfaction with those ecofeminists who are quick to dismiss Christianity and turn elsewhere for spiritual nourishment. At the same time, Christian ecofeminists are unanimous in their insistence that Christianity will have to change—a conviction upheld even by evangelical ecofeminists, as illustrated in the publication *Daughters of Sarah*.[26]

The effort by Protestant ecofeminists to inspire change is both practical and theological. On the practical level, there is much consideration on how to focus Christianity on doing something for ecology and for feminism. The particular proposals may seem trivial, but the implicit message of the entire effort is that these ecofeminists reject a Christianity that is not committed to concrete ecofeminist change and a re-formed Christianity.[27]

On the theological level, arguments move in a great many directions. Reconceptualizing God is particularly popular: emphasis falls on God as Creator and nature as sacred. Reinterpretations of the Bible that stress ecological themes are equally frequent. So are recast images for God's earth. The image of earth as Mother is famous, but there are other ideas as well. One suggests that the idea of earth as Mother is a mistake and that people should substitute the image of a child instead. People leave their mothers behind, while children, like the earth, always need love and nurturing.

Sallie McFague's *Models of God* has gotten special respect for its endeavor to reconceptualize God in ways that might transform Christian assumptions and prejudices for our age. McFague is much too much the postmodern thinker to maintain that any of the images she presents fully comprehends or captures God. Instead she insists that her conceptualizations are merely models that may or may not assist us as we seek and reflect on God. They are examples of what she describes as "metaphorical theology."[28] Similarly, for her the Bible becomes a set of "case studies, or a prime Christian classic, or a prototype." It is not, of course, "the authoritative text."[29] For a postmodern like McFague, the idea of authoritative texts is literally incomprehensible.

McFague understands her overall project as another postmodern "thought experiment," the value of which is not the illumination of truth, a concept she apparently does not recognize. Rather, it is an adventure in heuristic exploration that she hopes may yield insight for her readers. She grants that she is open to the accusation that her approach puts what she perceives to be the needs of our day over all other considerations. She denies that this is her prime motivation; at the same time, she underlines her conviction that no theology is, or should be, suitable for all time, including her own, no matter who asserts the contrary.[30]

Among the images that McFague commends to her readers are God as Lover, God as Friend, and God as Mother. Along the way she does not completely ignore the historical Jesus as the model but leans toward another route: she visualizes Christ as "illuminative and illustrative" of the Christian understanding of "the God-world relationship."[31]

What she means is that a good, ecologically sound understanding of Christ—that is, of the Incarnation—will take seriously the principle of embodiment. She perceives the Incarnation as the Christian affirmation of the body, the whole body of nature. It is about space, not just time (as has been common in traditional Christianity), and necessarily involves overcoming dualisms and dominations between the spirit and the flesh, man and woman, humanity and nature. This affirmation of God as incarnation and embodiment, McFague believes, should lead us to appreciate the idea that our home is not just (or not at all) in heaven. Humans are created, earthly, mundane beings, at home on the earth and properly concerned about the earth, our space, our home.[32]

McFague's discussions accord intentionally with a political agenda that is distinctly egalitarian and hostile to those places in the world that she contends are sexist, antinature, hierarchical, and dualistic. In this context she enunciates her disapproval of any "monarchical" model of God ("God the Father"). This concept has no value for her either as a thought experiment or in any other way. Unfortunately, it lures supporters just because "it makes us feel good about God and about ourselves," giving security and comfort rather than insight.[33] Moreover, it is "dangerous." It undermines McFague's egalitarian political agenda, which she believes will be better served by a Christian religion that is "a destabilizing, inclusive, non-hierarchical vision of fulfillment for all of creation." To get there, we must overthrow "monarchical" models of God.[34]

McFague places considerable emphasis on sin. For her, sin is real, and its nature is familiar enough: it is, as Christianity has always perceived, about selfishness. It is about people focusing on themselves over all else—over other people (such as the poor), over other living things, and over the rest of nature. She argues that human beings are not on the top of some ladder but are just one part of a web. They have their place, but so does all else in nature. Sin is appalling just because it involves people putting themselves into spaces that are not theirs.[35]

Roman Catholic Rosemary Radford Ruether is probably the most prominent Christian ecofeminist, and one much admired by others, both Protestants and Catholics.[36] The latest expression of her ecofeminism is in *Gaia and God: An Ecofeminist Theology of Earth Healing* (1992), but she has written often and extensively on the subject. One of her major themes is the need to understand both women and nature within a framework that acknowledges their patriarchal mistreatment by Christianity and Christians. As a Roman Catholic, Ruether acknowledges what she takes to be the extensive sins of Roman Catholicism, though she does not believe Catholicism to be uniquely guilty by any means.

Ruether is among the most vocal advocates of rethinking Christianity in the light of the ecofeminist agenda. What she seeks, as she and her critics agree, is literally a revolution in Christianity in general and Roman Catholicism in particular. The goal is a reborn Christianity that is egalitarian, inclusive, and caring (as she might want to describe it). In her view this means taking women and nature seriously and striking down symbols of God and aspects of human society that too often stand in the way. Hierarchy in the universe and in the church must be abolished. The concept of God and popes as patriarchal fathers must disappear. Androgyny must come to permeate all religion. Jesus, specifically, must be understood as an androgynous figure. People must also discover the feminine dimensions of God/dess. Finally, there must be an open-minded exploration of the pre-Christian world, of the status of its goddess religions and political matriarchies.

If this proposal seems sweeping and almost casual at the same time, Ruether does not mind. She believes there is no sense in hanging on too hard to any particular religious outlook from the past, including traditional Christianity. After all, she reassures her readers, "we must see Christology . . . as paradigmatic. We must accept its relativity to a particular people. . . . The Cross and the Resurrection are contextual to a particular historical community."[37] No wonder that in *Gaia and God*, Christ and the Incarnation all but disappear as Ruether undertakes to fashion a religion of ecological community and healing, united in affirming equality, responsibility, and inclusiveness and in repudiating competition, domination, and, of course, patriarchy.[38]

Ruether does not, however, abandon the possibility that Christianity may have relevance for her place and time. Christianity, she contends, offers much that serves valuable purposes, if it is properly understood or reconstructed. She maintains that in many ways the Bible honors "an ecological theology" and that many aspects of the Christian God/dess are feminine: supportive of equality, community-focused, and devoted to wisdom.[39]

Ruether also identifies other potentially constructive elements from the Bible and the Christian tradition. Examples include the sacramental tradition—seeing the created world as intimately connected with God—and the covenantal tradition—establishing in another form that intimate contact between God and the created world. But for Ruether, these elements have possibilities only if they are radically shorn of their patriarchal pasts and redesigned for the egalitarian and inclusive ethic that is central to her outlook. And she knows that accomplishing this objective will not be simple.[40]

While Ruether has urged an open-minded exploration of the pre-Christian religious world of goddess religions and putative matriarchies, she has been careful not to rush to embrace goddess religions, an important spiritual stream of ecofeminism. Her attitude here expresses a caution that has generated criticism from within the ecofeminist community. Ruether has walked a narrow line, urging study, even sympathy, for goddess religions, but at the same time articulating doubts about them.

She asks whether there ever were such worlds of goddess worship—or matriarchal rule in society—and, if so, how widespread they were. She asks whether they promoted gender or economic equality. In fact, she goes on to cast doubt on such putative historical societies in their idealized form, as models of female rule, gender equality, or peace and gentle happiness. She faults others such as Carol Christ and Mary Daly for their vulnerability to such romantic excursions. Ruether says she appreciates how inspiring the idea of such societies may be to feminists today, but such enthusiasm, she writes, has "to be sorted out from what we can prove or not prove about prehistory."[41]

For Ruether, announcing that religion and/or society was once matriarchal does not make it so—nor does such a claim establish that the matriarchy's consequences were all to the good.[42] Thus, even where Ruether does find the case convincing for "female-centered culture" in early societies, she argues that women exercised their influence through the family. Sometimes that did make for great influence by women, but that was different from real power in the realms of religion or politics or from a situation where women were genuinely equal or free. Even in such societies, tremendous limits on women and their roles existed, and it was more than possible for patriarchy to win control of both religion and politics. For this reason, Ruether concludes that these worlds are no model for women today. We "need to learn the lessons of weaknesses of the matricentric core . . . that made it vulnerable to patriarchy." And, in any case, there "can be no literal return to a Neolithic matricentric village as a basis for gender parity today."[43]

Whether Ruether shows herself to be a conventional Christian or Roman Catholic in her considerations is no longer of any particular importance to her. She argues that people should realize that tradition and orthodoxy are the problem, not the solution. Her intention—and that of other ecofeminists within the Christian camp—is not to salute the Christian past but to transform its legacy radically and pulverize the idols that have too long dominated the universe: God and man understood as rulers or oppressors. To put it another way, she is determined that the relationship between humans and God be healed. Abuse of women, of the poor, and of nature are all violations of a proper relationship with God, and they must cease.

In pursuing this cause, Ruether has been a prominent advocate of Women-Church—an interdenominational (but originally largely Catholic) movement of women seeking to carve out their own sphere of religious truth and human association within, and yet separated from, traditional faith structures. In particular, Ruether has argued for the creation of feminist communities of worship and religious experience—"communities of celebration and resistance"—founded on principles of liberation theology and similar to Christian base communities in Latin and South America. She hopes that they may help to liberate women spiritually, psychologically, economically, and politically.[44]

Liberated communities of all sorts are central examples of Ruether's conception of what creation should look like. Indeed, her core value is undoubtedly community, a theme many other Christian environmentalists also invoke (see chapter 10). Thus her vision of fulfilling spirituality is distinctly communal. It involves overcoming our narcissistic focus, living in caring interdependence with others, and appreciating each person—in community as well as in themselves.[45]

Ruether and other Christian ecofeminists do not make their case without opposition. We have observed that some opposition springs from those ecofeminists who reject Christian spirituality no matter how it is defined or reconstructed. There is also opposition from other Christians, of course, and this resistance is increasing in evangelical Protestant circles as concern over ecofeminism rises. Loren Wilkinson, for example, insists that

Christ and Christ alone is the basis for the Christian religion. Earth gods/goddesses, or the earth as god/goddess, cannot conceivably substitute for Christ.[46] Nor can Christians casually repudiate all dualisms. While God is still "nearer to us than we are to ourselves," nonetheless "God is "wholly *other* than us."[47] Thus "there *is* a fundamental dualism"— that between the universe and its Creator.[48]

Elizabeth Achtemeier recently joined the critique in the evangelical periodical *Christianity Today.* Part of her very Protestant argument was that we have to trust the Bible, which never identifies God as Mother or as female. To be sure, she grants that there are a few female references in connection with the divine (such as Isaiah 42:14), but she contends that they are nothing more than similes. For her, the Bible speaks of God in male language—though not because God is somehow one gender or another—and she insists that there can be no whitewashing of the fact that God revealed himself as a male in Jesus Christ.[49]

Ecofeminists can encounter indifference too, especially from some Christian feminists. Although they may not deny much that Ruether or evangelical feminists say, many of them are not especially interested in the ecofeminist argument. As these feminists explore questions of God, the ministry, their personal journeys or, sometimes, lesbian experience, ecofeminism sometimes slips very much into the background.[50]

Spirituality in Other Modes

Spirituality among ecofeminists does not any longer come in just the Christian or anti-Christian modes. There is simply no way to appreciate current ecofeminist discussion within Protestantism, and Christianity more generally, without a sense of its participants' recognition of the spiritual energy that lies outside Christianity. One prominent example is Charlene Spretnak, but she is far from alone in the crusade for a non-Christian spiritual ecofeminism and in the attack on Christian spirituality. For Spretnak, spirituality is vital and teaches the oneness of everything— what she believes every true feminist and ecologist already knows.

The particular form of spirituality does not matter, so long as it is in tune with wholeness as understood in the feminist ecological movement. According to ecofeminists like Spretnak, this proper spirit may manifest itself in a multitude of ways and in a variety of places. And to confine or to channel spirit is itself an act of domination, just the sort of practice that spiritual ecofeminists want humanity to abandon.

In this milieu as elsewhere, we encounter interest in "creation spirituality"—the conviction that people are, with God, co-creators of life; that spiritual realms are all of one piece; and that everything and everyone in the universe is interrelated. Adherents of this viewpoint also express a good deal of fascination with Native American spirituality. It attracts praise because it is held to celebrate integrated and integrating spirits in the universe; the attention it receives, though, is often highly generalized and sentimental. Buddhism is admired as well and has a positive image as an integrative and peaceful religion.

Other alternative spiritualities share an outlook their adherents proudly call pagan. All express genuine awe for the spiritual around us and in us, honor experience rather than creeds, and seek to be holistic and profoundly egalitarian. Few of their defenders operate from a dogmatic or sectarian frame of mind. As Charlene Spretnak says, ecofeminists should be eclectic, incorporating any and all spiritualities that speak to them and that coincide with truth as they experience it.[51]

Perhaps goddess religions are the most discussed alternative spiritualities among ecofeminists at present. Goddess worship has quite suddenly attracted much interest in the past decade or so, as illustrated in such classics as Carol Christ's *Laughter of Aphrodite: Reflections on a Journey to the Goddess*. How widespread any actual worship of goddesses is, however, is unknown. There is no data about numbers of adherents in any of the "new" ecofeminist spiritualities.

Most devotees of goddess religions insist that they are not in the Christian tradition and do not wish to be. To them, Christianity is hopelessly flawed in its inherent patriarchy, which has historically crushed both nature and women. Many ecofeminists either recall a lost, pristine era of harmony under the caring and holistic guidance of goddesses—a state where no one and nothing, including nature, was exploited—or envision such an ideal age for the future. To achieve or to recover that world is their objective.

Skeptics sometimes wonder how seriously proponents of goddess worship take their beliefs. On one level, this query is simply insulting to believers. More legitimately, questions arise about the historicity of claims that prehistory had goddess religions. Others wonder about how attractive this past, whether real or not, actually is. In the times of goddesses, they still see a patriarchal past in which women's roles were "naturally" family-oriented or focused on caring. Such conditions led inevitably to women's oppression and could do so again.[52] After all, nothing about being a mother or caring is, or has ever been, necessarily antihierarchical or egalitarian.

The ecofeminist answer is often an affirmation of women as caring creatures and a confidence that a society more directed to caring will prompt a diminution of hierarchy and a growth of equality. If it does not, blame can be attributed to the artificial constructions of gender that we experience in our time and place, constructions that should be done away with as soon as possible.

Witchcraft is another stream of women's spirituality that today often self-consciously identifies with environmentalism. Witchcraft may be defined as the practice of magic—"the art of changing consciousness at will"[53]—designed to direct events and people and employing special rituals. The practices of witchcraft come in many forms. Some are quite recent creations from the 1970s and 1980s, and many are variations on truly ancient traditions. There is no single leading representative, though Starhawk is the best-known contemporary voice. She has considerable status in the witchcraft movement and has written of her religion in such works as *Truth or Dare: Encounters with Power, Authority, and Mystery* as well as in briefer accounts contained in many collections.[54]

While there is much variation among witches, there is considerable agreement that all women are connected with spiritual forces in the universe that stand in opposition to the history of male domination, against which witches must struggle today as they did in the witch-burning past. Rituals are an important part of witchcraft worship because they are the outer signs of inner solidarity among witches, women as a whole, and nature.

Many expressions of witchcraft are self-consciously ecofeminist, anxious to close the gaps between humans and the rest of nature and between the material and spiritual realms. They contain considerable confidence that this goal can be accomplished. This is a theme, for example, of Starhawk's writings: "We really can turn the tide—we can survive the destruction of the Earth."[55] At the same time, some witches are lesbian separatists who appreciate witchcraft as a female spirituality, the origins and practices of which do not always include men.

Like all forms of spirituality, witchcraft has its tensions. For example, not all traditional witchcraft worshipers were terribly happy with the feminist infusion that occurred in the 1970s and thereafter. From this perspective, witchcraft was not and should not be a spirituality about feminism or for feminism. Nor have all participants in witchcraft been overly joyful about the political side of some contemporary witchcraft. Time has lessened some of these tensions, though, at least in the United States. There has been a growing acceptance of the new diversity in what, after all, has been a pluralist phenomenon for many years.[56]

While Protestant and general Christian ecofeminism have felt the fervor and influence of other ecofeminist spiritual paths, they are not the same and rarely pretend to be. Yet on one level, religious ecofeminists often agree about more than the need for a spiritual dimension to achieve a reborn earth. A certain confidence, a confidence in the power of spiritual forces, is a shared chord that unites spiritual ecofeminists. It undergirds their impulse toward a holistic universe and a world liberated from mechanistic reason, male rule, and patriarchal divinities. It underlies their considerable common interest in small, steady-state, egalitarian communities devoted to stewardship of the earth.[57]

Several significant philosophical problems will engage critics and ecofeminists alike in the years ahead. Much more attention must be given to the philosophical foundations for ecofeminism. If the foundation for ecofeminism is nature, then what is nature, how is it discerned, and how does it acquire normative status? On the other hand, if the foundation for ecofeminism is something other than nature, utility, or one or another religions or spiritualities, their connection to ecofeminism will need defense and development.

There is also this philosophical question: how can ecofeminism urge the view that nature is what matters and that humanity must be understood only in naturalistic terms? Doesn't the very fact that people are so concerned about nature show that human beings are not just another part of nature but are, in some important way, special or unique?[58] One can also perceive uneasy relations and questions of priorities among such ecofeminist goals as holism, gender equality, and the celebration of women as exemplification of the natural or as god(desses). Do all these go together? Could they do so pragmatically? How might any conflicts be amicably resolved?

Moreover, the expanding enthusiasm for an ecofeminist spirituality—whether through Christianity or outside of it—at times overshadows the serious issue of whether ecofeminist spiritualities rest in truth. The need for one or another truth obviously does not establish that such a truth exists. Critics sense that unusually strong pragmatic factors are at work in ecofeminist spirituality and that in this case there may be a "sacrifice of truth to utility."[59] And the usual form of ecofeminist spirituality, one that is vaguely pantheistic, also elicits sharp questions from skeptics. Is nature divine? And does merging women into nature abandon the basis of individual responsibility?

Far more controversial, of course, is the ecofeminist attitude toward science as a window to the nature they applaud. Ordinarily ecofeminists are at best ambivalent toward "normal" science. It is repeatedly classed with other rationalist, "male" activities whose history and methodology they conclude have been oppressive and patriarchal. For example, some feminist epistemological doubts about how much material world is really out there have had a major impact; for the teachings of normal science about the reality of the material world have worked to the detriment of women, according to some feminists; on the other hand, a socially constructed world might be changed to women's benefit. The work of such figures as Evelyn Fox Keller, Sandra Harding, and Donna Haraway is influential here.[60]

Such awareness is also directly related to arguments over the historical validity of some ecofeminist claims. These arguments are vigorous, but for some ecofeminists they are not quite on point. They contend that it is neither entirely relevant nor really possible to recapture such pasts. Often they are not much concerned whether "their" past ever existed. Inventing it or pretending it existed will do just as well. And if some critics find this stance objectionable, one response is that "knowledge about the world" is always and inexorably a matter of social construction, thus inevitably "historically contingent," and that we must accept this postmodern reality and move on.[61]

Ecofeminists who do offer enthusiastic affirmation of the historicity of ecofeminism in some early societies face strong disagreement.[62] Critics including Susanne Heine, Janet Biehl, and Mary Kassian assert that the history on which so much of some ecofeminist religion rests is hardly self-evident. Some deny the self-evidence for much matriarchy in human societies of the past. They point out that matrilinear family patterns should not be confounded with evidence for matriarchy, and they observe that goddesses of the Western past are a dubious model for today. Those goddesses were mostly fertility goddesses, a sharp contrast with what modern-day revivalists have in mind for the image of the goddess. Skeptics conclude that the field's abundant casual history and numerous generalizations across temporal and cultural boundaries simply will not work.[63]

Biehl in particular is uneasy with ecofeminism and analyzes it as a jumble of incoherent myth and imagination about nature, the past, and women, "a mystical mood language that is more shadowy than clear."[64] She believes it contains entirely too much sentimentalist affirmation of such concepts as wholeness, spirit, and community, with little clue offered as to what they might mean. Along with other critics, she asks what this is all about and what it does except to promote "blatant irrationality."[65]

Nevertheless, an impressive aura lingers around this subject. Ecofeminism is a creative effort that, as we have noted, breaks through many boundaries. To be sure, at this point it is very much another elite analysis and agenda, and how seriously it deserves to be taken, in the context of Protestant ecological thinking, is hardly obvious. Its critics often ridicule it as not serious, as "a kind of pseudo-mystical mixing and matching of symbols and ideas that have nothing in common with each other, . . . another exciting . . . shopping spree in the great mall of the world's traditions."[66]

Yet ecofeminism seeks to shed new light on religion and the universe, nature and spirituality, women and theology. Perhaps it will enrich Protestantism as neo-Platonism enriched Augustine's Christianity in the fourth and fifth centuries, though its "gender requirement for spiritual truth" conflicts with Protestantism's belief in the priesthood of all believers.[67] In any case, religious ecofeminism cannot be blithely ignored or casually repudiated. Along with process and creation spiritualities, it is a growing part of the debate within Protestant environmentalism.

THE PROTESTANT ENVIRONMENTALIST AGENDA

The practical implication of much of the discussion among Protestant thinkers about the environment is not immediately obvious. Arguments abound over the Bible's teachings regarding the ecosystem, and there are numerous and sometimes contradictory theological reflections about God, people, and nature. The topics Protestant environmentalists confront are diverse and enriching—stewardship, the Book of Genesis, creation, eco-feminism, process theology, end times, and much more. But at some point one has to wonder, what is the connection with action? When does Protestant environmentalism shift from theory to practice? Where is its effort to think about how to transform God's world in response to crisis? What agenda do green Protestants propose?

In this chapter and the next, this book turns directly to the green Protestant agenda. The focus of this chapter is Protestant environmentalist goals for change, granting from the start the diversity in this literature. The focus of the next chapter is on the proposed means of change.

Three directions appear, often in combination, in ecological Protestant agendas for change. First, there are many specific policy proposals, even long lists of proposals, that represent the most down-to-earth policy side of Protestant environmentalism. Second, one particular objective—the goal of a transformed ecological consciousness—represents, for its advocates, an essential end in itself and the key to other more structural changes. It reflects a consistent pattern in Protestant environmentalist thought, the conviction that ideas matter—even or especially when it comes to action. Finally, one branch concentrates on three main structural reforms—or revolutions?—that are the heart of the green Protestant action agenda: creating a sustainable society of limits; fostering an egalitarian community; and speeding the arrival of a world order of eco-justice.

Specific Policy Agendas

Protestant environmentalism can be quite policy-directed, typifying the entire green movement's inclination toward action. The down side, however, can be a neglect of reflective thought in the rush to action. In this instance, such a tendency is exaggerated, because so much of Protestant environmental effort has as its source an overpowering sense that time is short and the crisis overwhelming.

Thus the treasured beliefs are that we must act and that it is God who gives that summons: "I believe, deeply," Theodore Malloch writes, "that God wants us to help Him create a new kind of world."[1] Sometimes these exhortations are general and can be vapid. Calls to "follow God" beg the crucial question of what following God is supposed to mean except when tied to specific policy agendas.[2] Sometimes there are no such guidelines; at other times they are spelled out effectively.[3] What seems rare in this literature is any sense that one might not know what God intends.

The overarching assumption is always the urgency of the need for action, an unrelenting theme among Protestant environmentalists. Implicit in this assumption, of course, is a considerable faith in what action can accomplish. Few believe that action can magically solve all ecological problems, but many insist that action is possible, is valuable, and can make all the difference. Change is not going to be easy, but most Protestant environmentalism expresses confidence that humans have the potential to act wisely to assist creation. Moreover, green Protestants have faith that God will not forget creation, that God's grace will bless both it and those who act for it.[4]

Thus many Protestant denominations endorse and sometimes work for a variety, often a blizzard, of specific proposals for ecological action. This "list" approach has its limitations. It sometimes adds up to little more than a jumble of "good things" environmentalists should favor, a state of affairs far short of a coherent and empirically grounded Christian environmentalism. In this realm one may encounter undeveloped priorities, conflicting policies, and a lack of connections with Scripture or other Christian teachings. The lists of specific proposals, however, are testimonies to the desire to act before it is too late.[5]

Some approaches have focused on a single issue or concern. For example, attention to energy policy dominated Protestant environmentalism beginning in the middle 1970s. The energy crisis of those years stimulated an enormous response from parts of the Protestant religious community, as the mainstream culture came bursting through the church doors. The result was an awesome number of articles and essays devoted to energy policy and the environment.[6]

Typical discussions sought to be as specific as possible. Readers of Protestant periodicals learned exactly how to cut energy costs, especially in their churches, and numerous reports recounted how this or that church had succeeded in doing so. Articles told how Lutheran or Episcopalian or Methodist congregations had cut or could cut energy costs by combining church services in the winter, building solar panels, installing fans and insulation, carpooling to church and, in one case, by following a list of fifty-three ideas for reducing energy use in a church.[7] The strategy was and is obvious: exhortation and example were to lead to detailed changes at the local level. The larger movement's ethic—"act locally"—was alive within green Protestantism, and it remains alive today.

The energy crisis of the middle 1970s led Protestant environmentalists to consider energy policy alternatives. They tended to reject oil and gas as sources of energy, for example, and cast around for alternatives. Some praised solar energy, others synfuels; many argued the pluses and (mostly) minuses of nuclear energy; more than a few maintained that the real answer was to escape modern life and return to a simpler existence requiring less energy, whatever the kind.[8]

Money was definitely a concern in energy policy matters. Many essays in the Protestant denominational press made no bones that their aim was to reduce their suddenly soaring energy costs.[9] The focus was practical, but one might ask, was it too practical? It is not always obvious how Protestant discussions of energy policy, driven partly by just such practical concerns, differed from those of the larger environmental movement. At times there was only a glimmer of theological or other religious explanation for green Protestants' proposed energy policies. At other times, the language of Christian stewardship did play a noticeable role in justifying the energy policies proposed.[10]

A second policy area that has received attention is population control. While it has been the subject of innumerable Protestant discussions over the past twenty-five years, Protestant environmentalists have spoken about it in a decidedly muted voice. Specific policy concerns by no means always lead to articulated and shared policy agendas. Those Protestant activists who have enlisted in the cause of population control argue that there are too many people on Earth, overwhelming the environment and blocking social justice. Moreover, the prognosis is poor unless the "population timebomb" can be "defused."[11]

This theme received particular emphasis in the 1970s, when limiting human numbers was "clearly one of the tasks of Christian stewardship,"[12] but it has remained on the agenda in recent years. The language of alarm surrounding the topic of population growth is frequently dramatic, but when policy specifics arise, caution is typically the watchword. This caution reflects the activation of the abortion issue, which arose after *Roe v. Wade* in 1973. Of course, abortion is a terribly sensitive matter within a Protestantism severely divided over the issue. To this point, however, abortion as a means of population control has not attracted much support in Protestant environmentalism.[13]

When the argument over overpopulation has raged hotly, the agenda has been set from outside Christianity. Paul Ehrlich's flamboyant predictions of imminent world collapse due to overpopulation and Garrett Hardin's somber strictures about the terrible human choices required for species survival have stimulated a good deal of debate among environmentalist Protestants. So have Barry Commoner's claims that population control advocates are hostile to the Third World and economic justice because their focus on population control clashes with the practice and values of Third World cultures.[14]

In every policy discussion, Protestant environmentalists must confront the question of how their Christian values dovetail with their specific policy proposals. Some contend that there can never be a close fit between specific policy proposals and Christian truth. Christianity and the Bible may teach stewardship, they argue, but they do not delineate the specifics. Nor can the Bible tell us much more. The Bible is not "a textbook," and a Protestantism that promulgated detailed policies would not be wise anyway. The danger is an "environmental fundamentalism" that would impede a flexible and changing response to God's summons to stewardship.[15]

Such an analysis is plausible, yet the questions persist. How will "responsible stewardship" be defined in policy terms? What does the Bible teach? Should the answers be left up to subjective guesses and claims, or to "experts" who are often not Christians? Will the result be little more than another set of secular programs and policies? The answers are hardly clear.[16]

Green Values

A second green Protestant approach seeks transformed values through transformed consciousness. Many Protestant environmentalists insist that people desperately require a dramatic change in their values, above all else. Perhaps it is predictable that religious intellectuals and activists—so involved in the realm of belief, symbol, and myth—would conclude that a change in values is integral to any program of change.[17]

Values discussions among Protestant environmentalists usually start with the call for change, not disputations about the meaning of Christianity or the Bible. The reason may be that Protestant environmentalism proceeds from the prophetic sense that it is in conflict with the corrupt world around it. Despite the internal divisions within the Protestant ecological movement, there is a wide consensus that the greater enemy lies without, in the often uncaring or wrongly directed social order that is destroying God's creation. This is why a new consciousness is necessary.

The objective is an "immense change in habits of thought" regarding the earth and a commitment to act to effect this change in local churches, in national politics, and over the entire globe.[18] Some predict a flowering of spirituality as people learn to live in concert with God's wishes. Much more often, though, the aim is more down-to-earth: a new consciousness to help the environment survive. This attitude bothers critics. They suggest that it is not always clear what ultimately matters to green Protestants: religious truth or saving the environment. To the committed, however, this dichotomy is false and should be recognized as such.[19]

There is consensus, especially among many liberal Protestant writers, on what they oppose. They are almost automatically critical of what they hold to be central Western values, particularly of liberalism (defined as selfish individualism), oppressive hierarchies, economic development, profit-making, and income inequalities.[20]

They agree much less on what values to promote. Some Protestant thinkers do little more than announce the importance of a revamped set of values and leave readers adrift about questions of definition and coherence. Others do much better. The rest of this chapter analyzes the values Protestant environmentalists most often advance when considering "what to do." These values are the core of the Protestant ecological agenda; they go beyond both lists of specific policy proposals and a general enthusiasm for changed consciousness and new values.

Toward a Sustainable Society of Limits

Green Protestants seek a transformation of consciousness, but they also insist that society must change its institutions and modes of living. For most green Protestants, a sustainable social order of limits in concert with nature must be at the heart of a good, ecological society. What this oft-invoked model means is that humanity must fashion ways of living that operate in genuine cooperation with the earth's other living systems. We must live as one part of a natural world that we respect and with which we achieve integration.

Implicit and sometimes explicit in this ideal is green Protestantism's commitment to a society of limits—sometimes, in fact, to a kind of social asceticism.[21] As Thoreau might have wished, the cry is for simplifying one's life. Personal consumption and economic development must yield to simpler lifestyles driven by the values of conservation and recycling rather than the current addiction to consumption and "throwaway" practices.[22] Thus, while much environmentalist writing, religious and otherwise, has a reputation for utopianism, this is only even putatively true if utopianism means the reach for a society of somewhat ascetic limits.

In practice, the argument is that human appetites and institutions must be downsized in order to sustain life. People must learn that in every dimension of existence, smaller is the answer if we want to survive—if we want God's creation to survive. A typical recent article, "Respecting Creation's Integrity: Biblical Principles for Environmental Responsibility," cites 1 Timothy 6:6–9 and urges people to "practice contentment" and "not exploit creation beyond meeting your basic needs."[23]

While the argument here is that in a limited, sustainable society, the result in every dimension of existence will be survival, other thinkers also emphasize other benefits. People will come to appreciate that to go slower, listen longer, and restore a sense of peace in their lives can be a wonderful thing. They will discover that their dependence on conveniences and luxuries that hurt nature actually robs them of contact with the beauties around them. They will become more secure and will begin to grow more deeply as people; they will become literally more down-to-earth, closer to outer nature and to inner natures.[24] Meanwhile, a minimal "sustainable development" will allow humanity to provide for "successive generations."[25]

In its discussions about the sustainable society, green Protestantism's most common subtheme is that of achieving sustainability in economic life. This is particularly noticeable among liberal Protestants, who offer more economic (and more radical economic) analysis. Some stress organic farming; others favor a serious commitment to recycling; others demand production only for "basic human needs" and never for luxuries (always a term of disrepute in this occasionally puritanical outlook); for still others, production must be local and cooperative within nature. These thinkers perform a regular assault on traditional measures of economic health, such as

GDP (Gross Domestic Product); they maintain that such measures concern economic production and expansion, mocking the ethic of sustainability and thus threatening the earth.[26]

Garrett Hardin has argued that environmentalists have a religion of their own and that central to it is this orientation toward limits.[27] At the least, Protestant environmentalism's ethic of sustainability is its economic gospel. Thus, the larger goal in proposals for saving energy is to regularly spread the ethic of limits and thereby maximize a sustainable social order. As suggested in *101 Ways to Help Save the Earth*, by the National Council of Churches' Eco-Justice Working Group, societies must become self-sustaining by altering their energy use and much more. Acid rain, fading ozone layers, the greenhouse effect, overuse of energy at home and in cars, and many other problems promise to lead us quickly to the end. If we want to save the planet, we must turn to an economics that will speed the arrival of sustainability, not growth or expansion.[28]

Green Protestants invariably identify restriction of economic growth as the straightest channel to long-run sustainability. How stringent the limit to economic expansion should be provokes discussion, as does the question of whether the most militant versions of that goal are really a yearning for an ascetic primitivism. Most of these thinkers express confidence that economic down-scaling need not mean hurling society into a massive depression or a premodern economic life. But there is a need for much more detailed empirical discussion, explanation, and planning regarding this goal.

Opponents of growth economies often have a multitiered agenda. While the survival value and other social benefits of a sustainable economics form the major objection to a growth economy model, green Protestants can make a more personal argument as well. Many of them, such as Roger Shinn, have attacked a growth economy model because they believe it depersonalizes human existence. It neglects human (and divine) values in the rush toward economic growth and gain. It clashes with expanding human community as well. These critics charge that growth economics has no respect for bonds or bonding among people and cheerfully tears them up if development is at issue.[29]

A growth model also runs afoul of the numerous justice advocates within liberal Protestant environmentalist circles. Defining justice as economic equality, they charge that growth economics only respects a "merit" definition of justice, denying substantive equality, and that it creates huge economic inequalities. For this reason, denunciations of the growth model are routine in Protestant environmentalism. Rarely are there any doubts about this judgment—for example, doubts about whether the Third World can afford to spurn economic growth.[30]

The normative case for the sustainable economic model is often made, and some of the discussion of sustainability, growth, and economics does speak from carefully identified Christian premises. For example, some green Protestants argue against a growth economy and its predictable economic inequalities as a disgrace to a God who created all as moral equals and who loves all equally. Others interpret the Bible's statement that the earth and everything on it is God's as a warning against growth economics. For them, to manipulate God's creation in service of the idol of economic expansion is to deny God.[31]

It follows, not surprisingly, that hostility toward capitalism is pervasive in the green Protestant literature—especially among religious and political liberals. This sentiment is not unanimous, but it represents the orthodoxy. To be sure, much turns around how one defines capitalism. Insofar as capitalism includes approval of corporate business and a market economy, sympathy for economic growth, and a belief in the legitimacy of economic "gain or self-interest," however, disapproval is keen.[32] Indeed, Protestant environmentalist literature regularly attacks capitalism as a selfish, rapacious, want-creating, crass system, responsible for much of the desecration of God's Earth. And it rarely recommends capitalism or the market as viable instruments for realizing any environmental goals.

The attack is sometimes oblique, phrased as a critique of a market economy or the economics of growth. Why the approach is sometimes indirect is an interesting question. Perhaps the realistic explanation is that open repudiation of capitalism has gone out of fashion in capitalist America. Another reason may flow from the fact that few Protestant environmentalists are professional economists. The instincts of many green Protestants are anticapitalist, but making a case against capitalism in the terms of professional economics is something else again.[33] After all, neither earnest theology nor sincere political opinion is the same as serious economic analysis and argument. Their too-frequent absence in Protestant environmentalist discussion of the sustainable model of economic life is, in fact, its greatest weakness.

Some writers do tackle economic questions and the market system with sophistication. The prime recent example has been Herman Daly and John B. Cobb Jr.'s *For the Common Good*, which has already proven influential as a sustained reflection on economics, the environment, and the future. Its authors argue that our survival requires a "sustainable" economic society. To achieve this end, they suggest, the guiding norm should be long-run use value, not exchange value, the principle underlying capitalism. Long-run economic decisions must be made in terms of what helps global existence, not on what advantages particular individuals may obtain from things like economic growth.

Daly and Cobb are aware of what people can learn from market analysis as human beings move toward a more sustainable and cohesive community. They know that market realities are a powerful factor in economic life, a factor that cannot be wished away in enthusiasm for schemes to implement strict economic equality. For this reason, Daly and Cobb concede that employing modified market strategies will be the most effective means to accomplish selected policies and will carry distinct benefits. Ultimately, however, Daly and Cobb return to familiar ground in Protestant environmentalism. They are not sympathetic to capitalism, whatever its definition. Although it can teach people things, no one should emulate it. The market errs in anointing the individual while ignoring humanity's communal side and the means to achieve collective goods—including environmental goods.

Their alternative is a conventional one on the left: the model of worker participation and ownership in an economy firmly controlled and owned by a democratic government. They believe that worker participation will humanize the inevitable statist features of their economic ideal. It will bring people into the picture and respect their insights and their democratic rights. Daly and Cobb also see their model as helping to encourage other values they favor, especially community and greater social equality, in concrete strategic and institutional ways.[34]

For Daly and Cobb and most others who look to a sustainable ecological model, Marxism is not the answer; Protestant environmentalists have generally come to recognize that Marxist-inspired systems failed in practice in Eastern Europe and the former Soviet Union. Indeed, talk about socialism of any sort has recently quieted in Protestant environmentalist circles. Adherents of socialism remain,[35] but they are on the defensive, responding to criticisms that in practice socialism has proven to be another command- and production-oriented economy, ineffective in its own terms and clearly not conducive to a healthy environment.[36]

A more popular approach to the environmentally sustainable society speaks the language of holistic community. It endeavors to create a society that replicates much of the holistic realm of nature. Such a model avoids discussing either socialist or capitalist modes of production. According to its proponents, such as Wesley Granberg-Michaelson, it is a good deal more biblical and is rooted specifically in the Gospels of Jesus—such as

Jesus' admonitions to help the poor or his feedings of the five thousand—as well as early Christianity's commitment to an economy of sharing, as described in the Book of Acts.[37]

Rendering Justice

Some Protestant environmentalists' discomfort with capitalism and, of late, with Marxism derives partially from a strong respect for (a certain vision of) justice. The favored term, "eco-justice," combines (if not altogether felicitously) the two objectives that overlie all liberal Protestant ecological considerations: environmentalism and justice.[38]

Over the past twenty-five years, a good many Protestant eco-justice groups have arisen in service of these two ideals. The National Council of Churches' Eco-Justice Working Group and *The Egg: An Eco-Justice Quarterly* embody these twin goals both in name and in program: "environmental sustainability" and "economic justice."[39] While praise for justice is often lavish in such a setting, defenses of justice are harder to come by. A good part of the reason may be the wide consensus within liberal Protestant writings on what justice is all about. The most prominent feature is almost always substantive economic equality, based on the assumption that only this definition respects the moral equality people share as creatures of God. This agreement leads too many of its advocates to take this definition for granted, though justice is a contested concept around which fierce arguments have swirled for thousands of years.

At its best, as in the work of Larry Rasmussen, eco-justice merges into an environmental concept of community—in this instance, a community of the earth. It becomes an ethic that incorporates God and the entire universe and that differs, as Rasmussen rightly contends, from familiar Western egalitarianism. While egalitarianism remains central, communitarian holism replaces the often mechanical quality of standard egalitarianism. The goal is not a cold, formal secular equality but a living reality of equal sharing and experiencing in a vibrant, holy community of God.[40]

Impressive-sounding and sometimes hyphenated terms such as "eco-justice" speak of good intentions, but they do not resolve the inevitable tensions that lurk behind them. How to incorporate justice into environmentalism, and vice versa, is a major challenge for Protestants concerned about the earth. As the ecological movement advanced within liberal Protestantism during the 1960s and 1970s, this conundrum came to the surface. Uncertainty abounded over whether and how environmental and justice goals could go together. Some argued that ecological objectives must have priority; others feared that concentration on the green agenda could mean more Third World inequality and suffering at the behest of an already comfortably well-off First World.[41]

In more recent years, the question of where and how the ideal of justice fits in the Protestant environmental crusade has remained alive, and it will continue to do so. For some skeptics, a focus on egalitarian justice mostly promises enormous conflict—even wars—over resources that will not result in care for the planet. Meanwhile, some justice advocates wonder about whether the commitment of environmentalists extends beyond their affinity for wilderness areas, beautiful birds, or the upper middle class.

The common strategy today is to endorse both goals, though many such efforts are rhetorical and thin rather than tight, cogent arguments that make a serious case both philosophically and practically. It is one thing to support "a just, participatory and sustainable society," but it is another to argue how these objectives are compatible.[42] When liberal Protestant groups announce that "justice . . . is always eco-justice," one needs to know why this is so and what the argument looks like.[43] Similarly, it is great to declare that "justice to human beings is inseparable from right relationships with and within the natural order," but why would we assume this to be true, and how, in concrete policy terms, could we realize such a desire?[44]

Some analyses do make an argument for both goals. One perspective makes a largely biblical case. From this viewpoint, creation is God's; it is good and humanity must restore it (Genesis 2). At the same time, God is committed to social justice (Leviticus 25:10–12) and unites both concerns in the promise of liberation for the earth and all that is on it (Romans 8:19, 21). Therefore, concentrating on eco-justice is the way to proceed.

A second eco-justice view also makes a biblical case, this time grounded in the Bible's teaching about the duty to help the weak and vulnerable. Its proponents argue that such a Christian duty inevitably leads one to recognize how vulnerable nature and the poor are in our time. Such an awareness must lead Christians to help them and, in the process, to render them justice.[45] Overall, the message is that eco-justice is really one cause, biblically and in practice.[46]

As a goal, eco-justice has long had greater support among mainline Protestant writers than anywhere else within Protestantism. Though similar themes are now appearing among some green evangelicals, in liberal Protestantism eco-justice is a true gospel. The National Council of Churches' ecological arm states that it "regards ecological wholeness and . . . justice as inseparable."[47] The aim is to "abolish" poverty, hunger, and environmental abuse, as aspects of the same endeavor.[48] For liberal Protestant activists, eco-justice represents a happy marriage: justice as economic equality combined with a commitment to ecological objectives, brought together in the belief that they must be advanced as one.

Some green Protestants have made an effort to find practical projects that might promote both objectives. The National Council of Churches' Eco-Justice Working Group has singled out combating toxic poisoning as a salient example. This group believes that to oppose toxic waste mismanagement is to campaign for an improved environment *and* for relief for the poor. Toxic dumps and leaks of toxic materials are terrible for the earth, and they almost always occur in poor areas and punish impoverished people. Thus, to address toxic waste is to strike a blow both for the environment and for justice.[49]

The question remains, however, whether tackling poverty and preserving the environment are always or even often compatible. Sometimes they are, as the toxic waste example demonstrates. But how typical is this example? Applied in an international setting, the same question has long been raised, sometimes from within the green community itself. Can poverty be eliminated by an egalitarian environmentalism, or might it be that defeating poverty requires economic growth, which may not dependably advance egalitarianism—or, for that matter, environmentalism?[50]

From another angle, some skeptics have long contended that environmentalists' concern about social justice for the poor and neglected is thin. To such critics, environmentalism is more accurately understood as a safe harbor for selfish souls hiding in ecological dress, mostly concerned about protecting their romantic environmental values, and not really interested in the average person and his or her life situations. Such attitudes would be unacceptable for any Christian and would hardly promise a genuine dedication to justice for all.[51]

Social justice, however, is not an irrelevant or secondary matter in many Protestant reflections on the environment and justice. Indeed, justice frequently is the predominant concern, or at least a necessary prior concern. In fact, over the last twenty-five years green Protestantism has exhibited a distinct drift toward the social justice left, often with explicit confidence that U.S. Christianity is a "sleeping giant" that could have a tremendous impact for egalitarian justice if it were mobilized.[52] This is especially true among liberal Protestants and is reflected well in the name and agenda of the Justice, Peace, and the Integrity of Creation (JPIC) effort, sponsored by the World Council of Churches.

Yet here, too, challenges remain. One is the intersection of the eco-justice program with racial questions. Some time ago, Richard Baer Jr. raised the matter of environmentalism and social justice in racial contexts. He argued that Christian environmentalists in the United States should pay more attention to black people, especially poor African Americans, than to celebrations of nature that are relevant mostly to affluent whites. Putting his point bluntly, Baer urged that environmentalism not become a cause more engaged with polar bears than with Harlem. Yet the place that racial justice should hold in green Protestant eco-justice is, as yet, rarely discussed.[53]

The Goal of Community

Where goals are concerned, Protestant environmentalists offer more un-restrained support for community than for any other objective. The notion of community is a normative goal that provokes much less controversy than the ideal of egalitarian justice. What green Protestants mean by community is usually a holistic society of equals sharing common ends and close personal bonds. Some images of community fasten on local communities; others look to "global Gemeinschaft"; still others broaden their vision to the "planetary community." Sometimes the accent falls more on human community, sometimes on community with the natural world, sometimes on both. The directions are many, but enthusiasm for community is widespread.

Community is a perfect and predictable value for Protestants devoted to the ecological cause. Both the Christian tradition and environmentalism have long honored it. Both share the conviction that it will require great efforts to advance community in a world where the pursuit of economic gain and other forms of selfish individualism constantly thwart the creation of community.[54]

Green Protestants constantly return to the proposition that nature teaches community. The "ecological challenge to Christian ethics" appears in just this light. Respect for nature requires Christians to live the community ethic, as does faithfulness to what Jesus taught and lived long ago. Both demand that Christians teach holism, interrelatedness, and the vital importance of striving to maximize a common good.

For community-minded Protestants, the pragmatic case is also important. People need community with their fellow humans and with all of life if the earth is to endure and flourish. As Lynn White defined it, all we need is a solemn "conviction of man's comradeship with the other creatures," a community that nature models for us if we will but look.[55]

Daly and Cobb's *For the Common Good* articulates many of the themes of the search for community among Protestant environmentalists. The authors favor human community in settings that are as decentralized as possible. There, they believe, democracy has a chance and economic life can flourish with maximum worker participation. But like a good many others in the green Protestant literature, they are also interested in community at other levels. They accept the need for a national community, which may be better able than local communities to ensure that civil and other human rights are protected. They also have a strong desire for a world community—a goal well under way, they argue, if one looks at economic developments in our time. Finally, of course, they seek the great eco-community, the community of humans and the rest of nature.[56]

All these putative communities are popular with many Protestant environmentalists. But the question of how they might fit together in principle and in practice constitutes a puzzle. One of Cobb and Daly's strengths is that they appreciate this puzzle, though not everyone else does. Even rarer is someone like Wendell Berry, who argues that they cannot all be achieved together.[57] Casual comments or passing reassurances that it will all work out do not get us anywhere. In a movement where some simultaneously call for world government while defending opposition to local waste dumps, both in the name of community, some tough challenges lie ahead.[58]

Balancing community with other values, such as justice, is not going to be simple either. Such decisions will not come more quickly now than they have over the centuries. Furthermore, they will not be made at all without rigorous attention to the theoretical and practical exigencies the task poses. The broad celebration of community that is standard fare for a wide variety of intellectuals in our time does not make the task easier. The problem is that these celebrations of community have not always gotten us as far as we might like in understanding or advancing this ideal.[59]

It helps to have some sense of the dynamics and problems present today in intellectual thought about community outside the green Protestant world in order to gain perspective on thought about community. As the normative watchword of our age, community has attracted a good many intellectuals to its banner.

The resulting discourse about community is an exciting area in current intellectual life, and much of the discussion is of great importance and worth.[60] There are also, however, some definite problems. Currently the ideal of community sometimes serves more as a stick with which to beat contemporary society for assorted failings than as a topic receiving the serious attention it merits. Moreover, proposals for community are sometimes really journeys of nostalgia, focusing on particular past eras or communities, though skeptics contest that such times or realms do not come very close to present-day images of them.[61] Both attitudes direct us away from serious study of community for our time.

Other difficulties also exist. Procommunity writers can assume such values as equality rather than exploring their practical dimensions; awkward questions about authority, obligation, and duty in community can garner scant attention; and some thinkers avoid the less-than-pretty historical experiences some "communities" in human history might teach.[62] On the other hand, Protestant environmentalism can also find in today's intellectual discussions of community some models for exploration of its ideal—for example, the models contained in such master works as Michael Walzer's *Spheres of Justice* or Glenn Tinder's *Community.*

Last, it is important to return again to questions about the nature that is so preeminent in this Protestant thought; for green Protestantism often understands community as a human replication of the basic holistic patterns of nature. However, answers are not at all obvious to key questions— in what sense nature is holistic, for one, and perhaps even more crucial, whether at some basic level living forms are harmonious. For example, some people within the scientific community see a good deal more competition and instability in nature than community enthusiasts might like.[63] And there remains the fundamental postmodern question: whether nature (and all its debatable features) is anything but a social construction in the first place.[64]

The Human Species and Divine Hope

Green Protestant objectives concentrate on community, justice, and a sustainable economy. They flow from perceptions of God's will and from analyses of what the human being created in God's image is like. Of course, the importance of views of human nature or behavior for political thought represents an old story in human history. Their significance in Protestant environmentalism is merely one more chapter.

For some time now, even sympathetic critics such as John Passmore have noted what they term "the anti-human bias of so many ecologists."[65]

Others have complained about what they interpret as environmentalists' affection for all species except the human being, who can be dismissed as "something unnatural, a hateful mutant, spewed out and rejected by the natural order, a cancer besmirching Spaceship Earth's green and pleasant land."[66] Thomas Derr sums up this widespread impression by regretting that some environmentalists travel "the dangerous misanthropic route."[67]

In fact, a great deal of criticism of the human species stems from Protestant theologians and activists worried about the fate of the earth. Some of this criticism is harsh and seems somewhat curious coming from those who are often so laudatory about God's other creations. These green Protestants have made many statements that lament people's "conceit and arrogance," identify humanity's "basic disease" as a fundamentally "exploitative attitude," and hold that "the human species is like a cancer let loose upon the biosphere."[68]

Some conclude that the human being "has used his dominance over nature with arrogance and contempt for everything but himself. Nature has been an enemy to be conquered and enslaved."[69] Others state after a bleak analysis of our history that "there is reason to doubt that the human species has the requisite capacity to change."[70] One author declares that it "is an appalling thought to conceive a future made up of such men,"[71] and another defines his mission as "liberating the earth from humanity's bondage and oppressive exploitation."[72]

There are also those, especially within evangelicalism, who express their disappointment about humankind in the traditional vocabulary of Christianity, invoking the language of sin. William Dyrness remarks that although the Sierra Club may not be comfortable putting it this way, human damage to the ecosphere has its roots in human sin—that is, in human disobedience of God.[73] Loren Wilkinson is equally straightforward in acknowledging the powers of sin. For him, to say that humanity is responsible for the destruction of the environment means to acknowledge that people are sinners. They have cut themselves off from God and God's handiwork by their "human choices."

This negativity about mankind, which fairly bursts forth from much of the Protestant environmental literature, involves something of a paradox. Exactly how do such judgments fit with an agenda that often is quite radical in its embrace of community, equality, and harmony? Such an agenda takes for granted a tremendous human capacity to live together in ways that, arguably, are not particularly characteristic of the human experience to this point. It also raises again the specter of elitism: are these negative judgments really anything more than an elitist minority's expression of its dislike for ordinary people and the ways they have chosen to live?

These questions are relevant, but so is the broad range of assessments of the human species. For example, even as they insist that people are fallen, evangelicals also affirm that people are God's creations, with great capacity for change. The Incarnation of Jesus represents the potential for humanity to reconnect with God, and therefore with God's creation, through stewardship. Hope is therefore possible.[74]

This theme of hope breaks through in many places and pushes back the gloom that inhabits Protestant environmentalism. Hopeful green Protestants argue that much must be done, that much can be done, and that people have the ability to change, no matter how wrenching and painful change may be. As Richard Baer Jr. phrases it, if Christians believe in the "power" of the Gospel, they can be transformed.[75] As John Cobb Jr. writes, Christians believe in the power of God and God's grace, and "we can place no limits on the extent to which grace can make us into new men and new women."[76]

Such confidence is real and should not be dismissed. Many Protestant environmentalists believe that God can change people and that in turn these people can change the world. But they give other grounds for confidence as well. Some Protestants hold that people are a good deal better than their critics would have us believe. Joyce Blackburn, for example, discourages pessimism about people. She sees them as well-intentioned and capable creatures, equipped to make the revolution required to revive and then preserve God's creation. Roger Shinn praises the worth of human beings and counts them the most "valuable" of all elements of life. While humans have hurt the natural world, Shinn argues that they also have the capacity to redeem themselves for their damage to the environment.[77]

Determining what to do is a perplexing and problematic enterprise for any movement. This has been true for the highly diffuse world of Protestant environmentalism, which has wanted to make a difference in policy terms in this world. Its disputes over the meaning of the Bible and the Christian tradition and the value of alternative theologies are important. But green Protestantism has also made a great effort to reach beyond these disputes to affect the world.

In that aspiration, one is reminded again of the Protestant involvement in the civil rights movement of the 1960s, something of a successful day in Protestant endeavors to change the world. There black and white Protestants (and, at least for a time, not just elites) sought to pursue a somewhat familiar agenda. African Americans were the focus of attention, but the goals were, once again, equal justice and community. They were not fully achieved, but for a brief but significant time there was a real effort to translate them into specific policies by determined strategies.[78]

Of course green Protestants face difficulties in their effort to formulate basic goals, just as they did in the civil rights crusade. Environmental Protestantism sometimes involves too many unranked normative objectives, too little defense of the chosen goals, a confusion between exhortation and rigorous argument and analysis, lack of clarity about assumptions, and too little empirical data in support of too many ideas. But problems in themselves are never the issue; they are inevitable. The issue is how one responds to them.

And these problems, or challenges, should not obscure the main development that has taken place: a serious attempt to formulate basic goals in Protestant environmental thought—toward a new consciousness, a sustainable society of limits, community, and eco-justice. It is true that the larger environmentalist movement frequently proposes a quite similar normative agenda for a green society. Pleas for change and arguments for community and eco-justice are everywhere. One cannot escape the conclusion that green Protestantism's agenda sometimes looks like a copy of secular environmentalism's.

But although this larger world has no doubt had great influence on green Protestantism, the normative goals of Protestant environmentalism have their own integrity. They are set in distinct Christian perspectives, justified by the Bible and Christian theology, intertwined with images of Christ and creation, of the Bible and the Reformation, and of God's calling to stewardship, images that reflect Protestant worldviews. To put it another way, few specifically green Protestant or Christian normative objectives exist; and perhaps their absence helps to preserve the environmentalist movement's unity. But there is definitely a Christian context for green Protestantism, distinguishing it from the larger secular movement. The two movements are allies, but they are far from the same.

POLITICS AND THE MEANS TO CHANGE

How the church should act in the world is an age-old dilemma for Christians. Protestant environmentalists have faced this dilemma in developing an agenda for action. Part of the challenge has been in fashioning the strategies that will best accomplish their ecological agenda. But part engages a much broader matter, the setting in which modern Protestantism finds itself as it seeks to act in the world.

With every religion in every age, the moments of most common influence on a culture have come when a religion's voice was clear and strong and when it had enough authority in the culture that it could be heard and thus respected—or feared. Christianity in general does not hold such a place in the United States today, nor does Protestant Christianity in particular.

Today religion in the United States comes in an almost endless variety of forms, each in obvious and not-so-obvious competition with the others. This situation has, in truth, long characterized religion in the United States, where market competition describes much more of our culture than just some aspects of our economy. Protestantism is the perfect metaphor and expression of this competitive reality in its own competitive diversity and in its competition with other religions within the United States.[1]

As it grapples with the environment, moreover, Protestantism looks like just one more voice (or like several voices singing different keys at the same moment) among a great many. Even at its most cohesive—a rare condition—Protestant environmentalism is no more than one more perspective fighting to be heard in an incredibly complex political scene.

In addition, others have led the way in defining an agenda and a set of strategies for environmentalism. They include many of the scientists of modern ecology as well as eco-heroes of the past, such as John Muir or Aldo Leopold, who retain great influence today. Protestant environmentalism is no mere form of followership, swimming in the wake of secular environmentalism, but this image comes closest to the truth at the level of policy and strategy. This situation is not necessarily bad; the appraisal depends on whether or not what is shared with the larger movement makes sense in terms of policy and strategy.[2]

Protestant environmentalists have emphasized three main strategies: working through church and religion; government action; and politics, a choice permeated with ambivalence. This chapter will explore all three strategies as it considers the question of strategy and Protestant environmentalism. It will ask what various green Protestants mean by each of the three strategies, what their perceived strengths and limitations are, and how Christian environmentalists justify calling on them. Finally, the chapter will compare Protestant environmentalism with the Protestant experience in the civil rights movement to see what comparisons may be drawn and what lessons learned.

Strategies other than the three main ones might deserve as much attention. Attention to education is an example, since environmental education is an important goal among green Protestants. Some concentrate on education within the churches, while others stress work through the public schools. Many also praise events such as Earth Day for their educational potential. There is interest in more experiential approaches as well, such as the idea that exposure to the wonders of nature will prove to be the best education of all for the cause. However, education is best seen as one part of the enterprise of those who look both to religion and to government to transform people into stewards of creation.[3]

Overall, green Protestant strategic thinking can be radical in temper, but it is usually pragmatic, this-worldly, and uncertain about drastic change. Things need to be done, and major change must take place now, but Protestant environmentalists tend to have less interest in grand formulations, which are sometimes perceived as exercises in abstract theology or vacuous rumination. The watchword is Christian action, though the connections between the strategies of action and Christianity as a faith are not always clear.[4]

The Church as a Means of Change

Liberal Protestants and evangelical Protestants often join hands to identify the church as a crucial agent of change. Indeed, they take its importance for granted: "There is no question that the key to the environmental crisis is the power inherent in the churches. They have the potential to fire the conscience of their membership into renewed activity on behalf of the earth."[5]

Environmentally minded Protestants are religious, after all, and they believe that change must and can come through the church as an expression of their faith.[6] But whether churches will prove effective agents of environmental change in the long run is not so clear. Doubts arise immediately. How much can churches do to change themselves, much less the country or the world? What can they do, especially in light of the power of governments, business, labor, and politics? To what extent will they run into strong opposition because of the American ideology of the separation of church and state, religion and politics?

The emphasis is usually placed on churches, as distinguished from religion in general, with the understanding that religion is the essential backdrop to everything a church does. However, some Protestant environmentalists visualize religion itself as the key. For them, what humans face in the ecological crisis is a spiritual crisis above all else. People need a reinvigorated spiritual life, and this transformation will also be the best strategy for healing the environment. Spiritual rebirth will lead to new, caring attitudes toward creation—and a commitment to act on them.[7]

To grasp ecological Protestantism's frequent reliance on the church as a means to change, we must explore this choice in more detail. One argument is simply pragmatic. The claim is that churches can make a difference. Once mobilized, churches can make changes *and* can sustain the changes made, thus the "church may be the only institution that can save the earth from destruction."[8] What is less often present, though, is any systematic evidence for why one should repose such confidence in churches as agents of change. This "pragmatic" claim often looks like a claim of faith.

Other arguments focus more on the religious and less on the pragmatic. Through this lens, involvement by churches is a matter of Christian responsibility, regardless of its pragmatic value. The argument is that God expects the church to act to fulfill God's mandate for stewardship from Christians. More radically, God expects the church to be God's "community of hope," modeling God's values and thus transforming society.[9]

Some Protestant environmentalists discuss in great detail how they expect churches to assist in the remaking of God's sickly world. The favorite idea is that the church can serve to promote consciousness-raising— another reminder of Protestant ecologists' strong belief in ideas and what they can accomplish. Sometimes these people acknowledge that it will not be easy. Consciousness can be obdurate, and there is little evidence that most churches alter anyone's consciousness—a matter that, in any case, is hard to measure. Moreover, few deny that even if churches succeeded in transforming consciousness, other societal institutions would still stand in the way. Yet despite such potential problems, many green Protestants remain hopeful and insist that there is no point falling into what they consider the trap of pessimism.

Protestant environmentalism's reliance on ecological education by churches is another expression of the broader American faith that education is somehow much of the answer to our problems. No country spends more on education—public, business, and church education. Surely no country believes more firmly in education's moral power, despite its very mixed record. Such great faith in education does have its problems. It can keep one from confronting hard choices and painful realities in political life. Focusing on education is safely peaceful and pleasantly optimistic, but it does not always provide one with a realistic picture about what divides people from each other nor about how difficult serious change is to accomplish. It also may not encourage us to grapple with what else might be—or must be—done to promote change.[10]

Yet Christian environmentalists want to make a difference through religious education—even though many do understand that education alone cannot do the job. Innumerable denominational efforts have been made to educate the clergy and laity, especially among mainline and liberal Protestant bodies; often these efforts have been directed to pollution problems, conservation measures, environmentalist lifestyles, land stewardship, and population questions. Ten years ago, energy issues were central. Today, toxic waste concerns are a major entry on the long list.

Educational endeavors also exist outside the conventional denominations. The Au Sable Institute in Mancelona, Michigan, is the premier example. Its efforts to educate Christian students and adults to an environmental consciousness have garnered a good deal of publicity. Significant attention is also paid to college student conferences, and especially to Christian colleges, as important centers for consciousness formation. Fields like environmental science and ecology are increasingly present in these colleges and have been complemented by environmental teach-ins, ecology fairs, and celebrations of Earth Day. Once noteworthy because of their novelty, they are now well established.[11]

All this activity supplements education in what everyone grants is the most crucial arena, the local church. It is here that activists hope to make the greatest impact, fashion a proper eco-consciousness, and spread the gospel of an environmentally aware lifestyle. Recommendations on how to remake each local church into a "Creation Awareness Center" are numerous. Sunday school classes must deal with the environment; so must sermons; Bible study and discussion groups should focus on the environment; attention should be given to projects such as cleaning the church grounds or planting trees, projects that teach people to act to improve their environment; churches should sponsor ecology symposia that feature workshops like "Dances of Universal Peace," "Energy: Friend or Foe," and "War Toys."[12] Indeed, the most zealous green Protestants can find no end of ideas, as illustrated in such detailed publications as "Fifty-Two Weeks of Congregational Activities to Save the Earth."[13]

The Hymn Society of America, among other groups, has called for more music of godly environmentalism. In the same spirit, environmental prayers have come into vogue.[14] This prayer, for example, provides a fair illustration: "O God, who in thine infinite love has entrusted to us both the knowledge of thy truth and the care of the earth: Teach us to value the glory of thy orderly creation, that we waste not nor despoil the physical riches which thou hast placed in our hands, nor use them only for our own selfish ends; through thy Son, Jesus Christ, our Lord, who liveth and reigneth with thee and the Holy Ghost, one God, world without end. Amen."[15]

There has also been considerable interest in liturgies devoted to raising environmental consciousness, liturgies that acknowledge the sacredness of life in all its varieties. A mass held at the Cathedral of St. John the Divine in New York City celebrates animals and incorporates a number of them into the liturgy. Similar services have taken place at the liberal Protestant Riverside Church in New York City and have now spread to other Protestant churches.[16]

Of course, some Protestant environmentalists push harder and want more than parades of animals through churches. They insist on change in actual church institutions as well as in fundamental conceptions of the faith. Richard Baer Jr. contends, for instance, that the Christian church must change until it systematically honors God's creation in every aspect of its doctrines and practices. James Parks Morton agrees and, employing Paul's metaphor from First Corinthians, argues that the church as the body of Christ must concretely reflect the full (body of) creation. Ian Barbour speaks of the compelling duty of all churches to love and embrace the fullness of God's creation. This rhetoric has now become standard.[17]

Such critics repeatedly argue that the church must move beyond talk and give witness *in its own practice* to the changes it urges on others. Here is the point where the familiar environmentalist goal of "acting locally" enters Protestantism, sometimes dressed up in such theological jargon as "ecclesial praxis."[18] This mission involves an endless array of suggestions about what individual churches should do, overflowing from time to time in Protestant periodicals. Suggestions have included combining services on cold Sundays, carpooling and biking to church, recycling church materials, and using solar heat in churches.[19]

Such advice can seem trivial, but those who affirm the church as a significant agent for change contend that such programs can make a difference. They insist that small changes add up and that each act helps transform people's consciousness. Moreover, they expect that consciousness changed at the local church level will assist in generating the resources for change at the state and national levels. Others expect results from awakened Protestants who get involved in protest politics or other types of politics. There is always a common appreciation that transformed local churches and church people can make a difference in the mobilization needed for broader political effectiveness and ecological transformation. After all, green Protestants maintain, a more sustainable or a more just society will not happen otherwise.[20]

Yet there are reasons to doubt these expectations. Such beliefs assume that churches have (or can have) much impact on their members' consciousness; they assume that Protestant churches can really mobilize on environmental issues *and* form a united front on what to do about them; above all, they assume that Protestantism at the end of this century in the United States still has a powerful enough vision to transform the culture in a serious way. Each assumption is debatable today, and each requires the kind of supporting argument that is only rarely offered.

Moreover, the place of politics in this effort is far from self-evident. Concentrating on the church and altered consciousness as principal change agents may lead to an avoidance of politics. Change focused on churches and transformed souls and lifestyles among the faithful can become a self-contained and purist exercise rather than a political strategy. It can be a substitute for the pushing and shoving, compromising and trading, conflict and consensus that make up ordinary politics and that in the end will be necessary for a society to meet the threats God's creation faces.

In this context, it is valuable to compare the Protestant participation in 1960s crusade for civil rights with the environmental effort. Like the green movement, the Protestant involvement in the civil rights movement of the 1960s was activated by concerned Protestant elites; it was "an elitist effort initiated largely by ministers and church bureaucrats."[21] The National Council of Churches led the way in the early and middle 1960s by assiduously encouraging denominations and local churches to take action and to support national actions. Generally the dominant theology was the "servant church" or stewardship model, which, as we have seen, is also important in Protestant environmentalism.

Also crucial, however, was the local church support stimulated in part by both white and African American church leaders from the National Council of Churches, the Southern Christian Leadership Conference, and more informal groups. In fact, local support was crucial for the entire Protestant civil rights movement; this is perhaps the main lesson of the Protestant civil rights effort. Support among black Protestants grew over time, but by the late 1960s white Protestant support declined at the local level as the movement became more militant.

This decrease in support was symbolized by the sharply negative reaction among many white churches to the famous Black Manifesto, which demanded that white denominations produce $500 million dollars in recompense for past white injustices to blacks. The result was a noticeable decline in local support for national Protestant efforts, measured in quite concrete ways, including financial assistance. The Protestant crusade for civil rights never recovered, and the cause moved on in other directions, drawing on others' energies.

To this point, the environmentalist cause has not generated the same kind of focused attention from Protestant elites, though it is gaining strength. Clearly, this kind of leadership will be essential if the cause is to grow stronger. It may be, however, that there is already more local enthusiasm within the Protestant church world for this cause than there was among many Protestant laity for the civil rights cause in the early 1960s. Moreover, the example of the civil rights crusade has to some extent paved the way in legitimizing a more activist church, a legacy from which the green Protestant movement will surely build.

Government Action

Protestant environmentalists rank government action as another favorite strategy for change. Indeed, undisguised affection for government action is routine in green Protestant thinking. This preference has also been shared by the larger movement since the 1960s. It is, of course, one obvious explanation for the major expansion of government influence in the environment.[22] This preference is reflected, for example, in biological science textbooks. They "unvaryingly advocate a single political outlook. The values of liberal statist environmentalism are privileged over all others."[23]

Green Protestants' rationale for using government action speaks the language of American pragmatism. Their argument is that while the church and an inspired laity can do a great deal, they both have their limits. Laws will be needed, sometimes for technical and economic reasons (e.g., how else to direct and regulate water quality) and sometimes because only government has the authority or power to enforce real change. Typically, Christian environmentalists suggest that government is the best single means to build a sustainable society, or to control technology, or to educate people in ecological consciousness, or to discipline strip mining, or to institute long-term planning, or to redesign tax laws to benefit the environment.[24]

The list of proposed roles for the state is invariably lengthy, and the particular uses for government tend to receive far more discussion than do the occasional theological justifications for calling on the state. Such justifications stress that God expects people to act to preserve creation: there is "ample warrant in the Bible and so in Christianity for seizing conscious, intelligent control of our environment and thus of our destiny."[25] This judgment usually translates as a defense of government action. The issue is usually not on lauding government in principle but on getting things done. Government is strongly preferred as a key means of change because many Protestant Greens are convinced that it can accomplish what they want, not because they somehow love it.

The regular recourse to government is by far the most startling thing about strategic thinking among Protestant environmentalists. Robert Heilbroner, William Ophuls, Paul Ehrlich, Garrett Hardin, and a few other well-known environmental thinkers outside the Christian tradition grapple more with the dilemmas of state action as a means to ecological change than do almost all Protestant ecological writers put together. Perhaps as a consequence, it is rare to encounter any green Protestant who has significant doubts about government as a central and effective mechanism for change.[26]

The issue is not necessarily whether the government can be of great help. It may make sense to employ government institutions from all kinds of perspectives—pragmatic outlooks, secular liberal outlooks, views focused on the need for urgency, or whatever. Perhaps this case can frequently be made; and it always deserves a hearing. However, the scarcity of arguments for the often uncritical embrace of the state by Protestant environmentalism is problematic.

Granted, not everyone is enthusiastic. Some regard the statist direction of environmentalism with dismay. They visualize giant bureaucracies stifling life in the name of the environment, and they question the theological case for this strategic choice. Also, as Anna Bramwell points out, this direction runs toward "the ecologists' paradox: that living in a 'Natural Way' is seen as better . . . while the way to this new life is to be planned for us" by governments employing "scientific or pseudo-scientific" outlooks.[27]

Advocates of governmental action must also face the challenge that comes from politically conservative Protestantism, which often originates in the precincts of evangelical and fundamentalist Protestantism. From that perspective, government is a growing Leviathan, threatening human liberty under God. At its best, this analysis concedes that the choices are hard and that the market has problematic colorations that cannot be lightly air-brushed away. At its worst, it baldly generalizes that government always threatens human liberty and that no further discussion is necessary. But no one needs to be a conservative to ponder the bureaucracy, unintended consequences, waste, petty tyranny, and confusion that government often spawns. And green Protestantism could benefit from more contact with the debates over the strengths and weaknesses of the state that exist in modern social science literature.[28]

Serious matters are at stake here. How can Protestantism embrace the secular state warmly without raising the hard Pauline question about secular powers and principalities corrupting the human spirit? Moreover, it is reasonable to ask what specific grounds the Bible or Protestant theology offer for a partnership between Protestant environmentalism and government. While some of the larger, secular movement demands that the state "save" nature, green Protestantism cannot and does not proceed with the same analysis, because it holds that no earthly institution ultimately can save anything important, that salvation is God's province. But green Protestantism is nonetheless deeply invested in government. Questions about why this is so, what the case for it is, and what the limits of government action might be require much more attention.

The Protestant tradition of the social gospel, now strongly embedded within mainline Protestantism, has long involved a sympathy for government as a means of change. At the elite and bureaucratic level of mainline denominations, this tradition received a major stimulus during the 1960s civil rights struggle. The lesson learned in these experiences was that government action is essential for the creation of equal civil and political rights.[29] But the use of government power has not been as effective in fighting poverty or running successful school systems. Perhaps government is only a sometime ally, but such a view finds very little echo in the green Protestant literature.

Politics

Recourse to politics is a final but crucial dimension in the eco-Protestant strategic calculus for change. Within Protestant ecological circles there is considerable consensus on government and the church as necessary ingredients for change, but politics is quite another matter. It has its supporters—especially in theory—but many fewer genuine enthusiasts. The list of its virtues is usually short among green Protestants.

Politics should not be conflated with government. I take politics to be, in Harold Lasswell's formulation, about who gets what, when, where, and how. It is the contest among assorted groups and perspectives for position, influence, and gain; it involves agreement and disagreement in the public realm. Government, on the other hand, involves the application of state power.

To be sure, there is nothing peculiar about the considerable distaste for politics among many environmentally minded Protestants. Affection for politics is uncommon in the American political tradition, where politics has never occupied an exalted—or even a respected—status. Our history is one of suspicion and resistance to politics and politicians, and our current popular and intellectual culture is continuing that custom.

The Protestant tradition in America has rarely had an opposing judgment. This too is no surprise. Few religious traditions are comfortable with politics, regardless of whether they serve as zealous apologists of the status quo. Politics and truth, politics and purity, and politics and salvation are at best ill-sorted bedfellows. Moreover, in the American context Protestantism has long committed itself (in theory) to the separation of church and state, which often has meant the separation of religion and politics.

Some observers today complain that the entire environmental movement has little sympathy for or understanding of politics, despite its proclaimed endorsement of political involvement as a key strategy for change. Robert C. Paehlke argues that although the environmental movement is more heavily engaged with politics now than in the 1970s or 1980s, abundant signs of distaste for politics remain. He notes, moreover, that much of environmental politics is single-issue "politics"—such as saving the wetlands or the whales—and overflows with negativism toward ordinary politics and political processes. Thus, a good deal of the current "acceptance" of politics within environmentalism might be said to better illustrate the movement's hostility toward politics.[30]

Critics make several main points. One is that environmentalists are often just plain impatient with politics. Some are so obsessed with what they perceive as the approaching collapse of the ecosystem that interest in politics—and its follies—is necessarily problematic. The question they pose is, Do we have time for politics, or at least for politics in its conventional forms?

Other critics suspect that in their hearts many environmentalists would prefer a world ruled by their Truth accompanied by a kind of purity (or piety), a picture that just does not leave room for politics. Bob Pepperman Taylor contends that this wish is a tendency in green thought: environmentalists often want to leap toward a perfect universe, but such a disposition is hardly compatible with real-world politics.[31] Others agree, remarking that such an inclination provides little nourishment for politics' slow processes, uncertain results, and compromises. Political actualities can taint what for some Protestant environmentalists is something of a holy crusade for God's creation.[32]

In an explicitly religious argument, Thomas Derr has criticized environmentalists who are reluctant to deal with the real world. After all, he argues, it is the world God has given us, a world that includes abundant tensions and contradictions. In that spirit, Derr insists that people should accept the reality of mundane politics. It is part of God's world and can have its uses, which include avoiding the illusion of quick, escapist "solutions" to the challenges before us.[33]

From a historical viewpoint, critics note that distaste for politics is an old story among environmentalists. In fact, it is a well-established tradition, and its presence today should be understood in this context. Henry David Thoreau and John Muir are two classic cases in point. They celebrated nature and distinguished it often and favorably from society and politics.[34]

In a similar vein, Bob Pepperman Taylor identifies what he calls the "pastoral tradition" of environmentalism, a stream in which Thoreau and Muir are important and which he believes has opted for indulging in mystery, wonder, and aesthetics while turning its back on politics. This is part of what he means when he argues that the "story of American environmental theory in the twentieth century is primarily the story of an increasingly obscured political vision." In Taylor's view, too many environmentalists have abandoned politics for aesthetics.[35]

A similar aestheticism is present in some corners of Protestant environmentalism. Recall that many Protestant environmentalists today are swept up in celebrating the glories and beauty of nature and that some have gone on to controversial creation-centered theologies. As concentration on the beauties of nature takes over, this orientation can relegate politics to a rather remote background, though there is no necessary trade-off between the two.

Other critics charge that the green cause resists the give and take of politics because it is the home of many who (consciously or not) are hostile to democratic decision-making. This oft-heard criticism holds that some environmentalists prefer rule by elites—by fellow believers or ecological experts or both. To be sure, one seldom finds such a stance openly defended in the "democratic" United States. But critics believe it is evident in environmentalist contempt for the mass of people, that "great unwashed of humanity" so frequently convicted of wrecking the ecosystem.[36]

This attitude is often combined with great respect for science and scientific experts. Frederick H. Buttel has underlined how much of modern environmentalism is wedded to the authority of science, despite its torrent of complaints about science and scientism. Some critics hold that in practice, this union encourages elitist faith in science and scientists over politics and as an escape from politics.[37] Others maintain that it encourages the legitimacy of coercion.[38]

Yet as we know, green Protestantism also contains plenty of ambivalence about science, which is why science gets no attention as a serious means of change for the good. Science and scientists may emerge sometimes as more trustworthy than politics and politicians, but they are not fully trusted either and are never trusted in Protestant environmental literature when the alternative is religious truth and wisdom. Nor is science or scientific expertise honored in comparison with nature itself, an entity in which green Protestants place almost unlimited trust.

This is especially true within the holistic model of nature that environmentalists commonly see. In this setting, there really is little room for the give and take of ethical argument or political disagreements. In this world, matters are sometimes rather self-evident and the margin for differing individual perspectives uncomfortably narrows.[39]

The Case for Politics

Although many green Protestants are antagonistic toward politics, the story does not end there. If politics is defined as human action in the public sphere, many green Protestants defend the worth of politics. Christian environmentalist leaders issue many specific injunctions to stay informed, to vote, and, of course, to act for various policy proposals designed to help save the earth. This sort of thing is common in the writings of environmentally minded Protestants and hardly suggests hostility to politics.[40]

Beyond these general endorsements of standard political involvements, a fair number of green Protestants propose political strategies of the most practical and down-to-earth sort. They may put their efforts in lobbying, organizing citizen action networks (interest groups), forming political coalitions, or encouraging other kinds of political citizenship. They do not necessarily proceed from any elaborate theory about politics or from a spirit that is much in love with politics; nonetheless, their support for such political strategies reflects a modest acceptance of ordinary politics. And in some instances the acceptance is more unqualified.[41]

In this context, Vernon Visick's discussion of Jesus as a political model is unusual and interesting. It is unusual in part because it is too rare for green Protestants who respect politics to connect it to Christianity, and even more rarely do they link politics to the life of Jesus Christ. Visick describes a Jesus who is open, flexible, ready for new ideas and new paths to realize Christian goals—a voice far from fixed in his politics or his ideas regarding public institutions or policies. To be sure, Visick's Jesus is no ordinary politician, but he is also no practitioner of the rigidities of either holy politics or conservative status-quo politics.[42]

David Morgan is another exception and one even more committed to ordinary politics for his religious-based goals. He has pressed the case for "constitutional democracy," which he contends requires "a messy public sphere characterized by diplomacy, negotiation, and compromise," where there will continually be "communities balancing self-interest with public good." He concludes that "messy as it is," such a reality "remains our last best hope" to make the policy changes so badly needed by our ecosystem.[43]

But a perspective such as Morgan's is unusual. Those who accept politics as part of the world that must be lived with, if hardly adored, are more usual. Such Protestant environmentalist "realists" regularly affirm the value of a "responsible" politics that undertakes change, even dramatic change, but within the limited contours of what they contend is the possible. They argue that historical circumstances and personal capacities form boundaries that necessarily circumscribe what human politics can accomplish for the environment or for anything else. And they maintain that recognition of these limits will in the long run lead to more successful changes than any other strategy.

Some who share this outlook on politics are admirers of the twentieth-century Protestant "realist" Reinhold Niebuhr, who emphasized the importance of working in politics and government, acknowledging the power of human sin and the restrictions of human structures. James Wall, longtime editor of the liberal Protestant *Christian Century*, has often argued in the Niebuhrian idiom for a politics with "a sense of responsibility and an uneasy conscience." Others specifically identify Niebuhr as the model for environmental politics. To them, Niebuhr provides a guide for understanding the complex relations between people and nature, for spurning utopianism, and for gaining a determination to take what practical action is possible to heal the earth.[44]

Another form of "realistic" politics is intensely idealistic in its goals but operates with a formidable tough-mindedness. This version of Protestant environmental politics is about "righteous power," the determined and driven injection of what is "right" into the political system and, through it, the country. Here power is not evil or even problematic as long as it is "righteous."[45] At their best, some who seek "holy" change acknowledge, along with Paul Santmire, that it must be "complemented and fulfilled by" what he calls "the politics of reconciliation."[46]

Thus Protestant environmentalism has several different sides, attracted to politics of several sorts for accomplishing ecological goals. What is unclear even among politics' usual proponents, however, is what happens if public discourse fails, if people do not listen to the environmentalists or do not rally to the agenda. What if politics produces the wrong actions—or no action at all? What might then happen to the status of politics within Protestant environmentalism? How deep does commitment to politics—as opposed to temporary acceptance—go in Protestant environmentalism?

In both approaches to politics in ecological Protestantism—both the hostile and the sympathetic strains—there is a need for rigorous thought. Green Protestants need to address what politics is and should be, what values it implies, what it can and cannot accomplish, and where commitment to it does and should end. If these questions are not faced now, they will have to be faced later under what may be much less favorable circumstances. To explore such matters more systematically will be neither easy nor comfortable. After all, a long and understandable uneasiness has existed between Protestantism and the political process. Problems of compromise are real for any movement, and doubly so for green Protestantism.

But this issue has another dimension here as well. It is not clear exactly what an ecological Protestantism can bring to the larger political arena that is special or promises to make a particularly valuable contribution. Part of any judgment on this question turns around how derivative Protestant environmentalism is; part turns around whether it has any specially great capacity in or for ordinary politics. Nor have we seen any sign that green Protestantism is ready for a radical politics of confrontation and conflict, heroism, or even martyrdom. So the future of politics and ecological Protestantism remains uncertain.[47]

Once more, it may be useful to compare other Protestant experiences with politics in modern times. The civil rights crusade of the 1960s showed that some Protestant activists had something to learn about the rough and tumble of politics and were quite willing to advance a kind of uncompromising "holy" politics through civil disobedience. Yet the movement did learn a good deal about politics. Over time it employed politics well—for example, the politics of effective lobbying and skilled use of a sympathetic media. The record, overall, was mixed. At least while congregations were providing considerable mass support, the combination of "holy" and practical politics was effective. When mass sympathy declined as the 1960s faded, more radical voices came to the fore, and no form of politics seemed to work.[48]

On the other hand, the effort of the National Council of Churches and some leaders of mainline Protestant denominations to block the Persian Gulf War in 1990–91 largely spurned conventional political terms. If this endeavor represented any politics, it was the politics of witness. In this case, in the concrete terms of political effectiveness, the effort failed. Of course, this was a very different situation, one in which the effort had scant lay support; perhaps the circumstances called for an equally different strategy.[49]

Protestant environmentalists often wrestle with the directions and dilemmas of strategy. The challenges posed are real, and valuable and successful steps in the process of strategic thinking have been made over the past two decades in the considerations on church and religion, government and politics as strategies of change.

Yet some continuing problems suggest the need for more reflection on Protestant strategies to make a difference in the crusade to help God's earth. Much of green Protestant strategy is derivative. This is most obvious in its sometimes uncritical affection for government, but it is also on display in ecological Protestantism's ambivalence regarding politics. Both of these sentiments reflect attitudes in the larger environmental movement, and it is not clear how much thought has been given to their implications.

It is also problematic that little empirical or practical information accompanies many of the green Protestant strategic discussions. Evidence about the practical effects of a choice invariably proves relevant. No one can confidently predict the results of one strategic choice or another, but there are other, often comparable experiences to draw on, such as the Protestant civil rights efforts in the 1960s. Finally, there are too few connections between strategies selected and their putative foundations in Christianity. There are too few Vern Visicks addressing these connections directly. Here more than anywhere else, one looks to environmentally minded Protestants to make a contribution toward strategic thinking in terms different from those of the secular mainstream.

No matter what, however, green Protestants have some understanding that strategies for environmental change are not entirely up to humanity. Strategies matter, and one kind of politics or another may help to save the earth; moreover, people are called to act swiftly in this cause as God's servants. But the earth and all that is on it is finally God's and in the end depends on God's grace.[50]

❦ CONCLUSION ❦

The story of Protestant environmentalism over the past several decades in the United States is a remarkable one. I have argued in this study that it is the story of a major shift toward environmental concern within Protestantism, especially within Protestant thought. In fact, from grand theology to everyday churches, the cause of saving God's creation increasingly shows up on the Protestant agenda. The future direction of Protestant environmentalism in both theology and politics, of course, remains open, and the struggle over that future will represent a process as intriguing as it is important. Perhaps the journey this book describes will one day be no more than the first chapter in a much longer and inspiring account of green Protestantism as it entered the twenty-first century.

My argument has been that at all levels of Protestantism there is now a considerable consensus on the necessity of action by Christian people to address the environment. At the same time, we have seen that this consensus has its limits, especially among some fundamentalist Protestants, and that disagreements frequently occur over how to conceptualize and act on a Christian ecological agenda. As it faces the environment, Protestantism has proven once again that it deserves its reputation as a study in both unity and diversity.

While some are disappointed that Protestantism is not more united on environmental concerns, the degree of unity that exists is actually impressive given Protestantism's divergent doctrinal, organizational, and political tendencies—as well as similar tendencies in American culture as a whole. Moreover, division within Protestantism on this matter may not be entirely a bad thing. It is a testament to the continuing reality of Protestantism as a place for religious dissenters and a source of vitality, or at least controversy, that in its way energizes people. In any case, divisions are not likely to disappear soon.

Struggle has been a dominant motif in Protestant environmental thought from 1970 into the 1990s. One struggle, of course, has been over the Bible—how to understand its ecological teachings and how to assess their importance for Protestantism's response to environmental concerns. We have seen that there is abundant disagreement on these questions—

and these disputes will continue in the future. The same applies to issues over how to understand the Christian environmental record during the past two thousand years—and what to make of its significance for today.

The search within Protestantism for a satisfactory theological framework for a Protestant or Christian environmentalism has been equally challenging. This search has led in many directions, some of them cautious, others bold. It has never been a simple task to reinterpret—or reconstruct—Christianity in any new age or in the face of any great contemporary problem. Viewed intellectually or in terms of faith, discerning the face of God anew is always and everywhere a daunting intellectual and spiritual task.

At times, green Protestant struggles over varying interpretations, theologies, and readings of the Bible have led to exacerbated conflicts within Protestant thought. This problem has manifested itself in several ways, as this book notes, but it has been especially obvious in tensions between environmentalist Protestants and more religiously conservative Protestants. As acrimonious at times, and more troubling to many Protestant ecological thinkers, has been the green Protestant conflict with critics of Christianity from the larger environmental movement, critics who have received many an echo from within Protestant environmentalism. The main charges have come from those outside, who, as we have seen, often advance alternative worldviews. There are many competing visions about how to "save" the eco-system—and human beings as well.

Such conflicts and struggles toward clarity and direction constitute the heart of the story of Protestant environmentalism in recent decades, the story that this book addresses and analyzes. They sometimes cause considerable frustration to Protestants determined to base their actions to ease ecological crises on their religion. Nothing has turned out to be simple. The problems and challenges are numerous and daunting.

But it is not mere sentimentalism to suggest that in all the confusion, division, and struggles, we may also discern a process of creation. Since 1970 (or actually, as we know, beginning earlier), Protestant thinkers have been engaged in formulating a Protestant environmentalism. The process has ebbed and flowed in terms of interest and energy. It has not always been consensual and has rarely been smooth. Yet this book describes this birth process and salutes it as an important step forward.

Along the way, this study has considered the fledgling development of an ecological Protestantism in relation to the direction of the entire environmental movement. That movement has definitely permeated green Protestant thought, especially in liberal Protestantism, and increasingly in evangelicalism as well. But Protestantism has not been passive in the process. In this instance, to a considerable extent, Christ and culture have gone hand in hand.

Green Protestantism has maintained its own distinct integrity, and that integrity must be acknowledged. It has emerged as an outlook (a set of outlooks) inseparable from religious beliefs, categories, and languages, sometimes even conventional Christian ones. These elements remain the base of Christian environmentalism. Of course, there are those who appear to wear their Christianity lightly in their quest for environmental relevance, and others whose apparent mission is to reconceptualize Christianity as quickly as possible, mostly to speed an environmental agenda. The broader picture, however, is different. As this study indicates, one can find considerable evidence of a Protestant environmentalism that is deeply engaged with Christian theology, language, and history.

Everywhere in Protestant ecological thought one also finds broader religious concerns and understandings: the wrestling with what God is and requires, with the relationship between God and human beings, with the status of nature in terms of creation, with what stewardship means and whether this is the best way of understanding what God expects of humanity, and so much more. The major place accorded to the church and to religion as an instrument of change underlines the importance of religion in Protestant environmentalism as well.

Perhaps for this reason, the movement is at its best when it addresses the formulation of eco-theologies or confronts creation and stewardship in and out of the Bible. Here it is operating from a kind of home ground, and it proves to be often insightful in its reflections and sometimes tough and provocative in its analyses. While the directions within Protestant environmentalism are many, a definite strength is demonstrated in the faithfulness and creativity that characterize so much of the resultant Protestant environmental thought.

At the same time, green Protestant thought encounters problems in assisting God's creation, especially in the realm of political action. Perhaps the life and energy and promise that Protestant environmentalism's diversity reflects should also be read as a political liability. Sometimes Protestant environmentalism appears to be both everywhere and nowhere when it comes to propounding even a modestly unified theology, shared analysis of the Bible, or common attitude toward the broader, secular environmentalist coalition and its complaints. Much of green Protestantism's energy goes to addressing its divisions, a process that drains energy from a political focus.

Moreover, Protestant ecological thought faces the need to achieve more rigor in its philosophical outlook. This is regrettably true of its key concepts, logical analyses, limited empirical information, and general philosophical arguments. In these ways, Protestant environmental thought can do better. Often too much is taken for granted, perhaps under the assumption that ecological crisis trumps the importance of greater philosophical rigor or that "we are all agreed." But to address environmental crisis requires serious philosophical analysis and argument. So does the fact that we are not all agreed in Protestantism or anywhere else on any given ecological analysis or agenda. Some serious philosophical work and argument already exists, and perhaps even more will emerge soon.

I would also argue that green Protestantism should grapple more directly with some of the limitations of the thought that it shares with aspects of the larger intellectual culture of our time. For example, ecological Protestantism too often simultaneously attacks and worships science and its findings. It frequently does not recognize scientific theories that do not fit its holistic, steady-state model of the universe.

Moreover, green Protestantism, like much of American intellectual life, is routinely committed to a "community" model of the ethical life. But Protestant environmentalists have not sufficiently explored what this means and what the costs of such a choice might be. I respect the concern for community and I share it. But affirmation of community is not enough—in fact, it is hardly a start—and Protestant environmentalism can do much better. Getting one's framework and values straight—and working to defend them—is essential.

Finally, there is the matter of Protestant environmentalism and politics. This study has recounted the division and skepticism over politics as a means of change. While I maintain that this is an understandable situation, characteristic in our culture and in Protestantism as well, such attitudes are a costly and naive mistake. They betray a deep lack of realism about how the world—and thus change—actually happens. Moreover, if Protestant environmentalism is not to advocate a practical embrace of politics (an embrace out of convenience, not love), then it surely must perform a more intensive consideration of alternative means of change.

In addition, there definitely must be a much greater study of government and of what government has done and can do, and what it has failed to do and cannot do. Serious study of the realities of public administration, policy formulation, and the complexities of government as a change agent is rarely to be found in green Protestantism, and this is a major problem. This lack is evident in what can only be considered a sometimes uncritical and unaware enthusiasm for government action—an enthusiasm that is surprising from any religious perspective, not least from that of American Protestantism.

It is exactly at the point when ecological Protestantism turns to address societal goals and strategies to implement them that we can see some signs of a growing effort to think more rigorously. But the way is littered with much that is derivative and analytically soft. As an optimist, I employ a favorite concept of green Protestantism—the concept of process—and suggest that it is best to see the movement as in process in this area too. It is reaching out to fashion clearer, tighter, and more politically driven agendas and strategies—a development that should be strongly encouraged.

What may lie ahead in the greening of Protestantism is the emergence of new strains of Christian or Protestant political and social thought and a fresh engagement with the permanent quest to bring Christ into the culture. From this perspective, Protestant struggles with the social and political dimensions of Christian environmentalism represent a sign of Protestant life—and renewal. Someday they may become a cause for Protestant celebration.

Yet among Protestant environmentalists, as among others in the cause, pessimism looms. So much is terribly wrong. The dire consequences of the abuse of God's creation are now so great, and they promise to be much worse soon. Most judgments are grim, and they have to be.

Such a mood, nevertheless, does not always carry the day within green Protestantism. Nor is it obvious that it could be the final word for many Protestant Christians committed to environmentalism. Voices of hope do break through the gloom, even among those for whom the historical record offers little basis for optimism. Hope refuses to go away, even if its exponents rarely speak of it glibly and never want hope to encourage passivity.

The reason, of course, is that for much of Protestant environmentalism —unlike the larger ecological movement—hope has a basis in an eternal and loving God. Hope is a gift of God's grace, and the faith of much of the movement is faith that God will not fail creation. These days this affirmation of faith does not always sound loudly, much less confidently. Yet it is there, offering us another reminder that crucial differences exist between Protestant environmentalism and its secular companion as they confront their common enemy, the destruction of the earth.[1]

❧ NOTES ❧

INTRODUCTION

1. Robert Booth Fowler, *Unconventional Partners, Religion and Politics in the United States,* and *New Engagement.*

2. Train, "Religion and the Environment," 5.

3. Consider that excellent, major works act as if there is no religious environmental thought or action. A good illustration is Paehlke, *Environmentalism and the Future of Progressive Politics.* For Nash's discussion see *Rights of Nature,* chap. 4.

4. For a version of this interpretation, see Barbour, Foreword to *Cry of the Environment,* vii–viii.

5. For example, I used with profit Cooper's *Green Christianity,* which surveys environmentalist ideas and practice from all over the globe.

6. Neuhaus, *In Defense of People,* 180.

7. The best example of several that are used is Findlay's *Church People in the Struggle.*

8. Two classics are Merchant, *Death of Nature,* and Devall and Sessions, *Deep Ecology.*

9. This is the argument of John Meyer in his fascinating dissertation project, now under way at the University of Wisconsin–Madison.

10. Compare Regan, *Case for Animal Rights,* and Callicott, *In Defense of the Land Ethic.*

11. Bob Pepperman Taylor, *Our Limits Transgressed;* Roderick F. Nash, *Rights of Nature.*

12. Callicott, *In Defense of the Land Ethic;* Paul Taylor, *Respect for Nature;* Roderick F. Nash, *Rights of Nature,* epilogue; Foreman, *Confessions of an Eco-Warrior.*

13. Manes, *Green Rage;* Merchant, *Radical Ecology.*

14. Joe Bowersox first got me thinking about images of scientific reality in these literatures; I reflect on these images of science further in "Broader Settings" below.

15. Waldrop, *Complexity.*

16. Evelyn Fox Keller, *Secrets of Life, Secrets of Death;* Haraway, *Primate Visions.*

17. For example, see Herzog, *Without Foundations;* Rorty, *Contingency, Irony and Solidarity.*

18. MacIntyre, *After Virtue;* Sandel, *Liberalism and Its Critics.*

19. Sullivan, *Reconstructing Public Philosophy;* Lasch, *Haven in a Heartless World;* Bellah et al., *Habits of the Heart;* Wolfe, *Whose Keeper?*

20. Robert Booth Fowler, *Dance with Community.*

21. For example, see Moon, *Constructing Community.*

22. Dryzek, *Rational Ecology;* Elshtain, *Public Man, Private Woman;* Sale, *Human Scale;* Mansbridge, *Beyond Adversary Democracy.*

23. See Robert Booth Fowler, *Dance with Community*, chap. 7; MacIntyre, *After Virtue*; Bellah et al., *Habits of the Heart*; Pocock, *Machiavellian Moment*.

24. Barber, *Strong Democracy*; Bloom, *Closing of the American Mind*; Susan Griffin, *Woman and Nature*; Boyte and Riessman, *New Populism*.

25. For example, see Goldsmith, "Gaia," 64–74.

26. A fascinating study here is Phillips, *Looking Backward*.

27. Robert Booth Fowler, *Dance with Community*.

28. This political theme has been developed to some extent, regarding the larger, secular movement, by Bowersox, "The Moral and Spiritual Potential of Environmentalism," chaps. 6–7, and Bob Pepperman Taylor, *Our Limits Transgressed*, 134–35, 137.

CHAPTER ONE

1. Baer, "Higher Education, the Church, and Environmental Values," 485; Regenstein, *Replenish the Earth*, 131, 154; Cable, "Environmental Education at Christian Colleges," 165–68; Yaple, "Christian Church and Environmental Education," 139.

2. See Sittler, "Theology for Earth," 367–74; "Ecological Commitment as Theological Responsibility"; and *Ecology of Faith*. See also Hefner, *Sense of Grace*.

3. Joranson, "Faith-Man-Nature Group and a Religious Environmental Ethic," 175–79; Roderick F. Nash, *Rights of Nature*.

4. Of course, the NCC is not solely a Protestant organization, nor solely a liberal Protestant one, but this is its main strength and its main theological orientation.

5. Regenstein, *Replenish the Earth*, 155–56; Glenn C. Stone, *New Ethic for a New Earth*; Bruce C. Birch, "Energy Ethics Reaches the Church's Agenda," 1034–38. For example, see *The Egg: An Eco-Justice Quarterly*, vol. 11, Summer 1991; see also *Christian Social Action*, March 1989. Stapert and Murphy, "Earth Faces Crisis," 44.

6. The best single compendium of all kinds of denomination declarations is now in Ellingsen, *Cutting Edge*.

7. This note merely suggests some of the sources available. Writing to the denominations concerned will yield more helpful and up-to-date materials. Yaple, "Christian Church and Environmental Education," has many of the early resolutions and history. See also *The Egg: An Eco-Justice Quarterly*, vol. 11, Summer 1991; Editor, "UPUSA Deliberates in Rochester, N.Y.," 8, 10; Giles, "Restoring Creation," 25; Editor, "Social Principles Summary," 32–33; *Environmental Stewardship*; Editor, LCA Board of Social Ministry, "Ecology: We Must Act Now," 9–12; and Regenstein, *Replenish the Earth*, 137–45.

8. James A. Nash, *Loving Nature*; Hessel, *After Nature's Revolt*.

9. Some examples include Editor, "Social Issues That Call Christians to Respond," 32–33; Editor, "LCA Group Named to Study Human Crisis in Ecology," 34; Editor, "For Earth, Peace," 50; General Executive Board, "Environment Resources," 2:19; Achtemeier, "Understanding God's Relation to His Created World," 16–17; "New Video" announcements from Department of Environmental Justice and Survival, United Methodist Church, 1990; Bhagat, *Creation in Crisis*, 130.

10. Two views on this joint project are Lynch, "Two Worlds Join to 'Preserve the

Earth,'" 142–44, and "Religious Leaders Join Scientists in Ecological Concerns," 49; and "Are Evangelicals Warming to Earth Issues?," 63, 65.

11. Regenstein, *Replenish the Earth*, 160–63; McKindley-Ward, "Christian Ecologists Work toward Common Agenda," 11; Pat Stone, "Christian Ecology," 78–79; Stapert and Murphy, "Earth Faces Crisis," 44; Frame, "Planetary Justice," 74; Hope and Young, "Thomas Berry," 750–53.

12. These are strictly my conclusions, but the best book on the civil rights movement is Findlay, *Church People in the Struggle*.

13. Cooper, *Green Christianity*, 33.

14. McHarg, *Design with Nature*, 197; Roderick F. Nash, *Rights of Nature*, 91.

15. White, "Historic Roots of Our Ecologic Crisis," 1205.

16. For instance, see Shinn, "Eco-Justice Theories in Christian Ethics," 96–114; Hiers, "Ecology, Biblical Theology, and Methodology," 45; Cobb, "Theology and Space," 302.

17. For example, see Presbyterian Task Force on Eco-Justice, *Keeping and Healing the Creation*; Cobb, *Is It Too Late?*, chap. 1; Granberg-Michaelson, *A Worldly Spirituality*, chap. 1; Squiers, "Making of an Ethical Dilemma," 3–6; Wayne H. Davis, "Ecological Crisis"; "Ecology and the Church," 5–9; and *Christian Social Action*, March 1989.

18. Santmire, *Brother Earth*, 180; Joranson and Butigan, Introduction to *Cry of the Environment*, 3; Bhagat, *Creation in Crisis*, 9.

19. Austin, *Hope for the Land*, 195.

20. See the Presbyterian church discussion in Newsletter of the International Society for Environmental Ethics, vol. 1, Fall 1990, 23.

21. Moltmann, *Theology of Hope*.

22. See Carlson, "More than a Bad Smell," 15, for an early statement of what now is routine; for example, *Caring for God's Creation*.

23. For example, see Wall, "Getting Serious about the Environmental Threat," 371–72; Keehan, "The Energy Crisis and Its Meaning for American Culture," 756–59; Fagley, "Earth Day and After," 440–42; Fey, "Some Notes on 'Global 2000,'" 698–701.

24. Thomas Berry, *Dream of the Earth*, 116.

25. See, for example, a beautiful presentation of this sort in *Caring for God's Creation*.

26. See, for example, Bramwell, *Ecology in the Twentieth Century*, 227; Ray, *Trashing the Planet*, chap. 1; Dyrness, "Are We Our Planet's Keeper," 40–41; and for the announcement of the new direction, "It's Not Easy Being Green," 14.

27. For some discussion of the range of political ideas of evangelical and fundamentalist camps, see Skillen, *Scattered Voice*; Lepkowski and Lepkowski, "Opportunities and Obstacles in Relating Christian Salvation Belief to Ecological Renewal," 103.

28. Neuhaus, *In Defense of People*, 107, 70, 180, 259, 1–91; at this time Neuhaus was, of course, very much a Protestant.

29. There are numerous studies. For bibliographies for studies of 1980s and 1970s, see Milbrath, *Environmentalists*, and Watts and Wandesforde-Smith, "Postmaterial Values and Environmental Policy Change," 29–42. The most complete and current bibliography of studies and by far the most intelligent and searching discussion of public opinion studies may be found in Gundersen, *Finding the Kosmos in the Agora*.

Some other quite recent studies worth looking at are Eckersley, "Green Politics and the New Class," 205–23; Rohrschneider, "Citizens' Attitudes toward Environmental Issues," 347–67; Steger and Witt, "Gender Differences in Environmental Orientations," 627–49; and Dorceta E. Taylor, "Blacks and the Environment," 175–205. For this work Laura Olson did an original data analysis on Michigan National Election Survey data as discussed in text; this allowed me to have a comparative test of the many other studies.

30. Ornstein et al., *People, the Press, and Politics*, 30.

31. Gundersen, *Finding the Kosmos in the Agora*, vol. 2, chaps. 1 and 2.

32. Buttel and Finn, "Social Class and Mass Environmental Beliefs," 433–50; Steger, "Gender Differences"; Milbrath, *Environmentalists*, 76–78, 115; Dorceta E. Taylor, "Blacks and the Environment"; Mohai, "Public Concern and Elite Involvement in Environmental Conservation Issues," 820–38.

33. Hertzke, *Representing God in Washington*, 137–38; Gallup and Castelli, *People's Religion*, 214–15; Eckberg and Blocker, "Varieties of Religious Involvement and Environmental Concerns," 509–17; Hand and Van Liere, "Religion, Mastery-Over-Nature, and Environmental Concern," 555–70; Kanagy and Willits, "A 'Greening' of Religion?," 674–83; Shaiko, "Religion, Politics and Environmental Concern," 244–62.

34. Laura Olson did her data analysis for this study during the spring and summer of 1992. I am very grateful to her for her excellent and useful work.

35. See note 29 and, for activists, note 36 above.

36. Guth et al., "Faith and the Environment."

37. Ibid., 11.

38. Ibid.

39. See Kellstedt et al., "Theological Perspectives and Environmentalism among Religious Activists"; Kellstedt, "Letter to Respondents, June 1991."

40. See Guth et al., "Faith and the Environment," 4–6, for data on patterns of environmental thought among clergy.

CHAPTER TWO

1. For example, see David E. Engel, "Elements in a Theology of Environment"; McHarg, *Design with Nature*.

2. Glacken, *Traces on the Rhodian Shore*, 162–63; Passmore, *Man's Responsibility for Nature*, 9–10; Kay, "Concepts of Nature in the Hebrew Bible," 321–26.

3. Glacken, *Traces on the Rhodian Shore*, 161, 156.

4. Ibid., 165; Kay, "Concepts," 318.

5. Glacken, *Traces on the Rhodian Shore*, 157; Kaufman, "Problem for Theology," 337–66.

6. Kaufman, "Problem for Theology."

7. Hiers, "Ecology, Biblical Theology, and Methodology," 49, 48, 52–53; Kay, "Problem for Theology," 316; see also the non-U.S. scholar Robin Attfield, *Ethics of Environmental Concern*, 8, 16.

8. Hiers, "Ecology, Biblical Theology, and Methodology," 49–50; Kay, "Problem for Theology," 326; Regenstein, *Replenish the Earth*, 37.

9. Hiers, "Ecology, Biblical Theology, and Methodology"; George H. Williams, "Christian Attitudes toward Nature," 112.

10. Some examples include Roderick F. Nash, *Rights of Nature*, 90–91.

11. Wendell Berry, *Sex, Economy, Freedom and Community*.

12. A few illustrations include *Keeping and Healing the Creation*; Bonifazi, "Biblical Roots," 232; Austin, *Hope for the Land*; Editor, "Isaiah and Ecology," 15.

13. Some examples include Anderson, "Creation in the Bible"; Elder, *Crisis in Eden*, 84–86; Hendry, *Theology of Nature*, 172–73, 196; Barbour, *Technology*, 24–25; Abrecht, *Faith, Science, and the Future*, 42; Bratton, "Christian Ecotheology and the Old Testament," 64.

14. For instance, see Abrecht, *Faith, Science, and the Future*, 20; Austin, *Hope for the Land*, 58; Brockway, "Toward a Theology of the Sea," 16–23.

15. Glacken, "Man's Place in Nature," 167; Abrecht, *Faith, Science, and the Future*, 36; Derr, *Ecology and Human Need*, 17.

16. See, for example, these treatments: Austin, *Hope for the Land*, 103, 18–19; Derr, *Ecology and Human Need*, chap. 6; Brueggemann, "Earth Is the Lord's," 28–32.

17. For example, see Brockway, "Natural World," 23–4; Austin, *Hope for the Land*, chap. 19.

18. Derr, *Ecology and Human Need*, 21–25; Abrecht, *Faith, Science, and the Future*, 34, 40; Daniel Day Williams, "Philosophical and Theological Concepts of Nature," 15; Austin, *Beauty of the Lord*, 130; Brockway, "Toward a Theology of the Natural World," 25; Fracke, "Ecology and Theology," 121; Shinn, "Science and Ethical Decision," 149; Bratton, "Christian Ecotheology," 67–69; Hessel, "Preaching for Creation's Sake," 119; Hendry, *Theology of Nature*, 181; Bonifazi, "Biblical Roots," 206.

19. Brockway, "New Fad," 2; Bonifazi, "Biblical Roots," 207; Derr, *Ecology and Human Need*, 16.

20. Daniel Day Williams, "Philosophical and Theological Concepts of Nature," 16.

21. Austin, *Hope for the Land*, 24, 203, 210.

22. Rasmussen, "Road to Rio."

23. Imsland, *Celebrate the Earth*, 66.

24. Abrecht, *Faith, Science, and the Future*, 37–38; Imsland, *Celebrate the Earth*, 66; Brockway, "Natural World," 30; Bonifazi, "Biblical Roots," 217–20. Austin, *Hope for the Land*, has very little to say about the New Testament. Hendry, *Theology of Nature*, 214–21, is an especially good treatment from this point of view.

25. Cited passages include Matthew 6:25–34, John 1:3–4, and Mark 2:9–12; see Austin, *Hope for the Land*, 57; Hessel, "Preaching for Creation's Sake," 122; Bowman, *Beyond the Modern Mind*, 9; Bonifazi, "Biblical Roots," 220, 223, 228.

26. Humphreys, "Pitfalls and Promises," 114.

27. Ibid., 99.

28. Ibid., 105.

29. Derr, *Ecology and Human Need*, 50–51.

30. Ibid., 51–54; LaBar, "Biblical Perspective on Nonhuman Organisms," 76–93.

31. Derr, *Ecology and Human Need*, 68; Elder, *Crisis in Eden*, 89. Roger Shinn suggests that part of the reason for man being giving so much power over nature in the Bible was to remove the sacred from nature. Shinn, "Science and Ethical Decision," 147–48.

32. Stafford, "Animal Liberation," 19–23.

33. See, for example, "Scripture Index" in DeWitt, *Environment and the Christian*, 153–56.

34. "It's Not Easy Being Green."

35. DeWitt, "Respecting Creation's Integrity," 11; Wilkinson, *Earthkeeping*, 205–7; Stafford, "Animal Liberation," 21; Chewing, "State of the World 1991," 10.

36. Granberg-Michaelson, Introduction to *Tending the Garden*, 1.

37. Granberg-Michaelson, "Goodness of Creation," 10; Stafford, "Animal Liberation," 23, 21; Wilkinson, *Earthkeeping*, 208–14.

38. Wilkinson, *Earthkeeping*, 53, 21; Stafford, "Animal Liberation," 23; LaBar, "Message to Polluters from the Bible," 10–12.

39. Hindson, *End Times*, 47.

40. Wilkinson, "New Age," 28.

41. Van Leeuwen, "Christ's Resurrection."

42. A useful bibliography here is Wise, "Appendix."

43. Francis Schaeffer, *Pollution and the Death of Man*.

44. Granberg-Michaelson, *Worldly Spirituality*, especially 98–102.

45. Van Leeuwen, "Christ's Resurrection and the Creation's Vindication," 61.

46. Monahan, "Christ as the Second Adam"; Wilkinson, *Earthkeeping*, 217–18; Granberg-Michaelson, "Goodness of Creation," 12. See also Thomas Finger, "Modern Alienation and Trinitarian Creation," and "Summarizing Committee Report."

47. Thomas Finger, "Modern Alienation and Trinitarian Creation," 24.

48. Wilkinson, "Christ as Creator and Redeemer," 25–26, 30, 39–44; see also "Summarizing Committee Report."

49. Visick, "Creation's Care and Keeping"; Visick also kindly granted an interview to the author.

CHAPTER THREE

1. Lindsey, *1980s*; Lindsey, *Late, Great Planet Earth*, 174–76; Leilani Watt, *Caught in the Conflict*, 71; Voth, "Time in a Christian Environmental Ethic," 57–66; Hindson, *End Times*, 76–78.

2. Billingsley, Review of *Trashing the Planet*, 14.

3. Charles. "Environmentalists and Eco-Terror in the Gulf," 16.

4. Ron Arnold, *At the Eye of the Storm*; Leilani Watt, *Caught in the Conflict*.

5. Ibid.

6. Ron Arnold, *At the Eye of the Storm*, 10, 74–75, 86, 93; Leilani Watt, *Caught in the Conflict*, 82–83, 92, 97–99.

7. Ron Arnold, *At the Eye of the Storm*, 76–87; Leilani Watt, *Caught in the Conflict*, 83 and 94–97.

8. Leilani Watt, *Caught in the Conflict*, 163.

9. As Lindsey insists in *Late, Great Planet Earth*, chaps. 2 and 3; see also Walvoord, *Armageddon*, 19–20 and chap. 7.

10. Boyer, *When Time Shall Be No More*, 77–78.

11. Barkun, "Divided Apocalypse," 269; for Paul Boyer's read, see *When Time Shall Be No More*, 331–34.

12. Hindson, *End Times*; Lindsey, *Late, Great Planet Earth*; Walvoord, *Armageddon*.

13. Betzer, *Beast*; Pattison, *Left Behind*; Kirban, *666*.

14. "Goodbye Armageddon," 57; Wilkinson, "Theology of the Beasts," 21; Kenneth L. Woodward, "Final Days Are Here Again."

15. Lindsey, *Late, Great Planet Earth*, 76, 47, 177; Lindsey, *Armageddon*, 8 and chap. 3; italics in original.

16. Walvoord, *Armageddon*, 16, 128, 227, 24–25.

17. Betzer, *Beast*, chaps. 18 and 19.

18. Jeffrey, *Armageddon*, 194–95, 166, and chaps. 10 and 15.

19. Alnor, *Soothsayers of the Second Advent*, 202, 99, and chap. 15; Kenneth L. Woodward, "Final Days Are Here Again."

20. Hindson, *End Times*, 64 and chap. 9.

21. Alnor, *Soothsayers of the Second Advent*, 193–94 and chaps. 1–5.

22. For someone who takes both views, see Jeffrey, *Armageddon*, 166, 10, 44–45, and chap. 1.

23. Lutz and Santmire, *Ecological Renewal*, 77.

24. Wills, *Under God*, chap. 13; Neuhaus, *In Defense of People*, 180.

25. Barkun, *Divided Apocalypse*.

26. Schwarz, "Eschatological Dimension of Ecology," 325.

27. Rasmussen, "Care for the Earth," 42–43; Zencey, "Apocalypse Now?," 90–93.

28. Boyer, *When Time Shall Be No More*, 336–37.

29. Some discussions can be found in Lindsey, *1980s*, chap. 2; Jeffrey, *Armageddon*, chaps. 3 and 8; Walvoord, *Armageddon*, 201 and chaps. 2, 12–16; Lindsey, *Planet Earth*, 44 and chaps. 4–5, 9, 11, 13; Alnor, *Soothsayers of the Second Advent*, 20, 29, and chap. 13; Betzer, *Beast*, 318 and chaps. 5–6 and 15–16.

30. Some examples include Davidson, *Islam*, 95–98 and chap. 6; Walvoord, *Armageddon*, 146 and chaps 3–4.

31. Dyer and Hunt, *Rise of Babylon*.

32. Lasch, *True and Only Heaven*, 169–70.

CHAPTER FOUR

1. White, "Continuing the Conversation," 55–64.

2. Ibid., 58–64; Roderick F. Nash, *Rights of Nature*, 91; White, "Historic Roots of Our Ecologic Crisis," 1206.

3. White, "Historic Roots of Our Ecologic Crisis," 1206–7; Roderick F. Nash, *Rights of Nature*, 92–5.

4. Roderick F. Nash, *Rights of Nature*, 51. Tokar, *Green Alternative*, 18, is an especially harsh example.

5. Roderick F. Nash, *Rights of Nature*, 91, 17; Richard Knowles Morris, "Man and Animals," 30.

6. Roderick F. Nash, *Rights of Nature*, 91.

7. Ibid., 94.

8. Passmore, *Man's Responsibility for Nature*, 12; Toynbee, "Religious Background," 137–49.

9. Passmore, *Man's Responsibility for Nature*, 13; Roderick F. Nash, *Rights of Nature*, 90; McHarg, *Design with Nature*, 28.

10. Passmore, *Man's Responsibility for Nature*, 112.

11. McHarg, *Design with Nature*, 26, 24; Tokar, *Green Alternative*, 17–18.

12. An interesting discussion of this theme can be found in Moncrief, "Cultural Basis of Our Environmental Crisis," 31–42.

13. Imsland, *Celebrate the Earth*, 23.

14. Daly and Cobb, *For the Common Good*, 376.

15. Francis Schaeffer, *Pollution and the Death of Man*, 114; Joranson and Butigan, Introduction to *Cry of the Environment*, 6; Bonifazi, "Biblical Roots," 205.

16. Wilkinson, *Earthkeeping*, 104, 204.

17. Cobb, *Is It Too Late?*, 100; Hendry, *Theology of Nature*, 16–18, 20; Daly and Cobb, *For the Common Good*, 385.

18. Wilkinson, *Earthkeeping*, 219–20 and chap. 8; Hall, *Imaging God*, chap. 1; Santmire, *Travail of Nature*, 132.

19. Cobb, *Is It Too Late?*, 35; Barbour, *Technology*, 14.

20. Santmire, *Travail of Nature*, chap. 2; Freudenberger, *Global Dust Bowl*, 25; Bonifazi, "Biblical Roots," 223.

21. Santmire, *Travail of Nature*, chap. 4; Freudenberger, *Global Dust Bowl*, 25.

22. Santmire, *Travail of Nature*, chap. 5; Freudenberger, *Global Dust Bowl*, 25.

23. For example, see Wilkinson, *Earthkeeping*, 135; Granberg-Michaelson, "Why Christians Lost an Environmental Ethic," 22–23; Cobb, *Is It Too Late?*, chap. 4.

24. Bramwell, *Ecology in the Twentieth Century*, 17; Roderick F. Nash, *Rights of Nature*, 113–19; McDaniel, *Of God and Pelicans*, chap. 3.

25. See Ferkiss, *Future of Technological Civilization*, chap. 14.

26. See Roderick F. Nash, *Rights of Nature*. Other interesting skeptical discussions include Yandell, "Fundamentals of Environmental Ethics," 100–101, and Mary Anne Warren, "Rights of the Nonhuman World," 109–34.

27. Roderick F. Nash, *Rights of Nature*, epilogue.

28. Bob Pepperman Taylor, *Our Limits Transgressed*, chaps. 4 and 5.

29. Devall and Sessions, *Deep Ecology*; Manes, *Green Rage*; Foreman, *Confessions of an Eco-Warrior*.

30. Leopold, *Sand County Almanac*; Dubos, "Franciscan Conservation versus Benedictine Stewardship," 118; Leopold, "Land Ethic," 6–9; Leopold, "Conservation as a Moral Issue," 9–12; Callicott, *In Defense of the Land Ethic*. For an excellent biography of Leopold that considers his thought in detail, see Meine, *Aldo Leopold*.

31. See, for example, two excellent essays: Heffernan, "Land Ethic," 235–47, and

Rodman, "Four Forms of Ecological Consciousness Reconsidered," 82–92. On Leopold and those after him, see Bob Pepperman Taylor, *Our Limits Transgressed*, chap. 5.

32. Paul Taylor, *Respect for Nature*.

33. An excellent discussion of Callicott, one that differs somewhat from mine, is in Bob Pepperman Taylor, *Our Limits Transgressed*, chap. 5.

34. Callicott, *In Defense of the Land Ethic*, 7–8, 71, 93–98, and chap. 9; see Armstrong-Buck, "Whitehead's Metaphysical System," 245–46, for one interpretation of Callicott.

35. Callicott, *In Defense of the Land Ethic*, 114.

36. Bob Pepperman Taylor, *Our Limits Transgressed*, 115.

37. Ibid., 107, 78, 136–39, 154–55, and chaps. 10 and 11.

38. Ibid., 114.

39. Callicott, *In Defense of the Land Ethic*, 76 and chap. 7; Yandell, "Fundamentals of Environmental Ethics," 98–99; Armstrong-Buck, "Whitehead's Metaphysical System."

40. Callicott, "Traditional American Indian," 231–59.

41. Gundersen, "Native American Political Theory."

42. See, for example, Ames, "Taoism and the Nature of Nature," 317–50; Cheng, "Environmental Ethics," 351–70; Goodman, "Taoism and Ecology," 73–80.

43. For instance, see William R. Hoyt, "Zen Buddhism," 1194–96, and Jung, "Ecology," 1153–56.

44. Three examples are Sire, *Universe Next Door*, chap. 7; Passmore, *Man's Responsibility for Nature*, 32; and Derr, *Ecology and Human Need*, 62–64.

45. Santmire, "Reflections," 24.

46. See, for instance, Power, "Original Desert Solitaire," 1–53; Barbour, Introduction to *Western Man and Environmental Ethics*, 51–53; Attfield, *Ethics of Environmental Concern*, 34; Shinn, "Science and Ethical Decision," 146–68; and Ayers, "Christian Realism and Environmental Ethics," 154–71.

47. Passmore, *Man's Responsibility for Nature*, 13, 17.

48. Glacken, *Traces on the Rhodian Shore*, viii and 550.

49. George H. Williams, "Christian Attitudes toward Nature," 112–26.

50. Attfield, *Ethics of Environmental Concern*, 22; Derr, *Ecology and Human Need*, 31.

51. Tuan, "Our Treatment of the Environment," 244; Dubos, *God Within*, 158–60.

52. Tuan, "Our Treatment of the Environment," 244–45, 247.

53. White, "Historic Roots of Our Ecologic Crisis"; Glacken, *Traces on the Rhodian Shore*, 215–16; Francis Schaeffer, *Pollution and the Death of Man*, 115.

54. One source among many for this argument is Wilkinson, *Earthkeeping*, 221–22.

55. Some illustrations include Passmore, *Man's Responsibility for Nature*, 13; Elder, *Crisis in Eden*, 97; Freudenberger, *Global Dust Bowl*, 26; Attfield, *Ethics of Environmental Concern*, 45; Derr, *Ecology and Human Need*, 30; Francis Schaeffer, *Pollution and the Death of Man*, chap. 3.

56. Glacken, *Traces on the Rhodian Shore*, 707–9 and chap. 14; Wilkinson, *Earthkeeping*, 145–49; Hendry, *Theology of Nature*, 13–15; Granberg-Michaelson, *Worldly Spirituality*, chap. 3.

57. A rare, direct facing of the issue can be found in Attfield, *Ethics of Environmental Concern*, 22.

58. For instance, see Imsland, *Celebrate the Earth*, 148; Barnette, *Church and the Ecological Crisis*; "It's Not Easy Being Green," 14.

59. For instance, see Moncrief, "Cultural Basis for Our Environmental Crisis," 508–12; Barbour, Introduction to *Western Man and Environmental Ethics*, 1–17.

60. Two illustrations are Francis Schaeffer, *Pollution and the Death of Man*, 71, and Moncrief, "Cultural Basis for Our Environmental Crisis," 508–12.

61. See, for example, Hargrove, Preface to *Religion and Environmental Crisis*, xv.

62. Derr, *Ecology and Human Need*, 28.

63. Austin, *Hope for the Land*, 3; Shinn, "Science and Ethical Decision," 141–42; Barbour, *Technology*, chap. 3.

64. A point made by Calvin DeWitt during an informal presentation in Madison, Wisc., May 29, 1992.

65. Joe Bowersox first got me thinking about this problem.

CHAPTER FIVE

1. For current positions, one good place to start is to contact the denominations for their most recent statements and publications; for earlier ones, see Yaple, "Christian Church and Environmental Education," 279, 285. See Ellingsen, *Cutting Edge*, for the most comprehensive effort to bring together church statements on public issues.

2. A sampler of illustrations: Editor, "Pollution, Christian Faithfulness"; Editor, "The Steward-ship"; Editor, "Stewardship Is . . . ?"; Broyles, "We Are God's Partners"; Juleen Turnage, for The Assemblies of God, to Robert Booth Fowler, August 27, 1991; Chewing, "State of the World 1991"; Dobel, "Stewards of the Earth's Resources"; Faramelli, *Technethics*, 108–9.

3. Wilkinson, *Earthkeeping*, 26.

4. Elder, *Crisis in Eden*, 4–7; Abrecht, *Faith, Science, and the Future*, 35–36; Train, "Religion and the Environment," 5–8; Lowdermilk, "Eleventh Commandment," 12–15.

5. Compton, "Natural Resources Stewardship," 109–14; Elder, *Crisis in Eden*, 60; Barnette, *Church and the Ecological Crisis*, 70; Ehlers, "Christian Stewardship"; Abrecht, *Faith, Science, and the Future*, 42–43; Granberg-Michaelson, *Worldly Spirituality*.

6. Some examples include Fry, "Brown Boy," 21, 26; Butman, "Strange, Continuing Glory," 5–6; Hall, *Imaging God*, 167–74, 128, 68–75, 113, and chap. 2 and introduction.

7. Wilkinson, *Earthkeeping*, 231; Cobb, "Theology and Space," 183, 3–4.

8. Stafford, "Animal Liberation," 19; Anderson, "Creation and the Noachic Covenant"; Chewing, "State of the World 1991"; Regenstein, *Replenish the Earth*, 146–47.

9. Points raised in Laura Olson's telephone interview with Loren Wilkinson, August 6, 1992.

10. Hartt, "Faith," 73.

11. Some examples include Regenstein, *Replenish the Earth*, 26; Abrecht, *Faith, Science, and the Future*, 32; Wilkinson, *Earthkeeping*, 97–98.

12. For example, see Wilkinson, *Earthkeeping*, 26; Richardson, "New Look at Stewardship"; Hall, *Imaging God*, introduction, 148, 66–67; Barnette, *Christian*, appendix 1.

13. John A. Hoyt, "Matter of Choice," 13–16.

14. Tabscott, "To Build a New Earth," 29.

15. For example, see Heinegg, "Ecology and the Fall," 464; Hall, *Imaging God*, chap. 1; LaBar, "Message to Polluters."

16. Roderick F. Nash, *Rights of Nature*, 111.

17. Some of the major articles in the 1970s in *Christianity Today* include Editor, "Listening to God during Drought"; Edith Schaeffer, "God's Greatest Creation"; Bockmuhl, "Current Religious Thought"; Editor, "Living Better with Less"; Editor, "To Live Is to Pollute"; Edith Schaeffer, "Most Dangerous Pollution of All."

18. For instance, see Hall, *Imaging God*, 185–86; Wilkinson, *Earthkeeping*, 224; Rose, "World Won't Stop"; Abrecht, *Faith, Science, and the Future*, 20.

19. "It's Not Easy Being Green," *Christianity Today*, 14.

20. See, for example, Morken, *Pat Robertson*, 169–70.

21. Some celebrants of the caring or earthkeeping theme include Brockway, "Environmental Stewardship," 37; Presbyterian Eco-Justice Task Force, *Keeping and Healing the Creation*; Wilkinson, "Redeemers of the Earth," 45; Barnette, *Church and the Ecological Crisis*, 80–81.

22. For example, see Pollard, "God and His Creation," 70–71; Freudenberger, *Global Dust Bowl*, 111; Hessel, "Preaching for Creation's Sake," 125.

23. Abrecht, *Faith and Science in an Unjust World*, 2:161–62; Wall, "Animals in Research."

24. Au Sable Institute, *Official Bulletin*, overview.

25. Ibid., 1–3.

26. DeWitt, Introduction to *Creation in Crisis*, vii–viii; DeWitt, Introduction to *Environment and the Christian*; DeWitt, "Christian Stewardship."

27. Dickerson, interview of DeWitt; DeWitt, "Christian Stewardship"; DeWitt, Introduction to *Environment and the Christian*.

28. Dickerson, interview of DeWitt, 74.

29. Ibid., 76.

30. For instance, see Barnette, *Church and the Ecological Crisis*, 75–78; DeWitt, *Environment and the Christian*, 23.

31. Dickerson, interview of DeWitt, 76.

32. For instance, see Granberg-Michaelson, "Goodness of Creation."

33. Granberg-Michaelson, "At the Dawn of the New Creation," 13–16; Granberg-Michaelson, *Worldly Spirituality*, 115, 174, 132–34.

34. Granberg-Michaelson, "New Creation," 15.

35. Granberg-Michaelson, *Worldly Spirituality*, 62, 70, 127.

36. Meye, "Invitation to Wonder," 30–49.

37. The critical quotation is from Neuhaus, *In Defense of People*, 56; see Van Ham, "Praying with Trees"; Abrecht, *Faith, Science, and the Future*, 19, 34.

38. Austin, *Beauty of the Lord*, 182, 62.

39. Ibid., 163.

40. For instance, see Tuck, "Church and Ecological Action," 69–70; Butman,

"Strange Continuing Glory," 4–6; Palmer, "Prayer at Nature's Altar," 5; Kortrey, "Keeping a Good Green Earth," 13.

41. Austin, *Beauty of the Lord*, 128–29, 157, 11, 17, 22, 18, 33, 181.

42. Derr, *Ecology and Human Need*, 60–61.

43. For this almost unanimous official policy see such examples as Elder, *Crisis in Eden*, chap. 2; Baer, "Higher Education," 482; Mayo Y. Smith, "Subdue the Earth Didn't Mean Pollute It"; Fracke, "Ecology and Theology," 121; Owens, "Consider the Fingerprint of God."

44. Francis Schaeffer, *Pollution and the Death of Man*, 32–3.

45. Schilling, "The Whole Earth Is the Lord's," 113–22; Neuhaus, *In Defense of People*, especially 155.

46. Wilkinson, "Gaia Spirituality."

47. See, for example, Elder, *Crisis in Eden*, chap. 2; Baer, "Higher Education," 482; Mayo Y. Smith, "Subdue the Earth Didn't Mean Pollute It"; Fracke, "Ecology and Theology," 121; Owens, "Consider the Fingerprint of God."

48. Abrecht, *Faith, Science, and the Future*, 19; Derr, *Ecology and Human Need*, 75, 60, 71.

49. Schilling, "Whole Earth Is the Lord's," 111; Cobb, *Is It too Late?*, chap. 5.

CHAPTER SIX

1. Santmire, *Travail of Nature*, 175.

2. See, for example, Barnette, *Church and the Ecological Crisis*, chap. 5.

3. Passmore, *Man's Responsibility for Nature*, 184, 39–40.

4. Roderick F. Nash, *Rights of Nature*, 120.

5. Santmire, "In Him All Things Consist," 1–3.

6. This point was made by a number of those interviewed for this project.

7. H. Paul Santmire, telephone interview by Laura Olson, August 6, 1992.

8. Santmire, "In Him All Things Consist," 3.

9. Santmire, "Reflections," 46.

10. Santmire, *Travail of Nature*, 218.

11. Ibid., 7; Derr, *Ecology and Human Need*, chap. 2.

12. Santmire, "Catastrophe and Ecstasy," 76.

13. Santmire, "Reflections," 33.

14. Mark Thomas stressed this side of Santmire's perspective—which Santmire's writings fully support—in my interview with him, Madison, Wisc., 1992.

15. Santmire, *Travail of Nature*, 7, 24, 190, 182; Nelson, Review of *Travail of Nature*.

16. Santmire, *Travail of Nature*, 8–9.

17. Santmire, "Reflections"; Santmire, *Travail of Nature*, chap. 3.

18. Santmire, *Travail of Nature*, 73, 118, and chap. 6.

19. Ibid., chap. 7; Santmire, "Reflections," 24–31.

20. Santmire, "Reflections," 24, 32–33, 105–393; Santmire, *Brother Earth*, chap. 3; Santmire, *Travail of Nature*, 137.

21. Santmire, *Travail of Nature*, 133, 140, 152.

22. Santmire, *Brother Earth*, 17–34; Santmire, "Historical Dimensions of the American Crisis," 66, 89.

23. Santmire, *Brother Earth*, 149.

24. Santmire, "Reflections," 33, 45; Santmire, "Ecology, Justice and Theology"; Santmire, "Historical Dimensions," 74–80.

25. Stefferson, Herrscher, and Cook, *Ethics for Environment*, 103–6; Santmire, "Reflections," 34.

26. Santmire, "Catastrophe and Ecstasy," 77.

27. Santmire, "Historical Dimensions of the American Crisis," 90–91.

28. Santmire, *Brother Earth*, 99 (quote), 83, 104, 120, 124–27.

29. Ibid., 160 (quote), 81, 85, 98.

30. Santmire, "Liberation of Nature"; Roderick F. Nash, *Rights of Nature*, 104–5; Santmire, *Brother Earth*, 179; Derr, *Ecology and Human Need*, 36–37.

31. Santmire, *Brother Earth*, 90–91, 171–73, 176; Santmire, *Travail of Nature*, 199–205; Nelson, Review of *Travail of Nature*, 486. Santmire's high Christology was noted by several of those interviewed for this project.

32. Santmire, "In Him All Things Consist," 16.

33. Ibid., 18.

34. Ibid., 15.

35. Santmire, *Brother Earth*, 124, 192–200; Santmire, "Catastrophe and Ecstasy," 79.

36. Santmire, "In Him All Things Consist," 3.

37. Santmire, *Brother Earth*, 86, 160, 181, 184, 188; Roderick F. Nash, *Rights of Nature*, 105; Santmire, "Reflections," 36–38.

38. For example, see his agenda in Santmire, "Catastrophe and Ecstasy," 85–91.

39. Ibid., 110–17.

40. Lutz, "Interrelatedness," 254.

41. Presbyterian Eco-Justice Task Force, *Keeping and Healing the Creation*, 2; see also, for instance, Cobb, *Is It Too Late?*.

42. White, "Future of Compassion," 107.

43. A good well-argued example of this view is Granberg-Michaelson, *Worldly Spirituality*; or see Presbyterian Eco-Justice Task Force, *Keeping and Healing the Creation*, 2–3.

44. The mood started early and has continued strong. Consider a fairly typical early expression in Seaburg, "Man and Nature," 452.

45. An excellent presentation of the commonalities of the view is in Bowman, *Beyond the Modern Mind*, x, 34–44.

46. See, for instance, Seerveld, "Gospel of Creation," 18–19; Meyer and Meyer, *Earthkeepers*.

47. See also Matthew Fox, *Original Blessing*.

48. Matthew Fox, *Original Blessing*, Path 1; Granberg-Michaelson, "Why Christians Lost an Environmental Ethic," 22–23.

49. See these creation-minded discussions: Burhoe, "Cosmic Evolutionary Creation and Christian God," 218–52, and Joranson and Butigan, "Elements of Creation-Conscious Life Style," 436–40.

50. For example, see Matthew Fox, *Original Blessing*, especially 21. Two recent cases of criticism of Fox are Browning, Review of *Creation Spirituality*, and Streichen, *Ungodly Rage*, 219–42.

51. Hope and Young, "Thomas Berry," 753.

52. Thomas Berry, *Dream of the Earth*, 67.

53. Ibid., 81.

54. Matthew Fox, *Original Blessing*, 251 and theme 15.

55. Thomas Berry, *Dream of the Earth*, 81.

56. Matthew Fox, *Original Blessing*, 247 and theme 23.

57. Some examples include Elder, *Crisis in Eden*, chaps. 1 and 2; Bowman, *Beyond the Modern Mind*, chap. 1; Lutz, "Interrelatedness," 254; Joranson, "Prayer, Meditation, and Creation Consciousness," 347–54; Thomas Berry, *Dream of the Earth*, 21.

58. Hope and Young, "Thomas Berry," 750.

59. Thomas Berry, *Dream of the Earth*, 1, 116.

60. Matthew Fox, *Original Blessing*, theme 13. Streichen, *Ungodly Rage*, 230, is decidedly more skeptical about Fox's mysticism. Many of Fox's works deal with the history of spirituality and with mysticism in that context; a good example of this work is his *Western Spirituality*.

61. *Western Spirituality*, 121, 127–31, 160; Streichen, *Ungodly Rage*, 233–42.

62. Boulton, "Thoroughly Modern Mysticism of Matthew Fox," 428–32; Burhoe, "Cosmic Evolutionary Creation," 240; Matthew Fox, *Original Blessing*, 231 and themes 10 and 11.

63. Matthew Fox, *Original Blessing*, 121, 133, and themes 6 and 19.

64. Ibid., 123, 122–25.

65. Ibid., especially 166–72 and 239, themes 18 and 25.

66. Granberg-Michaelson, "Why Christians Lost"; Joranson and Butigan, "Elements of Creation-Conscious Lifestyle."

67. Bowman, *Beyond the Modern Mind*, 99 and chap. 4.

68. Thomas Berry, *Dream of the Earth*, 87 and chap. 11.

69. See Waldrop, *Complexity*.

CHAPTER SEVEN

1. See, for example, Imsland, *Celebrate the Earth*; Bonifazi, *Soul of the World*; Blackburn, *Earth Is the Lord's?*; Thomas Berry, *Dream of the Earth*; Barnette, *Church and the Ecological Crisis*.

2. Teilhard, *Phenomenon of Man*, 29.

3. Ibid., 244.

4. Ibid., 291–98.

5. Teilhard, *Phenomenon of Man*, 254–60, 306, 267–73, 291; Bonifazi, "Teilhard and the Natural Environment," 316, 319; Lischer, "From Faith to Heaven"; Hendry, *Theology of Nature*, 174.

6. Teilhard, *Phenomenon of Man*, 237–38, 243, and foreword.

7. Bonifazi, *Soul of the World*, 217–22, 233; Bonifazi, "Teilhard and the Natural

Environment," 318–20; Teilhard, *Phenomenon of Man*, 30, 303, 166, and book 3 ("Thought").

8. Birch and Cobb, *Liberation of Life*, 3–4; Santmire, *Travail of Nature*, 145–46 and chap. 8; Elder, *Crisis in Eden*, 63–67; Austin, *Hope for the Land*, chap. 20.

9. Teilhard, *Phenomenon of Man*, appendix.

10. Birch and Cobb, *Liberation of Life*, chap. 13; Cobb, *Is It Too Late?*, chap. 13.

11. David Griffin, "Whitehead's Contributions," 3.

12. Whitehead, *Process and Reality*, 27, 89, 94, and chap. 2; Dean R. Fowler, "Retrospective"; Armstrong-Buck, "Whitehead's Metaphysical System."

13. Whitehead, *Process and Reality*; David Griffin, "Whitehead's Contributions," 8; Wikenneth, "Process Theology and Eco-Justice," 86; Bonifazi, *Soul of the World*, 200–205; Dean R. Fowler, "Retrospective."

14. Whitehead, *Process and Reality*, 519–33; Hendry, *Theology of Nature*, 174; Dean R. Fowler, "Retrospective."

15. Armstrong-Buck, "Whitehead's Metaphysical System."

16. Ibid.

17. Yandell, "Protestant Theology and Natural Science," 466–67; Cobb, "Process Theology and an Ecological Model," 334–35.

18. Hartshorne, "How I Got That Way"; Birch and Cobb, *Liberation of Life*; Hartshorne, *Reality as Social Process*, 20–21 and chap. 14.

19. Hartshorne, *Reality as Social Process*, 17.

20. Cobb and Gramwell, *Existence and Actuality*; Hartshorne, *Reality as Social Process*, 18, 21, 34–35.

21. Hartshorne, *Reality as Social Process*, 133–34, 203–4, and chap. 9; Yandell, "Protestant Theology and Natural Science," 467.

22. Hartshorne, *Reality as Social Process*, 66.

23. Ibid., 23–24, 152; Yandell, "Protestant Theology and Natural Science," 466; Hartshorne, "How I Got That Way."

24. McDaniel, "Christian Spirituality," 37.

25. Cobb, "Process Theology," 334; Wikenneth, "Process Theology and Eco-Justice," 85; Loomer, "Process-Relational Corruption of Creation," 328.

26. McDaniel, *Of God and Pelicans*, 53; see also his *Earth, Sky, Gods, and Mortals*.

27. Bonifazi has made this his crusade; Bonifazi, *Soul of the World*, 6, 184, and chaps. 1, 3–4.

28. Charles Birch, "Creation, Technology, and Human Survival," 78–79; Birch and Cobb, *Liberation of Life*, chap. 1.

29. McDaniel, *Of God and Pelicans*, 17; Wikenneth, "Process Theology and Eco-Justice."

30. Malloch, "U.S. Energy Policy," 14.

31. McDaniel, "Christianity and the Need for New Vision," 188–212; Wikenneth, "Process Theology and Eco-Justice."

32. Cobb, "Process Theology," 335–36; Loomer, "Process-Relational Corruption of Creation," 321.

33. Cobb, *Is It Too Late?*, 135.

34. Morrison, "Process Philosophy," 77; Birch and Cobb, *Liberation of Life*; Cobb,

"Overcoming Reductionism"; Hartshorne, "Response by Charles Hartshorne"; Daly and Cobb, *For the Common Good*, 19.

35. Birch and Cobb, *Liberation of Life*, 138.

36. Ibid., 201.

37. Cobb, "Theology and Space," 303–4.

38. Birch and Cobb, *Liberation of Life*, 200.

39. Daly and Cobb, *For the Common Good*, 378, 301, 379, 376; Birch and Cobb, *Liberation of Life*, chap. 3.

40. Roderick F. Nash, *Rights of Nature*, 107.

41. Morrison, "Process Philosophy"; Wikenneth, "Process Theology and Eco-Justice," 86; Loomer, "Process-Relational Corruption of Creation," 324, 326; Cobb, "Process Theology."

42. McDaniel, *Of God and Pelicans*, is especially good in discussing process. See also Barbour, Foreword to *Earth Might Be Fair*, ix; Loomer, "Process-Relational Corruption of Creation," 321, 323; Wikenneth, "Process Theology and Eco-Justice," 90, 92; Charles S. McCoy, "Covenant, Creation, and Ethics," 355–65, 369; Birch and Cobb, *Liberation of Life*, 65; Hendry, *Theology of Nature*, 185–90; Bonifazi, *Soul of the World*, 15 and chap. 12.

43. Wikenneth, "Process Theology and Eco-Justice," 91; see Robert Booth Fowler, *Dance with Community*.

44. Daly and Cobb, *For the Common Good*, 377, 383; Cobb, "Process Theology," 330; Birch and Cobb, *Liberation of Life*, 175 and chap. 5.

45. Daly and Cobb, *For the Common Good*, 382; Cobb, "Is It Too Late?," 101; McDaniel, *Of God and Pelicans*, 79–80.

46. Daly and Cobb, *For the Common Good*, 379; Thomas Berry, *Dream of the Earth*, chap. 5; McDaniel, "Christian Spirituality."

47. McDaniel, *Of God and Pelicans*, 77.

48. Ibid., 38 and chap. 3; McDaniel, "Christian Spirituality."

49. Bonifazi, *Soul of the World*, 163, 231, and chap. 12; Birch and Cobb, *Liberation of Life*, 126.

50. Birch and Cobb, *Liberation of Life*, 205; Herman E. Daly, "Bios, Theos, Logos."

51. McDaniel, "Christianity and the Need for New Vision"; Cobb, "Process Theology," 332–33; McDaniel, "Christian Spirituality."

52. McDaniel, *Of God and Pelicans*, 15, 27, 30; Cobb, "Is It Too Late?," 133–34; Daniel Day Williams, "Changing Concepts of Nature," 58; Barbour, "Attitudes toward Nature and Theology," 152–59.

53. Daniel Day Williams, "Changing Concepts of Nature," 58; Charles S. McCoy, "Covenant, Creation, and Ethics," 367–69; McDaniel, *Of God and Pelicans*, 39, 66.

54. McDaniel, *Of God and Pelicans*, 15–16, 24.

55. Birch and Cobb, *Liberation of Life*, 117–22.

56. Daly and Cobb, *For the Common Good*, 386; Cobb, "Is It Too Late?," 124; Roderick F. Nash, *Rights of Nature*, 107; Cobb, "Theology and Space," 310; Joseph A. Sittler, "Ecological Commitment as Theological Responsibility," 172–81.

57. Hendry, *Theology of Nature*, 174, 206, 221; Roderick F. Nash, *Rights of Nature*, 107.

58. Discussions of this point include McDaniel, *Of God and Pelicans*, 46–49; Joranson and Butigan, "Elements of Creation-Conscious," 406–9; Sittler, "Ecological Commitment," 179; Charles Birch, "Creation, Technology, and Human Survival," 79.

59. McDaniel, *Of God and Pelicans*; Cobb, "Theology and Space."

60. Jay McDaniel, "Christian Spirituality"; Cobb, Review of *Theology of Nature*, 486; Cobb, Review of *Bent World*, 362; Cobb, "Theology and Space," 302–4.

61. Yandell, "Protestant Theology and Natural Science," 466–67; Arthus F. Holmes, "Why God Cannot Act," 194; Derr, *Ecology and Human Need*, 58.

62. Demarest, "Process Reduction," 59–90; Ronald H. Nash, "Process Theology and Classical Theism," 15. For a Roman Catholic view, see Himes, Reviews, 604.

63. Derr, *Ecology and Human Need*, 56–57; Peterson, "God and Evil in Process Theology," 117–39; Demarest, "Process Reduction"; Streichen, *Ungodly Rage*, 202–7.

64. Yandell, "Protestant Theology and Natural Science," 467; Ronald H. Nash, "Process Theology and Classical Theism," 22–23; Henry, "Stunted God," 374–75.

65. See Waldrop, *Complexity*.

CHAPTER EIGHT

1. See Grebe, "Witchcraft."

2. Diamond and Orenstein, *Reweaving the World*, xii.

3. Spretnak, "Ecofeminism," 3–14.

4. See, for example, Kassian, *Feminist Gospel*.

5. Merchant, "Ecofeminism and Feminist Theory," 100.

6. Gray, *Why the Green Nigger?*; Gray, *Green Paradise Lost*, 26; Ruether, *New Woman / New Earth*, 196; McDaniel, *Of God and Pelicans*, chap. 4; Iris Marion Young, Review of "Feminism and Ecology," 173–80; King, "Ecology of Feminism."

7. Diamond and Orenstein, *Reweaving the World*, introduction.

8. For example, see Ruether, *New Woman / New Earth*, 204; Spretnak, *Politics of Women's Spirituality*; Gray, *Green Paradise Lost*, 30.

9. More examples include Gray, *Green Paradise Lost*, 20; Willis, "Proclaiming Liberation," 55–70.

10. Gray, *Green Paradise Lost*, 23–24 and chap. 7; Ruether, "Mother Earth and the Megamachine," 267–72; Susan Griffin, *Woman and Nature*, especially Book 2; Iris Marion Young, Review of "Feminism and Ecology."

11. Merchant, *Death of Nature*, 1, 143.

12. Ibid., 131 and chap. 4.

13. Ibid., 131, 5, 288, 192, 228, 87, 132, and chaps. 2 and 6.

14. Ynestra King's discussion is interesting, especially its argument that socialism as an ideology incorporates approval of the domination of nature. See King, "Healing the Wounds," 106–21.

15. For instance, see Gray, *Green Paradise Lost*, chap. 10; Donald Davis, "Ecosophy," 155; McFague, "World as God's Body," 671–73.

16. Susan Griffin, *Woman and Nature*, 219; see also Plant, *Healing the Wounds*, part 4;

see also Susan Griffin, "Curves along the Road," 87–99; Gray, *Green Paradise Lost,* chap. 8.

17. Plant, *Healing the Wounds,* 1; see also Susan Griffin, "Split Culture"; Susan Griffin, *Woman and Nature,* 165.

18. Ruether, *Sexism and God-Talk,* 266 and postscript. See also, for example, Ward, "Story for Our Times," 18–21; Gray, *Why the Green Nigger?*; Plant, *Healing the Wounds,* part 2; Mary Daly, *Beyond God the Father.*

19. Donald Davis, "Ecosophy," 162.

20. Kheel, "Ecofeminism and Deep Ecology," 137.

21. Gray, *Green Paradise Lost,* 114, 111–12; Susan Griffin, *Woman and Nature,* 72–73; Merchant, *Death of Nature,* xvi, xix, 2.

22. Shute, "Review," 190; Binford, "Counter-Response," 558–59.

23. Zimmerman, "Feminism," 21–44.

24. Mary Daly, *Gyn/Ecology*; Chicago, *Dinner Party*; Card, *Feminist Ethics* (though in her book Card does not really address the environmental side—she speaks more to that side in her teaching); Iris Marion Young, Review of "Feminism and Ecology"; Karen J. Warren, "Feminism and Ecology."

25. Gray, *Green Paradise Lost,* 5, 19; Spretnak, *Spiritual Dimension of Green Politics*; Susan Griffin, *Woman and Nature.*

26. See vol. 16, May/June 1990.

27. For instance, see Raffensperger, "All God's Critters"; Schmitz, "Eucharist and Ecology"; Bagley, "Eco-Feminism and the Church"; McFague, *Models of God*; Bateson, "Caring for Children"; Catherine Keller, "Step beyond Metaphor."

28. McFague, *Models of God,* 29–31, 63, and chap. 4.

29. Ibid., 43.

30. Ibid., 35–36, 14.

31. Ibid., 46. Some of the images are described in chaps. 4–6.

32. McFague, Address to the Conference on Human Values and the Environment.

33. McFague, *Models of God,* 64 and chap. 5.

34. Ibid., 49, 27, 64–65.

35. McFague, Address to the Conference on Human Values and the Environment.

36. I draw on Ruether frequently here and elsewhere in this study. She is a serious and significant figure. See, for example, Ruether, "Biblical Vision of the Ecological Crisis"; Ruether, *Sexism and God-Talk*; or Ruether, *New Woman/New Earth.* For a stern critique of Ruether, see Streichen, *Ungodly Rage,* 32, 77–78, 162, 301–4; see also Kassian, *Feminist Gospel,* chaps. 5 and 20.

37. Ruether, *Disputed Questions,* 72–73.

38. Ruether, *Gaia and God,* especially 201.

39. Ibid., 31–34.

40. Ibid., chaps. 8 and 9.

41. Ibid., 154–55 and chap. 6.

42. Ibid., 137–39.

43. Ibid., 171.

44. Ruether, *Women-Church*; the quotation is from Ruether, *Gaia and God,* 269.

45. Ruether, *Gaia and God,* 251–52.

46. Wilkinson, "Gaia Spirituality," 16.

47. Ibid., 15.

48. Ibid., 13.

49. Achtemeier, "Why God Is Not Mother," 16–23.

50. For example, see Loades, *Feminist Theology.*

51. For example, see Spretnak, *Spiritual Dimension,* 41, 46–47, 54; Gray, *Green Paradise Lost,* 55–56; Spretnak, *Women's Spirituality,* xi–xxx.

52. Christ, *Laughter of Aphrodite,* 85.

53. Starhawk, "Power, Authority, and Mystery," 76.

54. See especially Starhawk, *Truth or Dare.*

55. Starhawk, "Power, Authority, and Mystery," 85.

56. Adler, *Drawing Down the Moon,* 197, 178, 184, 206–7, 213–14, 228–29, and chap. 8; Goldenberg, *Changing of the Gods,* chap. 7; Starhawk, "Witchcraft as Goddess Religion," 49–56; Plant, *Healing the Wounds,* part 3; Starhawk, "Feminist, Earth-based Spirituality, and Ecofeminism," 174–85; Grebe, "Witchcraft."

57. Blackburn, *Earth Is the Lord's?,* 110, 119; Marjorie Casebier McCoy, "Feminist Consciousness in Creation," 132–47; Merchant, *Death of Nature,* 288, xvi, 95, 252; Spretnak, *Spiritual Dimension,* 71; Ruether, *New Woman / New Earth;* Ruether, *Women-Church.*

58. Loren Wilkinson, interview by Laura Olson, August 6, 1992.

59. Biehl, *Rethinking,* 96.

60. Evelyn Fox Keller, *Secrets of Life;* Harding, *Science Question in Feminism;* Haraway, *Primate Visions.*

61. Haraway, *Primate Visions,* 111.

62. King, "Healing the Wounds."

63. Heine, *Matriarchs, Goddesses, and Images of God,* 48, 72, and chap. 3; Biehl, *Rethinking Ecofeminist Politics,* chap. 3; Kassian, *Feminist Gospel.*

64. Biehl, *Rethinking Ecofeminist Politics,* 84.

65. Ibid., 85, introduction, and chap. 1.

66. Lefkowitz, "Twilight of the Goddess," 29.

67. Ibid., 33.

CHAPTER NINE

1. Malloch, "U.S. Energy Policy," 15–16.

2. An example where the agenda is present is "Integrity: Biblical People for Environmental Responsibility," 10–11 and 20–21.

3. For some variety, see Blackburn, *Earth Is the Lord's?,* chap. 6; Howell, "Legislators Must Tip-Toe"; Shinn, "Science and Ethical Decision"; Squiers, *Environmental Crisis;* Vig and Kraft, *Environmental Policy in the 1990s.*

4. Some diverse examples include Presbyterian Eco-Justice Task Force, *Keeping and Healing the Creation,* chap. 4; Wayne H. Davis, "Ecological Crisis"; Cobb, "Christian Existence"; Daly and Cobb, *For the Common Good.*

5. Besides assorted denominational lists / statements, see, for example, the March

1989 issue of *Christian Social Action*, published by the United Methodist Church; Abrecht, *Faith, Science, and the Future*; Krueger, *Christian Ecology*, for a large section on practical ideas. Wilkinson, *Earthkeeping*, chap. 17, illustrates the variant of trying to be practical and detailed while exploring the ideal.

6. Douglas, "Wild Country and Wildlife."

7. Some of the many essays include Editor, "Churches Find Ways to Conserve Energy"; Editor, "N.C. Congregations Reduce Energy Use"; Pragnell, "ABC's of Church Energy Savings"; Editor, "Energy Conservation, Innovation Boosted"; Editor, "LCA Offices Cut Energy Use 17 Percent"; Editor, "Energy Conservation Steps Recommended by ALC Unit"; Judith L. Woodward, "Fuel Consumption"; Madison, "How Can You and Your Congregation Save Energy?"

8. Robert Hoyt, "Pragmatics of Energy"; Herman, "Powerful Vision with Flaws"; Sweeney, "Synfuels"; Shinn and Maxey, "NCC and Nuclear Power"; Corbett, "What Happened to President Carter's Energy Program?"; Editor, "Let Us Opt for Ecology Rather Than Energy."

9. Nyberg, "How Can You Help"; Berg, "Conservation"; Matthies, "Explore Your Church for Energy Leaks."

10. Nyberg, "Energy Conservation"; Lovins and Lovins, "Energy by the People"; Faramelli, "No Easy Choices on Energy Problems."

11. For example, see Imsland, *Celebrate the Earth*, 69; Hauerwas, "Ethics of Population and Pollution"; Lester R. Brown, "Defusing the Population Timebomb"; Shinn, "Population and the Dignity of Man"; Barnette, *Church and the Ecological Crisis*, 57; Cobb, *Is It Too Late?*, chap. 8; Editor, "What the Church Gathered in General Assembly Said."

12. Wilkinson, *Earthkeeping*, 48.

13. I just don't see it, despite the contrary argument of Neuhaus, *In Defense of People*, 196.

14. For instance, see Faramelli, "Religious Reconstruction," Fa7–8 and Fa12; Finnin, "Assessing Lifeboat Ethics"; Benjamin, "Challenge to the Eco-Doomsters"; Neuhaus, *In Defense of People*, chap. 7.

15. Wilkinson, *Earthkeeping*, 280, 251.

16. Kuby, "Day of Ecological Atonement?"; Watson, "International Storm over Acid Rain."

17. Faramelli, *Technethics*, 101–2.

18. Some examples include Malloch, "U.S. Energy Policy," 14; Elder, *Crisis in Eden*, chap. 8; Bowman, *Beyond the Modern Mind*; Joranson and Butigan, "New Road Ahead," 459–64; Carothers et al., *To Love or to Perish*, 108–36.

19. The following sources offer some variety: Platt, "Lord's Day"; Hargrove, *Religion and Environmental Crisis*, xii–xiii, xvii.

20. For example, see Wilkinson, *Earthkeeping*, 276; Ferkiss, *Future of Technological Civilization*, chaps. 2–4; Faramelli, *Technethics*, 111; Anderson, "Creation and the Noachic Covenant," 121–25.

21. As with my other examples, there is no unanimity here; I am merely illustrating some themes. Schwarz, "Eschatological Dimension of Ecology," 323–28; Cobb, "Christian Existence," 150; Abrecht, *Faith and Science in an Unjust World*, 2:147.

22. For example, see Cobb, "Ecological Disaster and the Church," 1185–87; Cobb, *Is It Too Late?*, chap. 7; Elder, *Crisis in Eden*, 144–55; Schneider, "Why 'Life-Style' Matters"; Kile, "Charting Economic Impact."

23. DeWitt, "Respecting Creation's Integrity," 20.

24. A few illustrations include Imsland, "Celebrate the Earth"; Warner, "God Called the Earth Good"; Lohman, "Theo-ecology of Diet"; Gibson, "Conundrum of Oil," 6.

25. World Evangelical Fellowship, "Summarizing Committee Report."

26. For example, Birch and Cobb, *Liberation of Life*, chap. 8; Daly and Cobb, *For the Common Good*, chap. 3; Cesaretti and Commins, *Let the Earth Bless the Lord*, chaps. 34–40; Presbyterian Eco-Justice Task Force, *Keeping and Healing the Creation*, chap. 5; Barnette, "Toward an Ecological Ethic," 31–32.

27. Hardin, "Ecology and the Death of Providence."

28. See *101 Ways to Help Save the Earth*.

29. Some relevant essays include Herman E. Daly, "Ecological and Moral Necessity," 212–30; Shinn, "Eco-Justice Theories in Christian Ethics," 106–7; Gibson, "Eco-Justice," 27; Cobb, "Theology and Space," 306–9; Birch and Cobb, *Liberation of Life*, 235 and chaps. 8–10; Schumacher, "Small Is Beautiful"; Elwood, "Primitivism or Technology."

30. Some relevant discussions include Abrecht, *Faith and Science*, 147; Faramelli, "Religious Reconstruction," Fa19–21.

31. For example, Faramelli, *Technethics*, 107–8; DeWitt, "Christian Stewardship"; Gerald Alonzo Smith, "Christian Ecological Economics."

32. The quotation comes from DeWitt, "Respecting Creation's Integrity," 21.

33. See, for example, Wilkinson, *Earthkeeping*, 274–75 and chap. 10.

34. Daly and Cobb, *For the Common Good*. See the whole book, but especially 151, 19–20, 159, 331, and chaps. 4 and 16.

35. Consider Bhagat, *Creation in Crisis*, chap. 12, and Thomas Berry, *Dream of the Earth*, chap. 7.

36. Shinn, "Eco-Justice Theories in Christian Ethics," 107.

37. For instance, see Hawksley, "Redefining the Family," 44–45; Granberg-Michaelson, *Worldly Spirituality*, chap. 10.

38. Hessel, *After Nature's Revolt*.

39. For an earlier NCC version of "ecological justice" see Cowap and Cowap, "Toward Ecological Justice," 250–52.

40. For example, see Wilkinson, *Earthkeeping*, 75, 215, 243, 264; Joranson and Butigan, *Cry of the Environment*, 8; Birch and Cobb, *Liberation of Life*, chap. 8; Rasmussen, "Creation," 120–22.

41. Shinn, "Eco-Justice Theories in Christian Ethics," 103.

42. Abrecht, *Faith and Science*, 120.

43. Gibson, "Eco-Justice," 26, 15–16.

44. Presbyterian Eco-Justice Task Force, *Keeping and Healing the Creation*, 2.

45. Dyrness, "Are We Our Planet's Keeper"; Hall, *Imaging God*, 165–67.

46. For instance, see Shoemaker, "Loving People, Loving Earth."

47. *The Egg: An Eco-Justice Quarterly* 11 (Summer 1991): 2.

48. Barbour, "Ecological Ethic."

49. See Eco-Justice Working Group of the National Council of Churches pamphlet on toxic poisoning.

50. Derr, *Ecology and Human Need*, 65 and chap. 6.

51. A classic example is Neuhaus, *In Defense of People*, 126, 130, and chap. 10; see also Stackhouse, Review of *In Defense of People*; McCloskey, *Ecological Ethics and Politics*.

52. For some interesting discussions on this theme, see Carothers, *To Love or to Perish*, 88; Earl Arnold, "Implications of Eco-Justice," 87; Diers, "Humanity and Environment," 146–47.

53. Baer, "Higher Education," 489.

54. For example, see Joranson and Butigan, "Elements of Creation-Conscious Life Style," 165; Au Sable Institute, *Official Bulletin*, 2; Presbyterian Eco-Justice Task Force, *Keeping and Healing the Creation*, chap. 5; Freudenberger, *Global Dust Bowl*, 40; Carothers, *To Love or to Perish*, 69.

55. For example, see White, "Future of Compassion," 106; Livingston, "Ecological Challenge to Christian Ethics"; Freudenberger, *Global Dust Bowl*, 41–42.

56. Daly and Cobb, *Common Good*, 14–15, 175, 178, 235, and 297.

57. Wendell Berry, *Sex, Economy, Freedom, and Community*.

58. Hatch, "When the Dump Is in 'Our' Backyard," 660.

59. For a discussion of community in contemporary American intellectual life, see Robert Booth Fowler, *Dance with Community*.

60. Ibid.

61. Phillips, *Looking Backward*.

62. See also Rosenblum, *Another Liberalism*; Cochran, "Thin Theory of Community."

63. For example, see Welden, "Intensity of Competition"; Goldsmith, "Gaia."

64. For example, see Haraway, *Primate Visions*; Harding, *Science Question in Feminism*.

65. Passmore, *Man's Responsibility for Nature*, 127.

66. Neuhaus, *In Defense of People*, 192.

67. Derr, *Ecology and Human Need*, 83–86; Neuhaus, *In Defense of People*, 188, 124, 138.

68. Ream, "Man and His Environment"; Shinn, "Science and Ethical Decision," 146; Bowman, *Beyond the Modern Mind*, ix.

69. Pollard, "God and His Creation," 67.

70. Cobb, "Christian Existence," 159.

71. Pollard, "God and His Creation," 69.

72. Bhagat, *Creation in Crisis*, chaps. 5–9; Willis, "Proclaiming Liberation," 68.

73. Dyrness, "Stewardship of Earth."

74. Wilkinson, *Earthkeeping*, 5–6, 183, 253, 257; see also, for example, Bhagat, *Creation in Crisis*, 131.

75. Baer, "Poverty," 49–57.

76. Cobb, "Christian Existence in a World of Limits," 152.

77. Blackburn, *Earth Is the Lord's?*, 67–68; Shinn, "Science and Ethical Decision," 159–63.

78. Findlay, *Church People in the Struggle*; Aldon D. Morris, *Origins of the Civil Rights Movement*; Garrow, *Bearing the Cross*.

CHAPTER TEN

1. The controversial market analysis is best articulated by Finke and Stark, *Churching of America*.

2. In thinking about these broader issues, my friend Charlie Anderson has been of great help to me.

3. For instance, see Editor, "Air Power and the Environmentalists"; Wilkinson, *Earthkeeping*, 307–8; Barnette, *Church and the Ecological Crisis*; Krueger, "Wilderness Retreats," 57.

4. Joe Bowersox and John Meyer both helped orient me here.

5. Bhagat, *Creation in Crisis*, 130.

6. See the discussion of Francis Schaeffer, *Pollution and the Death of Man*, 114–15.

7. Among others, Joranson and Butigan, *Cry of the Environment*, 4–5; Derr, *Ecology and Human Need*, chap. 5; see also Rasmussen, "Creation," 123–29.

8. Kirkland, "Church Activism," 106; Elder, *Crisis in Eden*, 155–62.

9. Some examples include Cauthern, *Christian Biopolitics*, chap. 6; Abrecht, *Faith and Science in an Unjust World*, 150–51; Daly and Cobb, *For the Common Good*, 20; Gelderloos, "Leadership in Environmental Ethics," 45–61.

10. The type of essays that skeptics wonder about include Trotter, "Spirituality in Environmental Education," and Barbieri, "Spirituality in Environmental Education."

11. See Yaple, *Christian Church and Environmental Education*, especially 139; Joranson and Butigan, *Cry of the Environment*, 441–46; Schicker, "Institute for 'Earth Keeping,'" 808–12; Cable, "Environmental Education at Christian Colleges," 165–68; Editor, "Global Datelines;" or Editor, "Presbyterians This Week," among a host of articles beginning in 1970 and going on from there.

12. For example, see Tuck, "Church and Ecological Action," 67, 70–71, 73–76; Barnette, *Church and the Ecological Crisis*, chap. 6; Bhagat, *Creation in Crisis*, 131; Dickerson, "Appropriate Ecological Programs," 101. The symposium called "Our Earth Family" took place at Orchard Ridge United Church of Christ, Madison, Wisc., 1991.

13. Hanson, "Fifty-Two Weeks."

14. Sources include Willis, "Proclaiming Liberation," 55–70; Editor, "May 7 to Be Observed as Environmental Sunday"; Meyer and Meyer, *Earthkeepers*, 20–23; Editor, "Hymn Society Calls for Ecology Songs."

15. Editor, "Collect for Environmental Sunday."

16. Despot, "All Creatures Great and Small"; Abrecht, *Faith and Science*, "Report 2."

17. Here are just three examples among many: Baer, "Church and Man's Relationship to his Natural Environment"; James Parks Morton, "Listen to the Earth"; Barbour, *Technology*, 311–13.

18. Willis, "Proclaiming Liberation," 56–58.

19. One interesting case is Adams, *Solar Church*. The Lutheran periodicals in

particular have had much discussion on this topic; there are a lot of Lutherans in the cold and energy-demanding Midwest; for instance, see Editor, "Churches Receive Energy Use Books"; Editor, "Saving Energy"; James M. Johnston, "They Bicycle."

20. See, for example, Kirkland, "Church Activism," 105–6; Carothers et al., *To Love or to Perish*, 104–5 and chap. 7.

21. Findlay, *Church People in the Struggle*, especially p. 223; see also Aldon D. Morris, *Origins of the Civil Rights Movement*.

22. Bramwell, *Ecology in the Twentieth Century*, 91; Lacey, *Governmental and Environmental Politics*; Paehlke, *Environmentalism*.

23. Killingsworth and Palmer, *Ecospeak*, 98.

24. These examples are from Shinn, "Science and Ethical Decision," 164; McCullough, "Death of a Mountain," 24–33; Wilkinson, *Earthkeeping*, 265; Derr, *Ecology and Human Need*, 142–56.

25. Derr, *Ecology and Human Need*, 79; Editor, "Lutheran Biologist Warns of Environmental Disaster"; Barnette, *Church and the Ecological Crisis*, 55–56.

26. See the discussions by Neuhaus, *In Defense of People*, and Paehlke, *Environmentalism*.

27. Bramwell, *Ecology in the Twentieth Century*, 234, 241.

28. For instance, Chewing, "State of the World 1991," 10; James G. Watt, *Courage of a Conservative*.

29. Findlay, *Church People in the Struggle*.

30. Paehlke, *Environmentalism and the Future*, 1–2.

31. Bob Pepperman Taylor, "Environmental Ethics and Political Theory."

32. Neuhaus, *In Defense of People*, 265, 163.

33. Derr, *Ecology and Human Need*, 76. For quite another perspective, see Chewing, "State of the World 1991," 10.

34. Derr, *Ecology and Human Need*, 160.

35. Bob Pepperman Taylor, *Our Limits Transgressed*, 137, 135.

36. Neuhaus, *In Defense of People*, 269, 124; for a more recent expression of similar worry, see Paehlke, "Environmental Values and Democracy."

37. Neuhaus, *In Defense of People*, 256; Buttel, "Environmentalism for the Long Term."

38. Worster, *Wealth of Nature*; Hardin, *Living within Limits*.

39. Joe Bowersox has made this argument in *Moral and Spiritual Potential of Environmentalism*, chap. 7.

40. For example, see Derr, *Ecology and Human Need*, 82–83; Wilkinson, *Earthkeeping*, 306–7 and appendix A; Hovey, "Questions after Earth Day," 139; Daniel Day Williams, "Philosophical and Theological Concepts of Nature," 21.

41. For instance, see Blackburn, *Earth Is the Lord's?*, 125–31; Cameron, "Hope for a Less Toxic Future"; Ensign, "Response of the Church"; Orgon and Paz, "Faith, Politics, and Ecology," 83.

42. Visick, "Creation's Care," 103.

43. Morgan, Review of *Rebirth of Value*, 406.

44. Typical sources include Wall, "Uncaged Vision of Nonhuman Creation"; or Ayers, "Christian Realism and Environmental Ethics."

45. Santmire, "Catastrophe and Ecstasy," 112–15.

46. Ibid., 104.

47. Charles Anderson helped me in reflecting on these concluding observations.

48. Findlay, *Church People in the Struggle*; Aldon D. Morris, *Origins of the Civil Rights Movement*.

49. Murphy, "Mainline Churches and Political Activism."

50. Some examples include Schilling, "Whole Earth Is the Lord's"; Fracke, "Ecology and Theology," 122–23.

CONCLUSION

1. Wilkinson, *Earthkeeping*, 293. Some expressions of hope, however modest, can be found in Daly and Cobb, *For the Common Good*, 400; Hessel, "Preaching for Creation's Sake," 121; Pollard, "God and His Creation," 74.

✖ BIBLIOGRAPHY ✖

Abrecht, Paul, ed. *Faith, Science, and the Future.* Philadelphia: Fortress, 1979.

——. *Faith and Science in an Unjust World: Report of the World Council of Churches' Conference on Faith, Science and the Future.* Vol. 2, "Reports and Recommendations." Geneva: World Council of Churches, 1980.

Achtemeier, Elizabeth. "Understanding God's Relation to His Created World." *Presbyterian Survey*, May 1976, pp. 16–17.

——. "Why God Is Not Mother." *Christianity Today*, August 16, 1993, pp. 16–23.

Adams, Jennifer A. *The Solar Church.* New York: Pilgrim Press, 1982.

Adler, Margot. *Drawing Down the Moon.* Boston: Beacon Press, 1986.

——. "The Juice and the Mystery." In *Healing the Wounds: The Promise of Ecofeminism*, ed. Judith Plant, pp. 151–154. Philadelphia: New Society, 1989.

Aeschliman, Gordon. *Global Trends.* Downers Grove, Ill.: InterVarsity, 1990.

Allen, Paula Gunn. "The Woman I Love Is a Planet; The Planet I Love Is a Tree." In *Reweaving the World: The Emergence of Ecofeminism*, ed. Irene Diamond and Gloria Feman Orenstein, pp. 52–69. San Francisco: Sierra Club, 1990.

Alnor, William M. *Soothsayers of the Second Advent.* Old Tappan, N.J.: Revell, 1989.

Ames, Roger T. "Taoism and the Nature of Nature." *Environmental Ethics* 8 (Winter 1986): 317–50.

Anderson, Bernhard W. "Creation and the Noachic Covenant." Chap. 2 in *Cry of the Environment*, ed. Philip N. Joranson and Ken Butigan. Santa Fe: Bear and Co., 1984.

——. "Creation in the Bible." Chap. 1 in *Cry of the Environment*, ed. Philip N. Joranson and Ken Butigan. Santa Fe: Bear and Co., 1984.

"Are Evangelicals Warming to Earth Issues?" *Christianity Today*, June 22, 1992, pp. 63 and 65.

Armstrong-Buck, Susan. "Whitehead's Metaphysical System as a Foundation for Environmental Ethics." *Environmental Ethics* 8 (Fall 1986): 241–59.

Arnold, Earl. "The Implications of Eco-Justice." In *Christian Ecology*, ed. Frederick W. Krueger. San Francisco: North American Conference on Christianity and Ecology, 1988.

Arnold, Ron. *At the Eye of the Storm: James Watt and the Environmentalists.* Chicago: Regnery Gateway, 1982.

Attfield, Robin. *The Ethics of Environmental Concern.* New York: Columbia University Press, 1983.

Au Sable Institute. *Official Bulletin.* Mancelona, Mich.: Au Sable Institute, 1991.

Austin, Richard Cartwright. *Beauty of the Lord.* Atlanta: John Knox, 1988.

——. *Hope for the Land.* Atlanta: John Knox, 1988.

——. "Three Axioms for Land Use." *Christian Century*, October 12, 1977, pp. 910–11 and 915.

Ayers, Robert H. "Christian Realism and Environmental Ethics." In *Religion and Environmental Crisis*, ed. Eugene C. Hargrove, pp. 154–71. Athens: University of Georgia Press, 1986.

Badke, William B. *Project Earth: Preserving the World God Created*. Portland, Ore.: Multnomah Press, 1991.

Baer, Richard A., Jr. "The Church and Man's Relationship to His Natural Environment." *Quaker Life*, January 1970, pp. 420–21.

——. "Higher Education, the Church, and Environmental Values." *Natural Resources Journal* 17 (July 1977): 477–91.

——. "Poverty, Pollution and the Power of the Gospel." *Engage/Social Action*, January 1975, pp. 49–57.

Bagley, Rachel. "Eco-Feminism and the Church: Part Three." In *Christian Ecology*, ed. Frederick W. Krueger. San Francisco: North American Conference on Christianity and Ecology, 1988.

Barber, Benjamin. *Strong Democracy*. Berkeley: University of California Press, 1984.

Barbieri, Charles. "Spirituality in Environmental Education, Part Two." In *Christian Ecology*, ed. Frederick W. Krueger, pp. 81–82. San Francisco: North American Conference on Christianity and Ecology, 1988.

Barbour, Ian G. "Attitudes toward Nature and Theology." In *Earth Might Be Fair: Reflections on Ethics, Religion, and Ecology*. Englewood Cliffs, N.J.: Prentice Hall, 1982.

——. *Christianity and the Scientist*. New York: Association Press, 1960.

——. *Earth Might Be Fair: Reflections on Ethics, Religion, and Ecology*. Englewood Cliffs, N.J.: Prentice Hall, 1982.

——. "An Ecological Ethic." *Christian Century*, October 7, 1970, pp. 1180–84.

——. "Foreword." In *Cry of the Environment*, ed. Philip N. Joranson and Ken Butigan, pp. vii–x. Santa Fe: Bear and Co., 1984.

——. Introduction to *Western Man and Environmental Ethics*. Reading, Mass.: Addison-Wesley, 1973.

——. *Technology, Environment, and Human Values*. New York: Praeger, 1980.

——, ed. *Western Man and Environmental Ethics*. Reading, Mass.: Addison-Wesley, 1973.

Barkun, Michael. "Divided Apocalypse: Thinking about the End in Contemporary America." *Soundings* 66 (Fall 1983): 257–80.

Barnette, Henlee H. *The Church and the Ecological Crisis*. Grand Rapids, Mich.: Eerdmans, 1972.

——. "Toward an Ecological Ethic." *Review and Expositor* 69 (Winter 1972): 23–35.

Bateson, Mary Catherine. "Caring for Children, Caring for the Earth." *Christianity and Crisis*, March 31, 1980, pp. 67–70.

Bellah, Robert, et al. *Habits of the Heart: Individualism and Commitment in American Life*. Berkeley: University of California Press, 1985.

Benjamin, Walter W. "A Challenge to the Eco-Doomsters." *Christian Century*, March 21, 1979, pp. 311–14.

Berg, James Vande. "Conservation: Survival or Stewardship." *Presbyterian Survey*, September 1980, pp. 38–39.

Berry, Thomas. *The Dream of the Earth.* San Francisco: Sierra Books, 1988.

Berry, Wendell. "God and Country." In *Christian Ecology*, ed. Frederick W. Krueger, pp. 15–17. San Francisco: North American Conference on Christianity and Ecology, 1988.

——. *Sex, Economy, Freedom and Community.* New York: Pantheon, 1993.

Betzer, Dan. *Beast: A Novel of the Future World Dictator.* Lafayette, La.: Prescott Press, 1985.

Bhagat, Shantilal P. *Creation in Crisis: Responding to God's Covenant.* Elgin, Ill.: Brethren Press, 1990.

Biehl, Janet. *Rethinking Ecofeminist Politics.* Boston: South End Press, 1991.

Billingsley, K. L. Review of *Trashing the Planet*, by Dixie Ray Lee. *World*, March 23, 1991, pp. 14–15.

Binford, Sally R. "Counter-Response." In *The Politics of Women's Spirituality*, ed. Charlene Spretnak, pp. 558–59. Garden City, N.Y.: Doubleday, 1982.

Birch, Bruce C. "Energy Ethics Reaches the Church's Agenda." *Christian Century*, November 1, 1978, pp. 1034–38.

Birch, Charles. "Creation, Technology, and Human Survival." *Ecumenical Review* 28, no. 1 (1976): 66–79.

Birch, Charles, and John B. Cobb, Jr. *The Liberation of Life: From the Cell to the Community.* Cambridge: Cambridge University Press, 1981.

Bird, Phyllis A. "Male and Female He Created Them." *Harvard Theological Review* 74 (1981): 129–59.

Blackburn, Joyce. *The Earth Is the Lord's?* Waco, Tex.: Word, 1972.

Bloom, Allan. *The Closing of the American Mind.* New York: Simon and Schuster, 1987.

Bockmuhl, Klaus. "Current Religious Thought: Destroyer or Provider." *Christianity Today*, June 6, 1975, pp. 49–50.

Bonifazi, Conrad. "Biblical Roots of an Ecologic Conscience." In *This Little Planet*, ed. Michael Hamilton, pp. 203–33. New York: Scribner's, 1970.

——. *The Soul of the World.* Washington, D.C.: University Press of America, 1978.

——. "Teilhard and the Natural Environment." In *Cry of the Environment*, ed. Philip N. Joranson and Ken Butigan, pp. 311–20. Santa Fe: Bear and Co., 1984.

Boulton, Wayne G. "The Thoroughly Modern Mysticism of Matthew Fox." *Christian Century*, April 25, 1990, pp. 428–32.

Bouma-Prediger, Steve. "Ecology and Social Justice: Toward an Integral Christian Theology of Nature and Human Liberation." Paper presented at the World Evangelical Fellowship/Au Sable Forum, 1992.

Bowersox, Joe. "Deep Ecology, Biocentrism, and Politics: The Specious Subordination of the Polis to 'Instinct'?" Paper presented at the annual meeting of the American Political Science Association, Chicago, Ill., September 1992.

——. *The Moral and Spiritual Potential of Environmentalism: Reclaiming the Historical Foundations of Western Liberal Philosophical and Religious Thought.* Ph.D. diss. draft, University of Wisconsin–Madison, 1989.

Bowman, Douglas C. *Beyond the Modern Mind: The Spiritual and Ethical Challenge of the Environmental Crisis.* New York: Pilgrim Press, 1990.

Boyer, Paul. *When Time Shall Be No More: Prophecy Belief in Modern American Culture.* Cambridge: Harvard University Press, 1992.

Boyte, Harry C., and Frank Riessman, eds. *The New Populism: The Politics of Empowerment.* Philadelphia: Temple University Press, 1986.

Braaten, Carl E. "Caring for the Future: Where Ethics and Ecology Meet." *Zygon* 9 (December 1974): 311–22.

———. "The Energy Crisis: A Blessing in Disguise?" *The Lutheran,* May 15, 1974, pp. 8–9.

Bramwell, Anna. *Ecology in the Twentieth Century.* New Haven: Yale University Press, 1989.

Bratton, Susan Power. "Christian Ecotheology and the Old Testament." In *Religion and Environmental Crisis,* ed. Eugene C. Hargrove, pp. 53–75. Athens: University of Georgia Press, 1986.

———. "The Original Desert Solitaire: Early Christian Monasticism and Wilderness." *Environmental Ethics* 10 (Spring 1988): B1–53.

Brockway, Allan R. "Environmental Stewardship." *Engage / Social Action,* January 1982, p. 37.

———. "The New Fad." *Engage / Social Action,* March 1970, p. 2.

———. "Toward a Theology of the Natural World." *Engage / Social Action,* July 1973, pp. 20–30.

———. "Toward a Theology of the Sea." *Engage / Social Action,* January 1978, pp. 16–23.

Brooke, Tal. *When the World Will Be as One: The Coming New World Order in the New Age.* Eugene, Ore.: Harvest Books, 1989.

Brown, Lester R. "Defusing the Population Timebomb." *Christian Century,* August 21, 1974, pp. 792–96.

Brown, Stephen. "Ecological Programs for the Local Church." In *Christian Ecology,* ed. Frederick W. Krueger, pp. 97–98. San Francisco: North American Conference on Christianity and Ecology, 1988.

Browning, Catherine. Review of *Creation Spirituality,* by Matthew Fox. *National Catholic Reporter,* September 6, 1991, p. 25.

Broyles, Vernon S., III. "We Are God's Partners in Preserving the World." *Presbyterian Survey,* October 1990, p. 13.

Brueggemann, Walter. " 'The Earth Is the Lord's.' A Theology of Earth and Land." *Sojourners* 15 (October 1986): 28–32.

Burhoe, Ralph Wendell. "Cosmic Evolutionary Creation and Christian God." In *Cry of the Environment,* ed. Philip N. Joranson and Ken Butigan, pp. 218–52. Santa Fe: Bear and Co., 1984.

Butman, Harry R. "The Strange, Continuing Glory." *Congregationalist* 149 (February/March 1989): 4–6.

Buttel, Frederick H. "Environmentalism for the Long Term: Beyond Global Warming." *The Egg: An Eco-Justice Quarterly* 11 (Summer 1991): 12–14.

Buttel, Frederick H., and William L. Finn. "Social Class and Mass Environmental Beliefs: A Reconsideration." *Environment and Behavior* 10 (July 1978): 433–50.

Cable, Ted T. "Environmental Education at Christian Colleges." *Perspectives on Science and Christian Faith* 39 (September 1987): 165–68.

Callicott, J. Baird. *In Defense of the Land Ethic: Essays in Environmental Philosophy.* Albany: State University of New York Press, 1989.

———. "Traditional American Indian and Traditional Western European Attitudes towards Nature: An Overview." In *Environmental Philosophy: A Collection of Readings*, ed. Robert Elliot and Arran Gare, pp. 231–59. University Park: Pennsylvania State University Press, 1983.

Cameron, Catherine M. "Hope for a Less Toxic Future." *Christian Century*, August 17–24, 1983, pp. 747–49.

Campolo, Tony. *How to Rescue the Earth without Worshipping Nature.* Nashville: Thomas Nelson, 1992.

Cannon, Katie G. *God's Fierce Whimsy: Christian Feminism and Theological Education.* New York: Pilgrim Press, 1985.

Card, Claudia. *Feminist Ethics.* Lawrence: University Press of Kansas, 1990.

Caring for God's Creation. Chicago: Evangelical Lutheran Church in America, 1989.

Carlson, Allan C. "Energy: The Crisis That Won't Go Away." *The Lutheran*, May 4, 1977, pp. 8–10.

Carlson, Donald F. "More Than a Bad Smell." *Lutheran Standard*, November 11, 1969, p. 15

Carothers, Edward J., Margaret Mead, Daniel D. McCracken, Roger L. Shinn, eds. *To Love or to Perish: The Technological Crisis and the Churches.* New York: Friendship Press, 1972.

Casebolt, Carl J., and Carol A. Robb, eds. *Covenant for a New Creation: Ethics, Religion and Public Policy.* Maryknoll, N.Y.: Orbis, 1991.

Caufield, Henry P. "The Conservation and Environmental Movements: An Historical Analysis." Chap. 2 in *Environmental Politics and Policy: Themes and Evidence*, ed. James P. Lester. Durham: Duke University Press, 1989.

Cauthern, Kenneth. *Christian Biopolitics.* Nashville: Abingdon, 1971.

Cesaretti, C. A., and Stephen Commins, eds. *Let the Earth Bless the Lord: A Christian Perspective on Land Use.* New York: Seabury, 1981.

Charles, J. Daryl. "Environmentalists and Eco-Terror in the Gulf: A Matter of Consistency." *World*, April 20, 1991, p. 16.

Cheng, Chung-ying. "On the Environmental Ethics of Tao and the Ch'i." *Environmental Ethics* 8 (Winter 1986): 351–70.

Chewing, Richard. "State of the World 1991, as Seen by Influential Environmentalists." *World*, March 16, 1991, p. 10.

Chicago, Judy. *The Dinner Party.* Garden City, N.Y.: Doubleday, 1979.

Christ, Carol P. *Laughter of Aphrodite: Reflections on a Journey to the Goddess.* San Francisco: Harper and Row, 1987.

———. "Why Women Need the Goddess." In *The Politics of Women's Spirituality*, ed. Charlene Spretnak, pp. 71–86. Garden City, N.Y.: Doubleday, 1982.

Christian Life Commission. *The Energy Crisis and the Churches.* Nashville, Tenn.: Southern Baptist Convention, 1977.

Cobb, John B., Jr. "Beyond Anthropocentrism in Ethics and Religion." In *On the*

Fifth Day: Animal Rights and Human Ethics, ed. Richard Knowles Morris and Michael W. Fox, pp. 137–53. Washington, D.C.: Acropolis, 1978.

——. "Christian Existence in a World of Limits." *Environmental Ethics* 1 (1979): 149–59; also in *Religion and Environmental Crisis*, ed. Eugene C. Hargrove, pp. 172–87. Athens: University of Georgia Press, 1986.

——. "Ecological Disaster and the Church." *Christian Century*, October 7, 1970, pp. 1185–87.

——. Review of *Bent World: A Christian Response to the Environmental Crisis*, by Ron Elsdon. *Environmental Ethics* 4 (Winter 1982): 359–62.

Cobb, John B., Jr. *Is It Too Late? A Theology of Ecology*. Berkeley, Calif.: Bruce, 1972.

——. "Overcoming Reductionism." In *Existence and Actuality: Conversations with Charles Hartshorne*, ed. John B. Cobb Jr. and Franklin Gramwell, pp. 149–64. Chicago: University of Chicago Press, 1984.

——. "Process Theology and an Ecological Model." In *Cry of the Environment*, ed. Philip N. Joranson and Ken Butigan, pp. 329–36. Santa Fe: Bear and Co., 1984.

——. Review of *Theology of Nature*, by George S. Hendry. *Zygon* 15 (December 1980): 436.

——. "Theology and Space." In *Beyond Spaceship Earth: Environmental Ethics and the Solar System*, ed. Eugene C. Hargrove, pp. 291–311. San Francisco: Sierra Club, 1986.

Cobb, John B., Jr., and Franklin Gramwell. *Existence and Actuality: Conversations with Charles Hartshorne*. Chicago: University of Chicago Press, 1984.

Cochran, Clarke. "The Thin Theory of Community." *Political Studies* 37 (September 1989): 422–35.

Commoner, Barry. *The Closing Circle*. New York: Knopf, 1971.

——. *Making Peace with the Planet*. New York: Pantheon, 1990.

Compton, Thomas L. "Natural Resources Stewardship: The Earth Is the Lord's." In *The Environmental Crisis*, ed. Edwin R. Squiers, pp. 109–14. Mancelona, Mich.: Au Sable Institute, 1982.

Cooper, Tim. *Green Christianity*. London: Hodder and Stoughton, 1990.

Corbett, J. Elliott. "U.S. Energy Program Passed by Congress." *Engage / Social Action*, January 1980, pp. 9–11.

——. "What Happened to President Carter's Energy Program?" *Engage / Social Action*, May 1980, pp. 36–39.

Craig, Robert H. *Religion and Radical Politics: An Alternative Christian Tradition in the United States*. Philadelphia: Temple University Press, 1992.

Daly, Herman E. "Bios, Theos, Logos" [Review of *The Liberation of Life*, by Charles Birch and John B. Cobb Jr.] *Christianity and Crisis*, July 12, 1982, pp. 216–18.

Daly, Herman E., and John B. Cobb Jr. *For the Common Good: Redirecting the Economy toward Community, the Environment, and a Sustainable Future*. Boston: Beacon Press, 1989.

Daly, Mary. *Beyond God the Father*. Boston: Beacon Press, 1973.

——. *Gyn/Ecology*. Boston: Beacon Press, 1978.

Davidson, Elisha. *Islam, Israel and the Last Days*. Eugene, Ore.: Harvest House, 1991.

Davis, Donald. "Ecosophy: The Seduction of Sophia." *Environmental Ethics* 8
(Summer 1986): 151–62.

Davis, Mary. "The Green Proposition." *Christian Century*, May 29, 1985, pp. 551–52.

Davis, Wayne H. "The Ecological Crisis." *Review and Expositor* 69 (Winter 1972): 5–
9.

Demarest, Bruce. "The Process Reduction of Jesus and the Trinity." In *Process
Theology*, ed. Ronald H. Nash, pp. 59–90. Grand Rapids, Mich.: Baker Book
House, 1987.

Derr, Thomas S. *Ecology and Human Need.* Philadelphia: Westminster, 1975.

Despot, Maggi. "All Creatures Great and Small." *Sojourners* 15 (February 1986): 50–
51.

Devall, Bill, and George Sessions. *Deep Ecology: Living as If Nature Mattered.* Salt
Lake City: G. M. Smith, 1985.

DeWitt, Calvin. "Christian Stewardship: Its Basis in the Cosmos, the Scriptures and
Spiritually." In *Christian Ecology*, ed. Frederick W. Krueger, pp. 20–21. San
Francisco: North American Conference on Christianity and Ecology, 1988.

———. Introduction to *Creation in Crisis: Responding to God's Covenant*, ed. Shantilal
Bhagat. Elgin, Ill.: Brethren Press, 1990.

———. Introduction to *The Environment and the Christian: What Can We Learn from the
New Testament?*, ed. Calvin B. DeWitt, pp. 13–23. Grand Rapids, Mich.: Baker,
1991.

———. "Postlude. A Hymn of Joy. A Steward's Hymn." In *Earthkeeping: Christian
Stewardship of Natural Resources*, ed. Loren Wilkinson, p. 293. Grand Rapids,
Mich.: Eerdmans, 1980.

———. "Respecting Creation's Integrity: Biblical Principles for Environmental
Responsibility." *Firmament*, Summer 1992, pp. 10–11 and 20–21.

———. "Statement." In *Christian Ecology*, ed. Frederick W. Krueger, p. 6. San
Francisco: North American Conference on Christianity and Ecology, 1988.

———, ed. *The Environment and the Christian: What Can We Learn from the New
Testament?* Grand Rapids, Mich.: Baker, 1991.

Diamond, Irene, and Gloria Feman Orenstein, eds. *Reweaving the World: The
Emergence of Ecofeminism.* San Francisco: Sierra Club, 1990.

Dickerson, Irene. "Appropriate Ecological Programs for Pastors and Churches." In
Christian Ecology, ed. Frederick W. Krueger, p. 101. San Francisco: North
American Conference on Christianity and Ecology, 1988.

———. "Protecting the Lord's Canvass" [interview of Calvin DeWitt]. *Christianity
Today*, November 18, 1988, pp. 74 and 76.

Diers, Judy. "Humanity and Environment: Precedence." *Christianity and Crisis*, May
14, 1990, pp. 146–47.

Dobel, J. Patrick. "Stewards of the Earth's Resources: A Christian Response to
Ecology." *Christian Century*, October 12, 1977, pp. 906–9.

Douglas, David. "Wild Country and Wildlife: A Spiritual Preserve." *Christian
Century*, January 4–11, 1984, pp. 11–13.

Dryzek, John S. *Rational Ecology.* Oxford: Basil Blackwell, 1987.

Dubin, Max. *Future Hype: The Tyranny of Prophecy.* New York: Viking, 1989.

Dubos, Rene. "Franciscan Conservation versus Benedictine Stewardship." In *Ecology and Religion in History*, ed. David Spring and Eileen Spring, pp. 114–37. New York: Harper, 1974.

——. *A God Within.* New York: Scribner's, 1972.

——. "A Theology of the Earth." In *Western Man and Environmental Ethics*, ed. Ian G. Barbour, pp. 43–54. Reading, Mass.: Addison-Wesley, 1973.

Dunlap, Riley E. "Public Opinion and Environmental Policy." In *Environmental Politics and Policy: Theories and Evidence*, ed. James P. Lester, pp. 87–134. Durham: Duke University Press, 1989.

Dyer, Charles H., and Angela E. Hunt. *The Rise of Babylon: Sign of the End Times.* Wheaton, Ill.: Tyndale House, 1991.

Dyrness, William. "Are We Our Planet's Keeper." *Christianity Today*, April 8, 1991, pp. 40–42.

——. "Stewardship of the Earth in the Old Testament." In *Tending the Garden: Essays on the Gospel and the Earth*, ed. Wesley Granberg-Michaelson, pp. 50–65. Grand Rapids, Mich.: Eerdmans, 1987.

Eckberg, Douglas Lee, and T. Jean Blocker. "Varieties of Religious Investment and Environmental Concerns: Testing the Lynn White Thesis." *Journal for Scientific Study of Religion* 28 (1989): 509–17.

Eckersley, Robyn. "Green Politics and the New Class: Selfishness or Virtue?" *Political Studies* 37 (June 1989): 205–23.

Eco-Justice Working Group of the National Council of Churches. Pamphlet on toxic poisoning.

"Ecology and the Church." *Review and Expositor* 69 (Winter 1972).

Editor. "Air Power and the Environmentalists." *Christian Century*, May 19, 1971, p. 613.

Editor. "Churches Find Ways to Conserve Energy." *The Lutheran*, May 21, 1980, p. 25.

Editor. "Churches Receive Energy Use Books." *Lutheran Standard*, November 20, 1979, p. 18.

Editor. "Churches Warned on Energy Crisis But Some See It as an Opportunity." *The Lutheran*, January 2, 1974, p. 18.

Editor. "A Collect for Environmental Sunday, May 7." *The Lutheran*, May 3, 1972, p. 5.

Editor. "Ecology Fair at CLC." *The Lutheran*, April 21, 1971, p. 45.

Editor. "Energy: Churches Combine Services for Conservation Witness." *The Lutheran*, January 16, 1980, p. 23.

Editor. "Energy Conservation, Innovation Boosted." *United Methodist Reporter*, February 16, 1979, p. 4.

Editor. "Energy Conservation Steps Recommended by ALC Unit." *Lutheran Standard*, February 5, 1980, p. 23.

Editor. "The Energy Crisis and Strip-Mining." *Christian Century*, April 25, 1973, pp. 467–68.

Editor. "Energy Weekend Set." *The Lutheran*, October 15, 1980, p. 19.

Editor. "For Earth, Peace." *Presbyterian Survey*, July / August 1990, p. 50.

Editor. "The Good Earth." *Lutheran Standard*, May 12, 1970, p. 38.

Editor. "Hymn Society Calls for Ecology Songs." *The Lutheran*, April 19, 1972, p. 34.

Editor. "Isaiah and Ecology." *Lutheran Standard*, June 9, 1970, p. 15.

Editor. "It's Not Easy Being Green." *Christianity Today*, May 18, 1992, p. 14.

Editor. "LCA Group Named to Study Human Crisis in Ecology." *The Lutheran*, June 2, 1971, p. 34.

Editor. "LCA Offices Cut Energy Use 17 Percent." *The Lutheran*, September 19, 1979, p. 18.

Editor. "LCA to Get Statements on Ecology." *The Lutheran*, April 19, 1972, p. 29.

Editor. "Let Us Opt for Ecology Rather Than Energy." *Engage / Social Action*, July 1975, pp. 2–4.

Editor. "Listening to God during Drought." *Christianity Today*, August 6, 1976, p. 25.

Editor. "Living Better with Less." *Christianity Today*, April 26, 1974, pp. 28–29.

Editor. "Lutheran Biologist Warns of Environmental Disaster." *The Lutheran*, February 21, 1973, p. 31.

Editor. "May 7 to be Observed as Environmental Sunday." *The Lutheran*, April 19, 1972, p. 32.

Editor. "N.C. Congregations Reduce Energy Use." *The Lutheran*, May 20, 1981, p. 30.

Editor. "NCC Sees Positive Value in Energy Crisis." *The Lutheran*, January 23, 1974, p. 19.

Editor. "Pastors' Conference Told of Environmental Crisis." *The Lutheran*, February 3, 1971, p. 36.

Editor. "Pollution, Christian Faithfulness." *United Methodist Reporter*, May 13, 1983, p. 2.

Editor. "Presbyterians This Week." *Presbyterian Survey*, September 6, 1971, p. 10.

Editor. "Religious Leaders Urge Cooperation on Energy." *The Lutheran*, February 20, 1980, p. 23.

Editor. "Saving Energy: Churches Combine Services for Conservation Witness." *Lutheran Standard*, February 5, 1980, p. 21.

Editor. "Social Issues That Call Christians to Respond." *Engage / Social Action*, December 1980, pp. 32–33.

Editor. "Social Principles Summary." *Engage / Social Action*, June 1972, pp. 32–33.

Editor. "The Steward-ship." *Presbyterian Survey*, July 1972, p. 17.

Editor. "Stewardship Is . . . ?" *Presbyterian Survey*, October 1987, p. 33.

Editor. "To Live Is to Pollute." *Christianity Today*, September 27, 1974, p. 38.

Editor. "UPUSA Deliberates in Rochester, N.Y." *Presbyterian Survey*, June 21, 1971, pp. 8, 10.

Editor, LCA Board of Social Ministry. "Ecology: We Must Act Now." *The Lutheran*, May 3, 1972, pp. 9–12.

"Education Models: Four Current Programs." In *Cry of the Environment*, ed. Philip N. Joranson and Ken Butigan, pp. 441–56. Santa Fe: Bear and Co., 1984.

Ehlers, Vernon J. "Christian Stewardship of Energy Resources—Twenty Theses." In *The Environmental Crisis*, ed. Edwin R. Squiers, pp. 331–42. Mancelona, Mich.: Au Sable Institute, 1982.

Ehrlich, Paul, and Anne H. Ehrlich. *The Population Explosion.* New York: Simon and Schuster, 1990.

Eisler, Riane. "The Gaia Tradition and the Partnership Future: An Ecofeminism Manifesto." In *Reweaving the World: The Emergence of Ecofeminism,* ed. Irene Diamond and Gloria Feman Orenstein, pp. 23–34. San Francisco: Sierra Club, 1990.

Elder, Frederick. *Crisis in Eden: A Religious Study of Man and Environment.* Washington, D.C.: Abingdon, 1970.

Ellingsen, Mark. *The Cutting Edge: How Churches Speak on Social Issues.* Grand Rapids, Mich.: Eerdmans, 1993.

Elliot, Robert, and Arran Gare. *Environmental Philosophy: A Collection of Readings.* University Park: Pennsylvania State University Press, 1983.

Elshtain, Jean Bethke. *Public Man, Private Woman.* Princeton: Princeton University Press, 1981.

Elwood, Douglas J. "Primitivism or Technology: Must We Choose?" *Christian Century,* December 1, 1971, pp. 1413–18.

The Energy Crisis and the Churches. Nashville, Tenn.: Southern Baptist Convention, Christian Life Commission, 1977.

Engel, David E. "Elements in a Theology of Environment." *Zygon* 5–6 (September 1970): 216–28.

Engel, J. Ronald. *Sacred Sands: The Struggle for Community in the Indiana Dunes.* Middletown, Conn.: Wesleyan University Press, 1983.

Ensign, Stewart E. "The Response of the Church to Shrinking Petroleum Availability." In *The Environmental Crisis,* ed. Edwin R. Squiers, pp. 315–30. Mancelona, Mich.: Au Sable Institute, 1982.

Environmental Stewardship. Washington, D.C.: The United Methodist General Board of Church and Society, 1990.

"Episcopalians Fail to Resolve Sexuality Issues." *Christianity Today,* August 19, 1991, p. 46.

Fagley, Richard M. "Earth Day and After." *Christian Century,* April 15, 1970, pp. 440–42.

Faramelli, Norman. "No Easy Choices on Energy Problems." *Engage / Social Action,* January 1977, pp. 6–11.

———. "Religious Reconstruction for the Environmental Future." In *Religious Reconstruction for the Environmental Future,* ed. Philip N. Joranson and C. Alan Anderson, Fa1–29. Storrs, Conn.: Office of Environmental Education, 1973.

———. *Technethics: Christian Mission in an Age of Technology.* New York: Friendship Press, 1971.

Faulkner, David. "Technology Isn't the Enemy." *World,* April 20, 1991, p. 21.

Ferkiss, Victor. *The Future of Technological Civilization.* New York: George Braziller, 1974.

Fey, Harold E. "Some Notes on 'Global 2000': Entering the Twenty-First Century." *Christian Century,* July 1–8, 1981, pp. 698–701.

Findlay, James F., Jr. *Church People in the Struggle: The National Council of Churches and the Black Freedom Movement, 1950–1970.* New York: Oxford University Press, 1993.

Finger, Rita. "Editorial." *Daughters of Sarah* 16 (May/June 1990): 2.

Finger, Thomas. "Modern Alienation and Trinitarian Creation." Paper presented at the World Evangelical Fellowship/Au Sable Forum, 1992.

Finke, Roger, and Rodney Stark. *The Churching of America, 1776–1990: Winners and Losers in Our Religious Economy.* New Brunswick: Rutgers University Press, 1992.

Finnin, William M., Jr. "Assessing Lifeboat Ethics." *Christian Century,* July 4–11, 1979, pp. 708–10.

Forbes, James A. "Preaching in the Contemporary World." In *For Creation's Sake,* ed. Dieter T. Hessel, pp. 45–54. Philadelphia: Geneva, 1985.

Foreman, Dave. *Confessions of an Eco-Warrior.* New York: Harmony, 1991.

Fowler, Dean R. "Retrospective: Alfred North Whitehead." *Zygon* 11 (March 1976): 50–69.

Fowler, Robert Booth. *The Dance with Community.* Lawrence: University Press of Kansas, 1991.

———. *A New Engagement: Evangelical Political Thought 1966–1976.* Grand Rapids, Mich.: Eerdmans, 1982.

———. *Religion and Politics in the United States.* Metuchen, N.J.: Scarecrow Press, 1985.

———. *Unconventional Partners: Religion and Liberal Culture in the United States.* Grand Rapids, Mich.: Eerdmans, 1989.

Fox, Matthew. *Creation Spirituality: Liberating Gifts for the Peoples of the Earth.* San Francisco: Harper, 1991.

———. *Original Blessing: A Primer in Creation Spirituality.* Santa Fe: Bear and Co., 1983.

———. *Western Spirituality: Historical Roots, Ecumenical Routes.* Santa Fe: Bear and Co., 1981.

———. *Whee! We, Wee All the Way Home: A Guide to a Sensual, Prophetic Spirituality.* Santa Fe: Bear and Co., 1981.

Fox, Thomas C. "Approach the Ecozoic Period of Earth History." *National Catholic Reporter,* September 6, 1991, p. 21.

Fracke, Gabriel. "Ecology and Theology." In *Western Man and Environmental Ethics,* ed. Ian G. Barbour, pp. 116–31. Reading, Mass.: Addison-Wesley, 1973.

Frame, Randy. "Planetary Justice." *Christianity Today,* November 18, 1988, p. 74.

Freudenberger, C. Dean. *Global Dust Bowl: Can We Stop the Destruction of the Land Before It's Too Late?* Minneapolis: Augsburg, 1990.

Fry, C. George. "Brown Boy." *Congregationalist* 148 (October/November 1988): 21, 26.

Gallup, George, Jr., and Jim Castelli. *The People's Religion: American Faith in the 1990s.* New York: Macmillan, 1989.

Garrow, David J. *Bearing the Cross: Martin Luther King, Jr., and the Southern Christian Leadership Conference.* New York: William Morrow, 1986.

Gelderloos, Orin G. "Leadership in Environmental Ethics." In *The Environmental Crisis,* ed. Edwin R. Squiers, pp. 345–61. Mancelona, Mich.: Au Sable Institute, 1982.

General Executive Board. "Environment Resources," Vol. 2. *Presbyterian Survey,* April 1974, p. 19.

Gibson, William E. "Beginning a 'turnaround decade'?" *Christianity and Crisis,* May 14, 1990, pp. 147–49.

——. "The Conundrum of Oil: Less Would Be Better." *The Egg: An Eco-Justice Quarterly* 11 (Summer 1991): 4–7.

——. "Eco-Justice: New Perspectives for a Time of Turning." In *For Creation's Sake,* ed. Dieter T. Hessel, pp. 15–31. Philadelphia: Westminster, 1985.

Giles, Jeanne. "Restoring Creation: Environment Paper Wins Approval." *Presbyterian Survey,* July / August 1990, p. 25.

Glacken, Clarence J. "Man's Place in Nature in Recent Western Thought." In *This Little Planet,* ed. Michael Hamilton, pp. 163–201. New York: Scribner's, 1970.

——. *Traces on the Rhodian Shore.* Berkeley: University of California Press, 1967.

Goldenberg, Naomi R. *Changing of the Gods: Feminism and the End of Traditional Religions.* Boston: Beacon Press, 1979.

Goldsmith, Edward. "Gaia: Some Implications for Theoretical Biology." *The Ecologist* 18 (1988): 64–74.

"Goodbye Armageddon." *Christianity Today,* May 27, 1991, p. 57.

Goodman, Russell. "Taoism and Ecology." *Environmental Ethics* 2 (Spring 1980): pp. 73–80.

Gottwald, Norman K. "The Biblical Mandate for Eco-Justice Action." In *For Creation's Sake,* ed. Dieter T. Hessel, pp. 32–44. Philadelphia: Geneva, 1985.

"Graham Group Fails Standards." *Christian Century,* January 31, 1979, p. 94.

Granberg-Michaelson, Wesley. "At the Dawn of the New Creation: A Theology of the Environment." *Sojourners* 10 (November 1981): 12–16.

——. "Earth Keeping." *Sojourners* 11 (October 1982): 20–24.

——. "The Ethics of Strip-Mining Coal in Montana." In *The Environmental Crisis,* ed. Edwin R. Squiers, pp. 293–307. Mancelona, Mich.: Au Sable Institute, 1982.

——. "The Goodness of Creation: A Biblical Framework for Addressing the Ecological Crisis." *Christian Social Action,* March 1989, pp. 8–12.

——. Introduction to *Tending the Garden: Essays on the Gospel and the Earth.* Grand Rapids, Mich.: Eerdmans, 1987.

——. "Why Christians Lost an Environmental Ethic." In *Christian Ecology,* ed. Frederick W. Krueger, pp. 22–23. San Francisco: North American Conference on Christianity and Ecology, 1988.

——. *A Worldly Spirituality: The Call to Redeem Life on Earth.* San Francisco: Harper and Row, 1984.

——, ed. *Tending the Garden: Essays on the Gospel and the Earth.* Grand Rapids, Mich.: Eerdmans, 1987.

Gray, Elizabeth Dodson. *Green Paradise Lost.* 2d ed. Wellesley, Mass.: Roundtable, 1981.

——. *Why the Green Nigger? Re-Mything Genesis.* Wellesley, Mass.: Roundtable, 1979.

Grebe, Margaret. "Witchcraft." Unpublished paper, 1993.

Greber, Brian, and K. Norman Johnson. "What's All This Debate about Overcutting?" *Journal of Forestry* 89, no. 11 (1991): 25–30.

Griffin, David. "Whitehead's Contributions to a Theology of Nature." *Bucknell Review* 20 (Winter 1972): 3–24.

Griffin, Susan. "Curves along the Road." In *Reweaving the World: The Emergence of Ecofeminism*, ed. Irene Diamond and Gloria Feman Orenstein, pp. 87–99. San Francisco: Sierra Club, 1990.

———. "Split Culture." In *Healing the Wounds: The Promise of Ecofeminism*, ed. Judith Plant, pp. 7–17. Philadelphia: New Society, 1989.

———. *Woman and Nature: The Roaring Inside Her.* New York: Harper, 1978.

Gundersen, Adolf. *Finding the Kosmos in the Agora.* Ph.D. diss., University of Wisconsin–Madison, 1990.

———. "Native American Political Theory: The Lesson for Contemporary Ecological Governance." Paper, Fourth Annual Symposium on Society and Resource Management, May 1992.

Guth, James L., John C. Green, Lyman A. Kellstedt, and Corwin E. Smidt. "Faith and the Environment: Religious Beliefs and Attitudes on Environmental Policy." Paper presented at the annual meeting of the Southern Political Science Association, Atlanta, Ga., November 1993.

Hall, Douglas John. *Imaging God: Dominion as Stewardship.* Grand Rapids, Mich.: Eerdmans, 1986.

Hamilton, Michael. *This Little Planet.* New York: Scribner's, 1970.

Hand, Carl M., and Kent D. Van Liere. "Religion, Mastery-Over-Nature, and Environmental Concern." *Social Forces* 63 (December 1984): 555–70.

Hanson, Jaydee. "Fifty-Two Weeks of Congregational Activities to Save the Earth." *101 Ways to Help Save the Earth.* New York: Eco-Justice Working Group of the National Council of Churches, 1990, pp. 27–35.

Haraway, Donna. *Primate Visions: Gender, Race, and Nature in the World of Modern Science.* New York: Routledge, 1989.

Hardin, Garrett. "Ecology and the Death of Providence." *Zygon* 15 (March 1980): 57–67.

———. *Living within Limits.* New York: Oxford University Press, 1993.

Harding, Sandra. *The Science Question in Feminism: Whose Science? Whose Knowledge?* Ithaca: Cornell University Press, 1986.

Hargrove, Eugene C. *Beyond Spaceship Earth: Environmental Ethics and the Solar System.* San Francisco: Sierra Club, 1986.

———. Preface to *Religion and Environmental Crisis*, ed. Eugene C. Hargrove. Athens: University of Georgia Press, 1986.

———, ed. *Religion and Environmental Crisis.* Athens: University of Georgia Press, 1986.

Harris Survey for the United Nations Environmental Program, 1989.

Hartshorne, Charles. "Foundations for a Humane Ethics." Richard Knowles Morris and Michael W. Fox, eds. *On the Fifth Day: Animal Rights and Human Ethics.* Washington, D.C.: Acropolis, 1978, pp. 154–72.

———. "How I Got That Way." In *Existence and Actuality: Conversations with Charles Hartshorne*, ed. John B. Cobb Jr. and Franklin Gramwell, pp. ix–xvii. Chicago: University of Chicago Press, 1984.

———. *Reality as Social Process.* Glencoe, Ill.: Free Press, 1953.

———. "Response by Charles Hartshorne." In *Existence and Actuality: Conversations with Charles Hartshorne*, ed. John B. Cobb Jr. and Franklin Gramwell. Chicago: University of Chicago Press, 1984.

Hartt, Julain N. "Faith and the Informed Use of Natural Resources." In *A New Ethic for a New Earth*, ed. Glenn Stone. New York: Faith-Man-Nature Group, 1971.

Hatch, Mark H. "When the Dump Is in 'Our' Backyard." *Christian Century*, July 7–12, 1989, p. 660.

Hauerwas, Stanley. "The Ethics of the Population and Pollution." *Engage*, August 1–15, 1970, pp. 8–11.

Hawksley, Richard Lee. "Redefining the Family in the 'Family Farm': Ecological Justice and the Biblical Call to Community." In *Christian Ecology*, ed. Frederick W. Krueger, pp. 44–45. San Francisco: North American Conference on Christianity and Ecology, 1988.

Heffernan, James D. "The Land Ethic: A Critical Appraisal." *Environmental Ethics* 4 (Fall 1982): 235–47.

Hefner, Philip, ed. *The Sense of Grace: Essays on Nature and Grace in Honor of Joseph Sittler*. Philadelphia: Fortress, 1964.

Heine, Susanne. *Matriarchs, Goddesses, and Images of God: A Critique of a Feminist Theology*. Minneapolis: Augsburg, 1988.

Heinegg, Peter. "Ecology and the Fall." *Christian Century*, May 12, 1976, p. 464.

Hendry, George S. *Theology of Nature*. Philadelphia: Westminster, 1980.

Henry, Carl F. H. "The Stunted God of Process Theology." In *Process Theology*, ed. Ronald H. Nash, pp. 357–76. Grand Rapids, Mich.: Baker, 1987.

Herman, Steward W. "A Powerful Vision with Flaws." *Christianity and Crisis*, September 17–October 1, 1979, p. 218.

Hertzke, Allen. *Representing God in Washington: The Role of Religious Lobbies in the American Polity*. Knoxville: University of Tennessee Press, 1988.

Herzog, Don. *Without Foundations*. Ithaca: Cornell University Press, 1985.

Hessel, Dieter T., ed. *For Creation's Sake, Preaching, Ecology, and Justice*. Philadelphia: Geneva, 1985.

———. "Preaching for Creation's Sake: A Theological Framework." In *For Creation's Sake: Preaching, Ecology, and Justice*, ed. Dieter T. Hessel, pp. 115–28. Philadelphia: Geneva, 1985.

———, ed. *After Nature's Revolt: Eco-Justice and Theology*. Minneapolis: Fortress, 1992.

Hiebert, Theodore. "Ecology and the Bible." *Daughters of Sarah* 16 (May/June 1990): 12–13.

Hiers, Richard H. "Ecology, Biblical Theology, and Methodology: Biblical Perspectives on the Environment." *Zygon* 19 (1984): 43–60.

Himes, Michael J. Reviews of *Religion in an Age of Science*, by Ian Barbour, *God and Creation: An Ecumenical Symposium*, edited by David B. Burrell and Bernard McGinn, and *The God Who Would Be Known*, by John Templeton and Robert L. Herrmann. *America*, June 1, 1991, p. 604.

Hindson, Ed. *End Times, The Middle East, and the New World Order*. Wheaton, Ill.: Victor Books, 1991.

Holmes, Arthur F. "Why God Cannot Act." In *Process Theology*, ed. Ronald H. Nash, pp. 177–95. Grand Rapids, Mich.: Baker, 1987.

Holmes, Stephen. *The Anatomy of Anti-Liberalism*. Cambridge: Harvard University Press, 1993.

Hope, Marjorie, and James Young. "Thomas Berry and a New Creation Story." *Christian Century*, August 16–23, 1989, pp. 750–53.

Hotchkiss, Wesley A. "Conservation of Natural Resources." *Advance*, June 15, 1955, pp. 21–23.

Hough, Joseph, Jr. "Land and People: The Eco-Justice Connection." *Christian Century*, October 1, 1980, pp. 910–14.

Houston, James M. "The Environmental Movement—Five Causes of Confusion." *Christianity Today*, September 15, 1972, pp. 8–10.

Hovey, Gail. "Questions after Earth Day." *Christianity and Crisis*, May 14, 1990, p. 139.

Howell, Leon. "Legislators Must Tip-Toe through a Minefield of Difficult Issues." *Engage/Social Action*, April 1982, pp. 41–46.

Hoyt, John A. "A Matter of Choice." *Congregationalist* 136 (March 1976): 13–16.

Hoyt, Robert. "The Pragmatics of Energy." *Christianity and Crisis*, September 17–October 1, 1979, p. 212.

Hoyt, William R. "Zen Buddhism and Western Alienation from Nature." *Christian Century*, October 7, 1970, pp. 1194–96.

Humphreys, W. Lee. "Pitfalls and Promises of Biblical Texts as a Basis for a Theology of Nature." In *A New Ethic for a New Earth*, ed. Glenn C. Stone, pp. 99–118. New York: Faith-Man-Nature Group, 1971.

Hunt, Dave. *Global Peace and the Rise of the Anti-Christ*. Eugene: Harvest, 1990.

——. *Peace, Prosperity, and the Coming Holocaust*. Eugene: Harvest House, 1983.

Imsland, Donald. *Celebrate the Earth*. Minneapolis: Augsburg, 1971.

——. "Celebrate the Earth." *The Lutheran*, July 21, 1971, pp. 12–13.

Ingram, Kristen Johnson. "Break Forth Together into Singing: A Christian Feminist Broods over Her Planet." *Daughters of Sarah* 16 (May/June 1990): 28–30.

Newsletter of the International Society for Environmental Ethics, Vol. 1.

Jackson, Martin Allan. "Turning Ecology Inside Out." *Lutheran Standard*, August 4, 1970, p. 3.

James, Edgar C. *Arabs, Oil and Armageddon*. Chicago: Moody Press, 1977.

Jeffrey, Grant R. *Armageddon: Appointment with Destiny*. New York: Bantam, 1990.

Johnston, James M. "They Bicycle, Recycle, Restructure, Petition, Educate and Clean Up for Ecology." *The Lutheran*, November 3, 1971, pp. 7–9.

Johnston, Robert K. "Wisdom Literature and Its Contribution to a Biblical Environmental Ethic." In *Tending the Garden: Essays on the Gospel and the Earth*, ed. Wesley Granberg-Michaelson, pp. 66–82. Grand Rapids, Mich.: Eerdmans, 1987.

Joranson, Philip N. "The Faith-Man-Nature Group and a Religious Environmental Ethic." *Zygon* 12 (June 1977): 175–79.

——. "Prayer, Meditation, and Creation Consciousness." In *Cry of the Environment*, ed. Philip N. Joranson and Ken Butigan, pp. 347–54. Santa Fe: Bear and Co., 1984.

Joranson, Philip N., and C. Alan Anderson, eds. *Religious Reconstruction for the Environmental Future*. Storrs, Conn.: Office of Environmental Education, 1973.

Joranson, Philip N., and Ken Butigan, eds. *Cry of the Environment*. Santa Fe: Bear and Co., 1984.

——. "Elements of Creation-Conscious Life Style." In *Cry of the Environment*, ed. Philip N. Joranson and Ken Butigan, pp. 436–40. Santa Fe: Bear and Co., 1984.

——. Introduction to *Cry of the Environment*. Santa Fe: Bear and Co., 1984.

——. "The New Road Ahead." In *Cry of the Environment*, ed. Philip N. Joranson and Ken Butigan, pp. 457–64. Santa Fe: Bear and Co., 1984.

Jordan, Peter A. "An Ecologist Responds." In *A New Ethic for a New Earth*, ed. Glenn C. Stone, pp. 86–98. New York: Faith-Man-Nature Group, 1971.

Jung, Hwa Yol. "Ecology, Zen, and Western Religious Thought." *Christian Century*, November 15, 1972, pp. 1153–56.

Kanagy, Conrad, and Fern Willits. "A 'Greening' of Religion?: Some Evidence from a Pennsylvania Sample." *Social Science Quarterly* 74 (1993): 674–83.

Kassian, Mary A. *The Feminist Gospel: The Movement to Unite Feminism with the Church*. Wheaton, Ill.: Crossway, 1992.

Kaufman, Gordon D. "A Problem for Theology." *Harvard Theological Review* 65 (1972): 337–66.

Kay, Jeanne. "Concepts of Nature in the Hebrew Bible." *Environmental Ethics* 10 (Winter 1988): 309–27.

Keehan, Boyd. "The Energy Crisis and Its Meaning for American Culture." *Christian Century*, July 18, 1973, pp. 756–59.

Keller, Catherine. "The Step beyond Metaphor." *Christianity and Crisis*, November 9, 1987, pp. 386–88.

Keller, Evelyn Fox. *Secrets of Life, Secrets of Death: Essays on Language, Gender and Science*. New York: Routledge, 1992.

Kellstedt, Lyman A. "Letter to Respondents: Report on 1990 Survey of Religious Activists." Wheaton, Ill.: Wheaton College, 1991.

Kellstedt, Lyman A., et al. "Theological Perspectives and Environmentalism among Religious Activists: A Preliminary Look." Paper presented at the Conference on Christian Political Activism, Calvin College, October 1992.

Kheel, Marti. "Ecofeminism and Deep Ecology: Reflections on Identity and Difference." In *Reweaving the World: The Emergence of Ecofeminism*, ed. Irene Diamond and Gloria Feman Orenstein, pp. 128–37. San Francisco: Sierra Club, 1990.

Kile, Frederick. "Charting Economic Impact." *Lutheran Standard*, September 6, 1977, pp. 31–33.

Killingsworth, M. Jimmie, and Jacqueline S. Palmer. *Ecospeak: Rhetoric and Environmental Politics in America*. Carbondale: Southern Illinois University Press, 1992.

King, Ynestra. "The Ecology of Feminism and the Feminism of Ecology." In *Healing the Wounds: The Promise of Ecofeminism*, ed. Judith Plant, pp. 18–28. Philadelphia: New Society, 1989.

——. "Healing the Wounds: Feminism, Ecology, and the Nature/Culture Dualism."

In *Reweaving the World: The Emergence of Ecofeminism*, ed. Irene Diamond and Gloria Feman Orenstein, pp. 106–21. San Francisco: Sierra Club, 1990.

Kirban, Salem. *666*. Wheaton, Ill.: Tyndale, 1970.

Kirkland, Les Ann. "Church Activism to Stop Toxic Pollution." In *Christian Ecology*, ed. Frederick W. Krueger, pp. 105–6. San Francisco: North American Conference on Christianity and Ecology, 1988.

Kjos, Berit. *Under the Spell of Mother Earth*. Wheaton, Ill.: Victor Books, 1992.

Kortrey, Walter A. "Keeping a Good Green Earth." *The Lutheran*, April 2, 1975, p. 13.

Kroll, LeRoy C. "Technology: Modern Ebal or Gerizim? A Chemist's Perspective." In *The Environmental Crisis*, ed. Edwin R. Squiers, pp. 177–86. Mancelona, Mich.: Au Sable Institute, 1982.

Krueger, Frederick W. *Christian Ecology, Being an Environmental Ethic for the Twenty-First Century: The Proceedings from the First North American Conference on Christianity and Ecology*. San Francisco: North American Conference on Christianity and Ecology, 1988.

——. "Wilderness Retreats, Part Three." In *Christian Ecology*, p. 57. San Francisco: North American Conference on Christianity and Ecology, 1988.

Kuby, Dennis G. "A Day of Ecological Atonement?" *Christian Century*, March 27, 1974, p. 335.

LaBar, Martin. "A Biblical Perspective on Nonhuman Organisms: Values, Moral Considerability, and Moral Agency." In *Religion and Environmental Crisis*, ed. Eugene C. Hargrove, pp. 76–93. Athens: University of Georgia Press, 1986.

——. "A Message to Polluters from the Bible." *Christianity Today*, July 26, 1974, pp. 8–12.

Lacey, Michael J. *Governmental and Environmental Politics*. Washington, D.C.: Wilson Center, 1989.

Lasch, Christopher. *Haven in a Heartless World*. New York: Basic Books, 1977.

——. *The True and Only Heaven: Progress and Its Critics*. New York: Norton, 1991.

Lee, Dixie Ray. *Trashing the Planet*. Washington, D.C.: Regnery-Gateway, 1990.

Lefkowitz, Mary. "The Twilight of the Goddess." *The New Republic*, August 3, 1992, pp. 29–33.

Leopold, Aldo. "Conservation as a Moral Issue." In *Ethics and the Environment*, ed. Don Scherer and Thomas Attig, pp. 9–12. Englewood Cliffs, N.J.: Prentice Hall, 1983.

——. "The Land Ethic." In *Ethics and the Environment*, ed. Don Scherer and Thomas Attig, pp. 6–9. Englewood Cliffs, N.J.: Prentice Hall, 1983.

——. *A Sand County Almanac*. New York: Oxford University Press, 1949.

Lepkowski, Helene, and Wil Lepkowski. "Opportunities and Obstacles in Relating Christian Salvation Belief to Ecological Renewal." In *Christian Ecology*, ed. Frederick W. Krueger, p. 103. San Francisco: North American Conference on Christianity and Ecology, 1988.

Lester, James P. *Environmental Politics and Policy: Theories and Evidence*. Durham: Duke University Press, 1989.

Lindsey, Hal. *The Late Great Planet Earth*. 1970. Reprint, New York: Bantam, 1981.

——. *The 1980s: Countdown to Armageddon*. New York: Bantam, 1981.

Linzey, Andrew. *Christianity and the Rights of Animals*. New York: Crossroad, 1989.

Lischer, Richard. "From Earth to Heaven: Teilhard's Politics and Eschatology." *Christian Century*, April 9, 1975, pp. 352–57.

Livingston, James C. "The Ecological Challenge to Christian Ethics." *Christian Century*, December 1, 1971, pp. 1409–12.

Loades, Ann, ed. *Feminist Theology*. Louisville: Westminster, 1990.

Lohman, Charles. "A Theo-ecology of Diet." In *Christian Ecology*, ed. Frederick W. Krueger, pp. 35–36. San Francisco: North American Conference on Christianity and Ecology, 1988.

Loomer, Bernard M. "A Process-Relational Conception of Creation." In *Cry of the Environment*, ed. Philip N. Joranson and Ken Butigan, pp. 321–28. Santa Fe: Bear and Co., 1984.

Lovelock, James. *Gaia: A New Look at Life on Earth*. New York: Oxford University Press, 1987.

Lovins, Amory, and Hunter Lovins. "Energy by the People, Energy for the People." *Christianity and Crisis*, March 17, 1980, pp. 51–57.

Lowdermilk, Walter C. "The Eleventh Commandment." *American Forests* 46 (January 1940): 12–15.

Loy, R. Philip. "Politics and the Environment: Toward a New Public Philosophy." In *The Environmental Crisis*, ed. Edwin R. Squiers, pp. 209–26. Mancelona, Mich.: Au Sable Institute, 1982.

Lutz, Paul. "An Interdependent World." In *Ecological Renewal*, ed. Paul Lutz and H. Paul Santmire, pp. 1–74. Philadelphia: Fortress, 1972.

——. "Interrelatedness: Ecological Pattern of the Creation." In *Cry of the Environment*, ed. Philip N. Joranson and Ken Butigan, pp. 253–74. Santa Fe: Bear and Co., 1984.

Lutz, Paul, and H. Paul Santmire, eds. *Ecological Renewal*. Philadelphia: Fortress, 1972.

Lynch, Timothy B. "Two Worlds Join to 'Preserve the Earth.'" *Christianity and Crisis*, May 14, 1990, pp. 142–44.

McAllister, Jo Ann. "Creation-Centered Spirituality: Healing Ourselves, Healing the Earth." In *Christian Ecology*, ed. Frederick W. Krueger, p. 26. San Francisco: North American Conference on Christianity and Ecology, 1988.

McCloskey, H. J. *Ecological Ethics and Politics*. Totowa, N.J.: Rowman and Littlefield, 1983.

McCoy, Charles S. "Covenant, Creation, and Ethics: A Federal Vision for Humanity and the Environment." In *Cry of the Environment*, ed. Philip N. Joranson and Ken Butigan, pp. 355–75. Santa Fe: Bear and Co., 1984.

McCoy, Marjorie Casebier. "Feminist Consciousness in Creation: Tell Them the World Was Made for Women, Too." In *Cry of the Environment*, ed. Philip N. Joranson and Ken Butigan, pp. 132–47. Santa Fe: Bear and Co., 1984.

McCullough, Harold. "The Death of a Mountain." *Engage/Social Action*, March 1973, pp. 24–33.

McDaniel, Jay B. "Christianity and the Need for New Vision." In *Religion and*

Environmental Crisis, ed. Eugene C. Hargrove, pp. 188–212. Athens: University of Georgia Press, 1986.

——. "Christian Spirituality as Openness to Fellow Creatures." *Environmental Ethics* 8 (Spring 1986): 33–46.

——. *Earth, Sky, Gods, and Mortals*. Mystic, Conn.: Twenty-Third Publications, 1990.

——. *Of God and Pelicans: A Theology of Life*. Louisville: Westminster, 1989.

McFague, Sallie. Address to the Conference on Human Values and the Environment, Institute for Environmental Studies, University of Wisconsin–Madison, October 1, 1992.

——. *Models of God: Theology for an Ecological, Nuclear Age*. Philadelphia: Fortress, 1987.

——. "The World as God's Body." *Christian Century*, July 20–27, 1988, pp. 671–73.

McHarg, Ian L. *Design with Nature*. Garden City, N.Y.: Natural History Press, 1969.

MacIntyre, Alasdair. *After Virtue: A Study in Moral Theory*. Notre Dame: University of Notre Dame Press, 1981.

McKindley-Ward, Steve. "Christian Ecologists Work toward Common Agenda." *Sojourners* 16 (November 1987): 11.

Madison, Norman. "How Can You and Your Congregation Save Energy?" *Lutheran Standard*, March 4, 1980, p. 37.

Malloch, Theodore R. "U.S. Energy Policy: Past, Present, and Future." In *The Environmental Crisis*, ed. Edwin R. Squiers, pp. 261–78. Mancelona, Mich.: Au Sable Institute, 1982.

Manahan, Ronald. "Christ as the Second Adam." Chap. 2 in *The Environment and the Christian: What Can We Learn from the New Testament?*, ed. Calvin B. DeWitt. Grand Rapids, Mich.: Baker, 1991.

Manes, Christopher. *Green Rage: Radical Environmentalism and the Unmaking of Civilization*. Evanston, Ill.: Times Change, 1989.

Mann, Dean, ed. *Environmental Policy Formation: The Impact of Values, Ideology, and Standards*. Lexington, Mass.: D. C. Heath, 1981.

Mansbridge, Jane. *Beyond Adversary Democracy*. Chicago: University of Chicago Press, 1983.

Matthies, Milo M. "Explore Your Church for Energy Leaks." *Congregationalist*, February/March 1986, pp. 6–7.

Maxwell, Joe. "Prophecy Books Become Big Sellers." *Christianity Today*, March 11, 1991, p. 60.

Meine, Curt. *Aldo Leopold*. Madison: University of Wisconsin Press, 1988.

Merchant, Carolyn. *The Death of Nature: Women, Ecology, and the Scientific Revolution*. San Francisco: Harper and Row, 1980.

——. "Ecofeminism and Feminist Theory." In *Reweaving the World: The Emergence of Ecofeminism*, ed. Irene Diamond and Gloria Feman Orenstein, pp. 100–105. San Francisco: Sierra Club, 1990.

——. *Radical Ecology: The Search for a Livable World*. New York: Routledge, 1992.

Meye, Robert P. "Invitation to Wonder: Toward a Theology of Nature." In *Tending the Garden: Essays on the Gospel and the Earth*, ed. Wesley Granberg-Michaelson, pp. 30–49. Grand Rapids, Mich.: Eerdmans, 1987.

Meyer, Art, and Joale Meyer. *Earthkeepers: Environmental Perspectives on Hunger, Poverty, and Injustice.* Scottsdale, Pa.: Herald Press, 1991.

Milbrath, Lester W. *Environmentalists, Vanguard for a New Society.* Albany: State University of New York Press, 1984.

Miller, Alan S. "The Environmental and Other Bioethical Challenges for Christian Creation Consciousness." In *Cry of the Environment*, ed. Philip N. Joranson and Ken Butigan, pp. 380–400. Santa Fe: Bear and Co., 1984.

Mitcham, Carl, and Jim Grote, eds. *Theology and Technology: Essays in Christian Analysis and Exegesis.* Lanham, Md.: University Press of America, 1984.

Mohai, Paul. "Public Concern and Elite Involvement in Environmental Conservation Issues." *Social Science Quarterly* 66 (December 1985): 820–38.

Moltmann, Jurgen. *On Human Dignity: Political Theology and Ethics.* Philadelphia: Fortress, 1984.

——. *Spirit of Life.* Minneapolis: Fortress, 1992.

——. *Theology of Hope.* New York: Harper, 1967.

Monahan, Ronald. "Christ as the Second Adam." In *The Environment and the Christian: What Does the New Testament Say about the Environment?*, ed. Calvin DeWitt, pp. 45–56. Grand Rapids, Mich.: Baker, 1991.

Moncrief, Lewis W. "The Cultural Basis for Our Environmental Crisis." *Science*, October 25, 1970, pp. 508–12.

——. "The Cultural Basis of Our Environmental Crisis." In *Western Man and Environmental Ethics*, ed. Ian G. Barbour, pp. 31–42. Reading, Mass.: Addison-Wesley, 1973.

Moon, J. Donald. *Constructing Community: Moral Pluralism and Tragic Conflicts.* Princeton: Princeton University Press, 1993.

Morgan, David. Review of *Rebirth of Value: Meditations on Beauty, Ecology, Religion, and Education*, by Frederick Turner. *Christian Century*, April 10, 1991, p. 406.

Morris, Aldon D. *The Origins of the Civil Rights Movement.* New York: Macmillan, 1984.

Morris, Richard Knowles. "Man and Animals: Some Contemporary Problems." In *On the Fifth Day: Animal Rights and Human Ethics*, ed. Richard Knowles and Michael W. Fox, pp. 26–44. Washington, D.C.: Acropolis Books, 1978.

Morris, Richard Knowles, and Michael W. Fox, eds. *On the Fifth Day: Animal Rights and Human Ethics.* Washington, D.C.: Acropolis Books, 1978.

Morrison, Roy D., II. "Process Philosophy, Social Thought, and Liberal Theology." *Zygon* 19 (March 1984): 65–81.

Morton, Hubert. *Pat Robertson: Where He Stands.* Old Tappan, N.J.: Revell, 1988.

Morton, James Parks. "Listen to the Earth." *Christianity and Crisis*, February 4, 1980, pp. 10–12.

Murphy, Andrew. "The Mainline Churches and Political Activism: The Continuing Impact of the Persian Gulf War." *Soundings* 76 (Winter 1993): 525–50.

Nash, James A. *Loving Nature: Ecological Integrity and Christian Responsibility.* Nashville: Abingdon, 1992.

Nash, Roderick F. *The Rights of Nature: A History of Environmental Ethics.* Madison: University of Wisconsin Press, 1989.

Nash, Ronald H. "Process Theology and Classical Theism." In *Process Theology*, ed. Ronald H. Nash, pp. 3–29. Grand Rapids, Mich.: Baker, 1987.

———, ed. *Process Theology*. Grand Rapids, Mich.: Baker, 1987.

Nelson, James S. Review of *The Travail of Nature*, by H. Paul Santmire. *Zygon* 23 (December 1988): 484–86.

Neuhaus, Richard John. *In Defense of People: Ecology and the Seduction of Radicalism*. New York: Macmillan, 1971.

"New Politics of the Environment." *Christian Century*, January 14, 1970, p. 36.

Nyberg, John R. "Energy Conservation: A Moral Imperative." *Lutheran Standard*, March 20, 1981, pp. 12–13.

———. "Environmental Safeguards Urged." *Lutheran Standard*, May 28, 1982, p. 29.

———. "How Can You Help Fight This Dollar Drain on Your Congregation's Pocketbook—Save Energy!" *Lutheran Standard*, October 2, 1981, pp. 4–7.

101 Ways to Help Save the Earth. New York: Eco-Justice Working Group of the National Council of Churches, 1990.

Ophuls, William. *Ecology and the Politics of Scarcity: Prologue to a Political Theory of the Steady State*. San Francisco: W. H. Freeman, 1977.

Orgon, Joan, and Maria Paz Artazo. "Faith, Politics, and Ecology, Part One." In *Christian Ecology*, ed. Frederick W. Krueger, p. 83. San Francisco: North American Conference on Christianity and Ecology, 1988.

Ornstein, Norm, Andrew Kohut, and Larry McCarthy. *The People, the Press, and Politics: The Times-Mirror Study of the American Electorate*. Reading, Mass.: Addison-Wesley, 1988.

"Our Earth Family." Brochure. Madison, Wisc.: Orchard Ridge United Church of Christ, 1991.

Owens, Virginia Stem. "Consider the Fingerprint of God." *Christianity Today*, November 17, 1978, pp. 14–17.

Paehlke, Robert C. *Environmentalism and the Future of Progressive Politics*. New Haven: Yale University Press, 1989.

———. "Environmental Values and Democracy: The Challenge of the Next Century." In *Environmental Policy in the 1990s*, ed. Norman J. Vig and Michael E. Kraft, pp. 349–67. Washington, D.C.: Congressional Quarterly, 1990.

Palmer, Albert W. "A Prayer at Nature's Altar." *Advance*, August 18, 1952, p. 5.

Paradise, Scott. "The Vandal Ideology." *The Nation*, December 29, 1969, pp. 729–32.

Passmore, John. *Man's Responsibility for Nature: Ecological Problems and Western Traditions*. New York: Scribner's, 1974.

Pattison, O. R. B. *Left Behind*. Old Tappan, N.J.: F. H. Revell, 1969.

Peerman, Dean. "Gertrude Blom: Prophet Crying *for* a Wilderness." *Christian Century*, December 11, 1985, pp. 1146–50.

Peters, Ted F. "Creation, Communication, and the Ethical Imagination." In *Cry of the Environment*, ed. Philip N. Joranson and Ken Butigan, pp. 401–29. Santa Fe: Bear and Co., 1984.

Peterson, Michael L. "God and Evil in Process Theology." In *Process Theology*, ed. Ronald H. Nash, pp. 117–39. Grand Rapids, Mich.: Baker, 1987.

Phillips, Derek L. *Looking Backward: A Critical Appraisal of Communitarian Thought.* Princeton: Princeton University Press, 1993.

Plant, Judith. *Healing the Wounds: The Promise of Ecofeminism.* Philadelphia: New Society, 1989.

Platt, Charles A. "The Lord's Day and the Energy Crisis." *Presbyterian Survey,* March 1974, p. 31.

Pocock, J. G. A. *The Machiavellian Moment: Florentine Political Thought and the Atlantic Republic Tradition.* Princeton: Princeton University Press, 1975.

Pollard, William G. "God and His Creation." In *This Little Planet,* ed. Michael Hamilton, pp. 43–76. New York: Scribner's, 1970.

Pragnell, Walter L. "The ABC's of Church Energy Savings." *Episcopalian,* May 1982, pp. 10–11.

Presbyterian Eco-Justice Task Force. *Keeping and Healing the Creation: A Resource Paper.* Louisville: Presbyterian Church, 1989.

Raffensperger, Carolyn. "All God's Critters Got a Place in the Choir." *Daughters of Sarah* 16 (May/June 1990): 4–6.

Ranck, Lee. "Earthian, Be an Earthbuilder!" *Engage/Social Action,* February 1, 1971, p. 2.

Rasmussen, Larry L. "Creation, Church, and Christian Responsibility." In *Tending the Garden: Essays on the Gospel and the Earth,* ed. Wesley Granberg-Michaelson, pp. 114–31. Grand Rapids, Mich.: Eerdmans, 1987.

———. "Review: Care for the Earth." *Sojourners* 14 (June 1985): 42–43.

———. "The Road to Rio: A Christian Perspective." Address to the Conference on Human Values and the Environment, sponsored by the Environmental Studies Institute, University of Wisconsin–Madison, October 1992.

Ream, Norman S. "Man and his Environment." *Congregationalist* 130 (January 1970).

Regan, Tom. *The Case for Animal Rights.* Berkeley: University of California Press, 1983.

Regenstein, Lewis G. *Replenish the Earth: A History of Organized Religion's Treatment of Animals and Nature.* New York: Crossroad, 1991.

"Religious Leaders Join Scientists in Ecological Concerns." *Christianity Today,* August 19, 1991, p. 49.

Richardson, Robert P. "A New Look at Stewardship." *Presbyterian Survey,* October 1977, p. 2.

Rifkin, Jeremy. *Biosphere Politics: A New Consciousness for a New Century.* New York: Crown, 1991.

———. *The Emerging Order.* New York: Putnam, 1979.

Riggan, George A. "Reconstructions of Scientific and Religious Consciousness for a Better Environmental Future." In *Religious Reconstruction for the Environmental Future,* ed. Philip N. Joranson and C. Alan Anderson, R1–19. Storrs, Conn.: Office of Environmental Education, 1973.

Riggs, Dianne. "Wilderness Retreats, Part Two." In *Christian Ecology,* ed. Frederick W. Krueger, p. 56. San Francisco: North American Conference on Christianity and Ecology, 1988.

Rodman, John. "Four Forms of Ecological Consciousness Reconsidered." In *Ethics and the Environment*, ed. Don Scherer and Thomas Attig. Englewood Cliffs, N.J.: Prentice Hall, 1983.

Rohrschneider, Robert. "Citizens' Attitudes toward Environmental Issues: Selfish or Selfless?" *Comparative Political Studies* 21 (October 1988): 347–67.

Rolston, Holmes, III. "Can and Ought We to Follow Nature?" *Environmental Ethics* 1 (Spring 1979): 7–30.

Rorty, Richard. *Contingency, Irony and Solidarity*. Cambridge: Cambridge University Press, 1989.

Rose, David J. "The World Won't Stop and We Can't Jump Off." *The Episcopalian*, June 1979, pp. 6–7.

Ruether, Rosemary Radford. "The Biblical Vision of the Ecological Crisis." *Christian Century*, November 22, 1978, pp. 1129–32.

——. *Disputed Questions: On Being a Christian*. Maryknoll, N.Y.: Orbis, 1988.

——. *Gaia and God: An Ecofeminist Theology of Earth Healing*. New York: HarperCollins, 1992.

——. "Mother Earth and the Megamachine." *Christianity and Crisis*, December 13, 1971, pp. 267–72.

——. *New Woman, New Earth*. New York: Seabury, 1975.

——. *Sexism and God-Talk: Toward a Feminist Theology*. Boston: Beacon Press, 1983.

——. *Women-Church: Theology and Practice of Feminist Liturgical Communities*. San Francisco: Harper, 1985.

Rust, Eric C. "Nature and Man in Theological Perspective." *Review and Expositor* 69 (Winter 1972): 11–22.

Ryali, Ragagopal. "Eastern-Mystical Perspectives." In *Ethics for Environment: Three Religious Strategies*, ed. Dave Stefferson, Walter J. Herrscher, and Robert S. Cook, pp. 47–56. Green Bay: University of Wisconsin–Green Bay, 1973.

St. John, Donald P. "Creation and the Churches: A Call for a New Reformation." In *Christian Ecology*, ed. Frederick W. Krueger, p. 50. San Francisco: North American Conference on Christianity and Ecology, 1988.

Sale, Kirkpatrick. *Human Scale*. New York: Coward, McCann, and Geoghegan, 1980.

Sandel, Michael. *Liberalism and Its Critics*. New York: New York University Press, 1984.

Santmire, H. Paul. *Brother Earth: Nature, God and Ecology in Time of Crisis*. New York: Thomas Nelson, 1970.

——. "Catastrophe and Ecstasy." In *Ecological Renewal*, ed. Paul E. Lutz and H. Paul Santmire. Philadelphia: Fortress, 1972, pp. 75–152.

——. "Ecology, Justice and Theology: Beyond the Preliminary Skirmishes." *Christian Century*, May 12, 1976, pp. 460–64.

——. "Historical Dimensions of the American Crisis." In *Western Man and Environmental Ethics*, ed. Ian G. Barbour, pp. 66–92. Reading, Mass.: Addison-Wesley, 1973.

——. "In Him All Things Consist: Christology, Ecology, and Ethics (1)." Mencosta, Mich.: World Evangelical Fellowship Theological Commission/Au Sable Forum, 1992.

——. Interview by Laura Olson, April 6, 1992.

——. "The Liberation of Nature: Lynn White's Challenge Anew." *Christian Century*, May 22, 1985, pp. 530–33.

——. "Reflections of the Alleged Ecological Bankruptcy of Western Theology." In *Ethics for Environment: Three Religious Strategies*, ed. Dave Stefferson, Walter J. Herrscher, and Robert S. Cook, pp. 23–46. Green Bay: University of Wisconsin, 1973.

——. *The Travail of Nature: The Ambiguous Ecological Promise of Christian Theology*. Philadelphia: Fortress, 1985.

Scarce, Rik. *Eco-Warriors: Understanding the Radical Environmental Movement*. Chicago: Noble Press, 1990.

Schaeffer, Edith. "God's Greatest Creation." *Christianity Today*, January 2, 1976, pp. 26–27.

——. "The Most Dangerous Pollution of All." *Christianity Today*, August 16, 1974, pp. 26–27.

Schaeffer, Francis A. *Pollution and the Death of Man: The Creation View of Ecology*. Wheaton, Ill.: Tyndale, 1970.

Scherer, Don, and Thomas Attig, eds. *Ethics and the Environment*. Englewood Cliffs, N.J.: Prentice Hall, 1983.

Schicker, Glenn E. "An Institute for 'Earth Keeping.' " *Christian Century*, September 14–21, 1988, pp. 808–12.

Schilling, Harold K. "The Whole Earth Is the Lord's." In *Earth Might Be Fair: Reflections on Ethics, Religion, and Ecology*, ed. Ian G. Barbour, pp. 100–122. Englewood Cliffs, N.J.: Prentice Hall, 1972.

Schmitz, Barbara G. "The Eucharist and Ecology: A Sacramental Look at Creation." *Daughters of Sarah* 16 (May/June 1990): 11.

Schneider, Edward D. "Why 'Life-Style' Matters." *Lutheran Standard*, September 6, 1977, pp. 27–28.

Schumacher, E. F. "Small Is Beautiful: Toward a Theology of 'Enough.' " *Christian Century*, July 28, 1971, pp. 900–902.

Schwarz, Hans. "The Eschatological Dimension of Ecology." *Zygon* 9 (December 1974): 323–38.

Seaburg, Alan. "Man and Nature." *Christian Century*, April 15, 1970, p. 452.

Seelman, Katherine, and Chris Cowap. "Toward Ecological Justice." *Christianity and Crisis*, October 16, 1978, pp. 250–52.

Seerveld, Calvin. "The Gospel of Creation." *Christianity Today*, November 17, 1978, pp. 18–19.

Shaiko, Ronald. "Religion, Politics and Environmental Concern." *Social Science Quarterly* 68 (1987): 244–62.

Shinn, Roger L. "Eco-Justice Theories in Christian Ethics since the 1960s." In *For Creation's Sake*, ed. Dieter T. Hessel, pp. 96–114. Philadelphia: Geneva, 1985.

——. "Ethics and the Family of Man." In *This Little Planet*, ed. Michael Hamilton, pp. 127–59. New York: Scribner's, 1970.

——. *Faith, Science in an Unjust World: Report of the World Council of Churches' Conference on Faith, Science and the Future*. Geneva, Switzerland: World Council of Churches, 1980.

——. "Population and the Dignity of Man." *Christian Century*, April 15, 1970, pp. 442–48.

——. "Science and Ethical Decision: Some New Issues." In *Earth Might Be Fair: Reflections on Ethics, Religion, and Ecology*, ed. Ian G. Barbour, pp. 123–45. Englewood Cliffs, N.J.: Prentice Hall, 1982.

Shinn, Roger L., and Margaret Maxey. "The NCC and Nuclear Power." *Christianity and Crisis*, May 10, 1976, pp. 105–11.

Shoemaker, Dennis E. "Loving People, Loving Earth." *Christianity and Crisis*, August 3, 1987, pp. 260–63.

Shute, Sara. Review of *Why the Green Nigger*, by Elizabeth Dodson Gray. *Environmental Ethics* 2 (Summer 1980): 187–91.

Sire, James W. *The Universe Next Door*. Downers Grove, Ill.: InterVarsity Press, 1976.

Sittler, Joseph A. "Ecological Commitment as Theological Responsibility." *Zygon* 5 (June 1970): 172–81.

——. *The Ecology of Faith*. Philadelphia: Fortress, 1961.

——. "A Theology for Earth." *The Christian Scholar* 37 (1954): 367–74.

Skillen, James W. "Ethics and Justice: What Should Governments Do for the Environment?" In *The Environmental Crisis*, ed. Edwin R. Squiers, pp. 227–34. Mancelona, Mich.: Au Sable Institute, 1982.

——. *The Scattered Voice: Christians at Odds in the Public Square*. Grand Rapids, Mich.: Zondervan, 1990.

Smith, Gerald Alonzo. "Christian Ecological Economics." In *Christian Ecology*, ed. Frederick W. Krueger, p. 71. San Francisco: North American Conference on Christianity and Ecology, 1988.

Smith, Mayo Y. "Subdue the Earth Didn't Mean Pollute It." *Presbyterian Survey*, May 1989, p. 47.

Somplatsky-Jarman, William. "For a More Inclusive Environmental Agenda." *Christianity and Crisis*, May 14, 1990, pp. 144–45.

Spretnak, Charlene. "Ecofeminism: Our Roots and Flowering." In *Reweaving the World: The Emergence of Ecofeminism*, ed. Irene Diamond and Gloria Feman Orenstein, pp. 3–14. San Francisco: Sierra Club, 1990.

——. Introduction to *The Politics of Women's Spirituality*. Garden City, N.Y.: Doubleday, 1982, pp. xi–xxx.

——. *The Spiritual Dimension of Green Politics*. Santa Fe: Bear and Co., 1986.

——, ed. *The Politics of Women's Spirituality*. Garden City, N.Y.: Doubleday, 1982.

Spring, David, and Eileen Spring, eds. *Ecology and Religion in History*. New York: Harper, 1974.

Squiers, Edwin R. "The Making of an Ethical Dilemma." In *The Environmental Crisis*, pp. 3–6. Mancelona, Mich.: Au Sable Institute, 1982.

——, ed. *The Environmental Crisis*. Mancelona, Mich.: Au Sable Institute, 1982.

Stackhouse, Max L. Review of *In Defense of People*, by Richard John Neuhaus. *Zygon* 7 (March 1972): 70–74.

Stafford, Tim. "Animal Liberation." *Christianity Today*, June 18, 1990, pp. 19–23.

Stapert, John, and Joan Murphy. "Earth Faces Crisis." *Presbyterian Survey*, April 1989, p. 44.

Starhawk. "Power, Authority, and Mystery: Ecofeminism and Earth-Based Spirituality." In *Reweaving the World: The Emergence of Ecofeminism*, ed. Irene Diamond and Gloria Feman Orenstein, pp. 73–86. San Francisco: Sierra Club, 1990.

———. *Truth or Dare: Encounters with Power, Authority, and Mystery*. San Francisco: Harper, 1990.

———. "Witchcraft as Goddess Religion." In *The Politics of Women's Spirituality*, ed. Charlene Spretnak, pp. 49–56. Garden City, N.Y.: Doubleday, 1982.

Steger, Mary Anne E., and Stephanie L. Witt. "Gender Differences in Environmental Orientations: A Comparison of Publics and Activists in Canada and the United States." *Western Political Quarterly* 42 (December 1989): 627–49.

Stewart, Claude Y., Jr. "Factors Conditioning the Christian Creation Consciousness." Chap. 5 in *Cry of the Environment*, ed. Philip N. Joranson and Ken Butigan. Santa Fe: Bear and Co., 1984.

Stone, Glenn C., ed. *A New Ethic for a New Earth*. New York: Faith-Man-Nature, 1971.

Stone, Merlin. "The Great Goddess: Who Was She?" In *The Politics of Women's Spirituality*, ed. Charlene Spretnak. Garden City, N.Y.: Doubleday, 1982.

Stone, Pat. "Christian Ecology." *Utne Reader* 31, no. 6 (November/December 1989): 78–79.

Streichen, Donna. *Ungodly Rage: The Hidden Face of Catholic Feminism*. San Francisco: Ignatius Press, 1991.

Sullivan, William. *Reconstructing Public Philosophy*. Berkeley: University of California Press, 1982.

Sweeney, Patrick. "Synfuels: Uncertain Promise." *Christianity and Crisis*, September 17–October 1, 1979, p. 229.

Tabscott, Robert. "To Build a New Earth." *Presbyterian Survey*, July 1977, p. 29.

Taylor, Bob Pepperman. "Environmental Ethics and Political Theory." *Polity* 23 (Summer 1991): 567–83.

———. *Our Limits Transgressed: Ecological Political Thought in America*. Lawrence: University Press of Kansas, 1992.

Taylor, Dorceta E. "Blacks and the Environment: Toward an Explanation of the Concern and Action Gap between Blacks and Whites." *Environmental Behavior* 21 (March 1989): 175–205.

Taylor, Paul. *Respect for Nature*. Princeton: Princeton University Press, 1986.

Teilhard de Chardin, Pierre. *The Phenomenon of Man*. New York: Harper, 1959.

Thomas, Mark. Interview by Robert Booth Fowler, Madison, Wisc., 1992.

Tinder, Glenn. *Community: Reflections on a Tragic Ideal*. Baton Rouge: Louisiana State University Press, 1980.

Todd, Judith. "On Common Ground: Native-American and Feminist Spirituality Approaches in the Struggle to Save Mother Earth." In *The Politics of Women's Spirituality*, ed. Charlene Spretnak, pp. 430–45. Garden City, N.Y.: Doubleday, 1982.

Tokar, Brian. *The Green Alternative: Creating an Ecological Future.* San Pedro, Calif.: R. and E. Miles, 1987.

Toynbee, Arnold. "The Religious Background of the Present Environmental Crisis." In *Ecology and Religion in History*, ed. David Spring and Eileen Spring. New York: Harper, 1974.

Train, Russell. "Religion and the Environment." *Renewable Resources Journal* 8 (Summer 1990): 5–8.

Trexler, Edgar R. "Organizing to Save the Earth." *The Lutheran*, July 21, 1971, pp. 14–16.

Trickett, David. "Needed: A Transformed Stewardship of the Earth." In *101 Ways to Help Save the Earth*, pp. iii–iv. New York: Eco-Justice Working Group of the National Council of Churches, 1990.

Trotter, Kathy. "Spiritualities in Environmental Education, Part One." In *Christian Ecology*, ed. Frederick W. Krueger, p. 80. San Francisco: North American Conference on Christianity and Ecology, 1988.

Tuan, Yi-Fu. "Our Treatment of the Environment in Ideal and Actuality." *American Scientist* 58 (May–June 1970): 244, 247–49.

Tuck, William P. "The Church and Ecological Action." "Ecology and the Church." *Review and Expositor* 69 (Winter 1972): 67–76.

Turnage, Juleen, of The Assemblies of God, Springfield, Mo. Letter to author, August 27, 1991.

Van Ham, Lee. "Praying with Trees." *Christian Century*, July 12, 1989, pp. 839–40.

Van Leeuwen, Raymond C. "Christ's Resurrection and the Creation's Vindication." Chap. 3 in *The Environment and the Christian: What Can We Learn From the New Testament?*, ed. Calvin B. DeWitt. Grand Rapids, Mich.: Baker, 1991.

Vig, Norman J., and Michael E. Kraft, eds. *Environmental Policy in the 1990s.* Washington, D.C.: Congressional Quarterly, 1990.

Visick, Vernon. "Creation's Care and Keeping in the Life of Jesus." Chap. 5 in *The Environment and the Christian: What Can We Learn from the New Testament?*, ed. Calvin B. DeWitt. Grand Rapids, Mich.: Baker, 1991.

Voth, Elver H. "Time in a Christian Environmental Ethic." In *The Environmental Crisis*, ed. Edwin R. Squiers, pp. 57–66. Mancelona, Mich.: Au Sable Institute, 1982.

Waldrop, M. Mitchell. *Complexity.* New York: Simon and Schuster, 1992.

Wall, James M. "Animals in Research: A Conflict in Caring." *Christian Century*, October 12, 1988, pp. 883–84.

———. "Getting Serious about the Environmental Threat." *Christian Century*, April 12, 1989, pp. 371–72.

———. "An Uncaged Vision of Nonhuman Creation." *Christian Century*, October 25, 1989, pp. 947–48.

———. "Words of Faith from Jimmy Carter." *Christian Century*, January 17, 1979, pp. 38–39.

Walvoord, John F. *Armageddon, Oil and the Middle East Crisis.* Grand Rapids, Mich.: Zondervan, 1990.

Wandesforde-Smith, Geoffrey. "Moral Outrage and the Progress of Environmental

Policy: What Do We Tell the Next Generation about How to Care for the Earth?" In *Environmental Policy in the 1990s*, ed. Norman J. Vig and Michael E. Kraft, pp. 325–47. Washington: Congressional Quarterly, 1990.

Ward, Charlotte R. "A Story for Our Times." *Daughters of Sarah* 16 (May/June 1990): 18–21.

Warner, Mary Elizabeth. "God called the Earth Good, But Man Messed It Up." *The Lutheran*, June 17, 1970, pp. 15–17.

Warren, Karen J. "Feminism and Ecology: Making Connections." *Environmental Ethics* 9 (Spring 1987): 3–20.

Warren, Mary Anne. "The Rights of the Nonhuman World." In *Environmental Philosophy: A Collection of Readings*, ed. Robert Elliot and Arran Gare, pp. 109–34. University Park: Pennsylvania State University Press, 1983.

Watson, Albert G. "An International Storm over Acid Rain." *Christian Century*, May 7, 1986, pp. 452–53.

Watt, James G. *The Courage of a Conservative*. New York: Simon and Schuster, 1985.

Watt, Leilani. *Caught in the Conflict: My Life with James Watt*. Eugene, Ore.: Harvest House, 1984.

Watts, Nicholas, and Geoffrey Wandesforde-Smith. "Postmaterial Values and Environmental Policy Change." In *Environmental Policy Formation: The Impact of Values, Ideology, and Standards*, ed. Dean E. Mann, pp. 29–42. Lexington, Mass.: D. C. Heath, 1981.

Welden, C. W., and William L. Slauson. "The Intensity of Competition and Its Importance." *Quarterly Review of Biology* 61 (1986): 23–44.

Wenz, Peter S. *Environmental Justice*. Albany: State University of New York Press, 1988.

Wheaton, Roger. "Wilderness Retreats, Part One." In *Christian Ecology*, ed. Frederick W. Krueger, p. 55. San Francisco: North American Conference on Christianity and Ecology, 1988.

White, Lynn, Jr. "Continuing the Conversation." In *Western Man and Environmental Ethics*, ed. Ian G. Barbour, pp. 55–64. Reading, Mass.: Addison-Wesley, 1973.

———. "The Future of Compassion." *Environmental Review* 30 (April 1978): 99–109.

———. "The Historic Roots of Our Ecologic Crisis." *Science*, March 10, 1967, pp. 1203–7.

Whitehead, Alfred North. *Process and Reality: An Essay in Cosmology*. 1927. Reprint, New York: Humanities Press, 1957.

Wikenneth, Cauthen. "Process Theology and Eco-Justice." In *For Creation's Sake*, ed. Dieter T. Hessel, pp. 84–95. Philadelphia: Geneva, 1985.

Wilkinson, Loren. "Christ as Creator and Redeemer." Chap. 1 in *The Environment and the Christian: What Can We Learn from the New Testament?*, ed. Calvin B. DeWitt. Grand Rapids, Mich.: Baker, 1991.

———. "Gaia Spirituality: A Christian Critique." World Evangelical Fellowship Theological Commission/Au Sable Forum, 1992.

———. Interview by Laura Olson, June 15, 1992.

———. "New Age, New Consciousness, and the New Creation." In *Tending the Garden:*

Essays on the Gospel and the Earth, ed. Wesley Granberg-Michaelson, pp. 6–29. Grand Rapids, Mich.: Eerdmans, 1987.

———. "Redeemers of the Earth." In *The Environmental Crisis*, ed. Edwin R. Squiers, pp. 39–56. Mancelona, Mich.: Au Sable Institute, 1982.

———. "A Theology of the Beasts." *Christianity Today*, June 18, 1990, p. 21.

———, ed. (in collaboration with Peter De Vos, Calvin De Witt, Eugene Dykeman, Vernon Ehlers, Derk Pereboom, and Aileen Van Beilen). *Earthkeeping: Christian Stewardship of Natural Resources*. Grand Rapids, Mich.: Eerdmans, 1980.

Williams, Daniel Day. "Changing Concepts of Nature." In *Earth Might Be Fair: Reflections on Ethics, Religion, and Ecology*, ed. Ian G. Barbour, pp. 48–61. Englewood Cliffs, N.J.: Prentice Hall, 1982.

———. "Philosophical and Theological Concepts of Nature." In *A New Ethic for a New Earth*, ed. Glenn C. Stone. New York: Faith-Man-Nature Group, 1971.

Williams, George H. "Christian Attitudes toward Nature." *Christian Scholar's Review*, Fall/Winter 1971–72, pp. 112–26.

Willis, E. David. "Proclaiming Liberation for the Earth's Sake." In *For Creation's Sake*, ed. Dieter T. Hessel, pp. 55–70. Philadelphia: Geneva, 1985.

Wills, Garry. *Under God: Religion and American Politics*. New York: Simon and Schuster, 1990.

Wilson, E. O. *Sociobiology*. Cambridge: Harvard University Press, 1975.

Wise, David S. "Appendix. A Review of Environmental Stewardship Literature and the New Testament." In *The Environment and the Christian: What Can We Learn from the New Testament?*, ed. Calvin B. DeWitt, pp. 117–34. Grand Rapids, Mich.: Baker, 1991.

Wolfe, Alan. *Whose Keeper? Social Science and Moral Obligation*. Berkeley: University of California Press, 1989.

Woodward, Judith L. "Fuel Consumption: Can the Church Lead the Way?" *Engage/Social Action*, November 1976, pp. 29–31.

Woodward, Kenneth L. "The Final Days Are Here Again." *Newsweek*, March 18, 1991, p. 55.

World Evangelical Fellowship. "Summarizing Committee Report." Mancelona, Mich.: Theological Commission/Au Sable Forum, 1992.

Worster, Donald. *The Wealth of Nature*. New York: Oxford University Press, 1993.

Yandell, Keith E. "Fundamentals of Environmental Ethics: East and West." In *The Environmental Crisis*, ed. Edwin R. Squiers, pp. 91–105. Mancelona, Mich.: Au Sable Institute, 1982.

———. "Protestant Theology and Natural Science in the Twentieth Century." In *God and Nature: Historical Essays on the Encounter between Christianity and Science*, ed. David C. Lindberg and Ronald C. Numbers, pp. 448–71. Berkeley: University of California Press, 1986.

Yaple, Charles H. *The Christian Church and Environmental Education: A Study of Involvements in the United States*. Ph.D. diss., State University of New York, College of Environmental Science and Forestry, 1982.

Young, Iris Marion. Review of "Feminism and Ecology" (special issue of *Heresies: A*

Feminist Journal of Art and Politics [1981]). *Environmental Ethics* 5 (Summer 1983): 173–79.

Young, Louise B. *The Unfinished Universe.* New York: Simon and Schuster, 1986.

Young, Norman. *Creator, Creation and Faith.* Philadelphia: Westminster, 1976.

Zencey, Eric. "Apocalypse Now? Ecology and the Peril of Doomsday Visions." *Zygon* 24 (January/February 1989): 90–93.

Zimmerman, Michael E. "Feminism, Deep Ecology, and Environmental Ethics." *Environmental Ethics* 9 (Spring 1987): 21–44.

Zylstra, Uko. "Ecological Aspects of Food Production: Biblical Directives for Agriculture." In *The Environmental Crisis,* ed. Edwin R. Squiers, pp. 135–50. Mancelona, Mich.: Au Sable Institute, 1982.

✖ SCRIPTURE INDEX ✖

Page numbers are in italics.

♨ GENERAL INDEX ♨

238